Liberation of Theology

Liberation of Theology

JUAN LUIS SEGUNDO

TRANSLATED BY JOHN DRURY

ORBIS BOOKS

MARYKNOLL, NEW YORK

Translator's note: Italics in quoted passages from other works should be regarded as the italics of this book's author. It is his emphasis that counts in the present thread of argument. Where both the original author and Segundo italicize the same passage or word, this fact is noted. Where Segundo does not italicize something that is italicized in quoted works, I have removed the italics to avoid confusion on the part of the reader. If a given case seems critical to the reader, he or she may consult the cited work for clarification.

ORIGINALLY PUBLISHED BY EDICIONES CARLOS LOHLÉ, BUENOS AIRES, © 1975

COPYRIGHT © 1976, ORBIS BOOKS, MARYKNOLL, NEW YORK 10545

MANUFACTURED IN THE UNITED STATES OF AMERICA

Library of Congress Cataloging in Publication Data
Segundo, Juan Luis.
   Liberation of theology.

   Translation of liberatión de la teología.
   Includes bibliographical references.
   1. Liberation theology.   2. Sociology, Christian.
3. Theology—20th century.   I. Title.
BT83.57.S4413   230   76-7049
ISBN 0-88344-285-X
ISBN 0-88344-286-8 pbk.

Contents

Acknowledgment

These pages represent an ampler version of a course given at Harvard Divinity School during the spring semester of 1974. The reader will readily realize that many of the examples presented and the criterion governing their selection were dictated by the audience for that course.

My deep-felt thanks go to the theology faculty of Harvard University. In particular I want to thank its dean, Krister Stendahl, who not only gave me the opportunity to develop these ideas in that center of learning but also offered me his warm and affectionate help during my stay.

I also want to extend a special word of thanks to several others who were unselfish in their help. Matilde E. de Lorena, Paul W. Boyd, and my co-worker in the course, Clinton P. Wilkins, greatly helped me to correct and revise the English version that served as the basis for this book.

Finally, I want to extend a special word of thanks to the SPIM Community at Cambridge, which took me in as its guest and helped me to find my way around Harvard.

Liberation of Theology

Introduction

What will remain of the "theology of liberation" in a few short years? The question may seem to be pessimistic in tone, suggesting that liberation theology was a superficial thing or a passing fad. That is certainly not the case. My question should be approached in a positive and hopeful spirit.

It is my opinion that the "theology of liberation," however well or poorly the name fits,[1] represents a point of no return in Latin America. It is an irreversible thrust in the Christian process of creating a new consciousness and maturity in our faith. Countless Christians have committed themselves to a fresh and radical interpretation of their faith, to a new re-experiencing of it in their real lives. And they have done this not only as isolated individuals but also as influential and sizeable groups within the Church.

While the process is irreversible, it is also broad in scope and varied within itself. Therefore it is not easy to say what the exact content of the theology of liberation is for all the Christians involved in it. Certain basic points, however, are clearly shared by all. They would maintain that the longstanding stress on individual salvation in the next world represents a distortion of Jesus' message. He was concerned with man's full and integral liberation, a process which is already at work in history and which makes use of historical means. They would maintain that the Church does not possess any sort of magical effectiveness where salvation is concerned but rather liberating factors in its faith and its liturgy; that the victory of the Church must be viewed in functional terms rather than quantitative or numerical terms, insofar as the Church's specific and proper means manage to exercise a truly powerful impact on human history. They would also maintain that there are not two separate orders—one being a supernatural order outside history and the other being a natural order inside history; that instead one and the same grace raises human beings to a supernatural level and provides them with the means they need to achieve their true destiny within one and the same historical process.

3

The situation changes somewhat if we try to predict the future impact of liberation theology on classical theology and on the internal and pastoral structures of the Church, outside of Latin America in particular. Here our optimism must be toned down considerably. Indeed it may give way to diffidence or dismay with regard to the short-term situation. For the *content* of liberation theology is jeopardized by three tendencies which, working separately or together, could destroy it.

The first tendency derives from the fact that ecclesiastical authorities have learned rather quickly that even the minimum content of liberation theology, the mere repetition of the basic declarations that were voiced without any great difficulty at the Medellín Conference, literally constitute a political crime today. They can entail imprisonment and torture for lay people. And though they may not entail exactly the same things for priests and bishops, they threaten to jeopardize something which the latter regard as just as important and critical: i.e., the privileged status of religious activity and even the basic right of its free exercise. Since the Medellín Conference we have witnessed a growing gap between the poor countries and the rich countries, and also an inevitable growth of political awareness in the former. Bit by bit this has led to the replacement of democratic governments, of even the most stable ones, by military dictatorships which can keep discontent under control though they may not be able to control its causes. Liberation theology, even when reduced to its most minimal content, has been singled out by these dictatorships as something as potentially explosive as the existence of Marxist groups and political parties.

The second tendency stems from the fact that ecclesiastical authorities themselves have adopted the terminology of liberation. Gradually this has led to a watering down of its content, so that the language of liberation is emptied of all real meaning. Everyone mouths the words, only to go on as before. Classical Catholic education describes itself as an education in liberation, and even the most extreme right-wing ideology makes frequent use of the idiom of liberation. And so we are confronted with a paradox that is readily comprehensible in ideological terms: on the one hand the authentic theology of liberation is persecuted as subversive; on the other hand its terminology is adopted in watered-down form to front for ideas and attitudes that have no connection whatsoever with truly liberative changes.

The third tendency is more subtle, but no less real and effective. Indeed it may be the most solidly rooted of the three by virtue of the mechanisms by which it operates. From its very inception liberation theology was a theology rising out of the urgent problems of real life. Faced with those problems and deeply influenced by them, it resorted to the traditional means of theologizing: that is, to biblical tradition and to dogmatic tradition. It did this seriously and earnestly, feeling a responsibility towards both the problems of real life and the canons of worldwide theology. But it did this, as it had to, with the means at its disposal. It did not move in a precipitate, hare-brained way to meet some inescapable pragmatic necessity, but it did move forward without the erudite exploration and attention to detail which is evident when a new line of theological thought is introduced into present-day European or North American theology. In affirming certain essential points, moreover, it left aside other points which may have been important in their consequences.

As a result, liberation theology evoked two reactions at the same time. It aroused interest among the noninitiate, but it also clearly evoked a certain amount of academic disdain from the great centers of theological thought around the world. Now the fact is that the everyday theology of Latin America, the theology that is passed on to priests in the seminaries and thus eventually to lay people in universities and churches, continues to be the erudite theology of textbooks. And if this latter theology continues to view liberation theology as a well-intentioned but rather naive and uncritical effort, it is clear that Latin Americans will not be immune to the influence of this outlook.

These three negative tendencies are being felt more and more keenly by Latin American theology. Perhaps it is now time to attack them head on. Gustavo Gutiérrez did that in his book, *A Theology of Liberation,* proving rather convincingly that liberation theology is not provincial or fundamentalist, whatever else one might think about it. Now, however, it may be time to get down to epistemology. By that I mean it may be time to get down to analyzing not so much the content of Latin American theology but rather its methodological approach and its connection with liberation. The fact is that only a study of our method of theologizing vis-à-vis the reality of Latin America, and an agreement on that methodology, can successfully challenge the mechanisms of oppression and the efforts of the oppressor system to expropriate the terminology of liberation.

Perhaps the time has come to go on the offensive even, to frontally attack the third tendency mentioned above. Perhaps we should now challenge theological methodology as it is practiced in the great centers of learning. I am not championing a partisan attack of a nationalistic or regional nature. I am suggesting that we hurl down a challenge that is authentically and constructively theological in nature. Every Latin American knows from personal experience that any struggle or combat of this sort is a rematch of David against Goliath. But that knowledge does not excuse us from the fight. Perhaps subsequent critiques and criticisms of Latin American theology, if they are sufficently *erudite,* will be forced to begin by justifying themselves. And that in itself could mark the start of a dialogue.

NOTE

1. When one wants to offer guidance to a reader who is not familiar with a given topic, it is difficult to avoid the dangerous shoals of bibliographies that are based on titles rather than on content or methodology. The average bibliography tends to list books and articles in which the word "liberation" shows explicitly in the title. In the best instances it is associated with terms that are political in content, terms such as "dependence," "politics," and "ideology." But even that is to mutilate and distort a theology which has a range of content as vast as theology itself on the one hand, and a much more restricted methodology (and methodological problematic) on the other hand. My task here is not to provide any such bibliography. This is all the more true insofar as we are dealing here with methodology rather than with content. In such a case, a work of little value insofar as content is concerned, indeed even one opposed to the theology of liberation, could be more illustrative than a work on liberation theology that followed the general lines of classical theological methodology.

CHAPTER ONE

The Hermeneutic Circle

We cannot start with the chicken and the egg, so let us start with the reality of everyday life and consider whether it is possible to differentiate the attitudes of a liberation theologian from those of some other theologian on that basis.

My past and present experience has taught me that theology, for all the changes that may have taken place, continues to be taught in an autonomous way. And this is true not only with respect to future professors of theology but also with respect to average people who will only use theology vis-à-vis the real-life problems that face ordinary people.

In mentioning this autonomy of theology I am referring to a long tradition in the Christian churches. Christianity is a *biblical* religion. It is the religion of a *book*, of various books if you will, for that is precisely what the word "bible" means. This means that theology for its part cannot swerve from its path in this respect. It must keep going back to its book and reinterpreting it. Theology is not an interpretation of mankind and society, not in the first place at least.

Attached as it is to a book, theology does not assert its independence from the past or from the sciences which help it to understand the past: e.g., general history, the study of ancient languages and cultures, the history of biblical forms, and the history of biblical redaction. On the other hand theology does implicitly or explicitly assert its independence from the sciences that deal with the present.

For example, a theologian as progressive as Schillebeeckx can arrive at the conclusion that theology can never be ideological—in the Marxist sense of the term—because it is nothing but the application of the divine word to present-day reality.[1] He seems to hold the naive belief that the word of God is applied to human realities inside some antiseptic laboratory that is totally immune to the ideological tendencies and struggles of the present day.

Now a liberation theologian is one who starts from the opposite end.

7

His suspicion is that anything and everything involving ideas, including theology, is intimately bound up with the existing social situation in at least an unconscious way.

Thus the fundamental difference between the traditional academic theologian and the liberation theologian is that the latter feels compelled at every step to combine the disciplines that open up the past with the disciplines that help to explain the present. And he feels this necessity precisely in the task of working out and elaborating theology, that is to say, in the task of interpreting the word of God as it is addressed to us here and now.

Without this connection between past and present there is no theology of liberation in the long run. You might get a theology which *deals with* liberation, but its methodological naiveté would prove to be fatal somewhere along the line. It would eventually be reabsorbed by the deeper mechanisms of oppression—one of these being the tendency to incorporate the idiom of liberation into the prevailing language of the status quo.

In this book I am going to try to show that an approach which attempts to relate past and present in dealing with the word of God has to have its own special methodology. I shall give this special methodology a pretentious name and call it the *hermeneutic circle*. Here is a preliminary definition of the hermeneutic circle: it is the continuing change in our interpretation of the Bible which is dictated by the continuing changes in our present-day reality, both individual and societal. "Hermeneutic" means "having to do with interpretation." And the circular nature of this interpretation stems from the fact that each new reality obliges us to interpret the word of God afresh, to change reality accordingly, and then to go back and reinterpret the word of God again, and so on.

The term "hermeneutic circle" is used in a strict sense to designate the method used by Bultmann in interpreting the Scriptures, and the New Testament in particular. At first glance it might seem that my use of the term here is less rigorous. But I hope to show, and the reader will be able to judge this, that my "hermeneutic circle" deserves that designation far more strictly than does Bultmann's. But first I must spell out in greater detail what I am referring to in concrete terms.

I think that two preconditions must be met if we are to have a hermeneutic circle in theology. The first precondition is that the questions rising out of the present be rich enough, general enough, and basic enough to force us to change our customary conceptions of life, death, knowledge, society, politics, and the world in general. Only a change of this sort, or at the very least a pervasive suspicion about our ideas and value judgments concerning those things, will enable us to reach the theological level and force theology to come back down to reality and ask itself new and decisive questions.

The second precondition is intimately bound up with the first. If theology somehow assumes that it can respond to the new questions without changing its customary interpretation of the Scriptures, that immediately terminates the hermeneutic circle. Moreover, if our interpretation of Scripture does not change along with the problems, then the latter will go unanswered; or worse, they will receive old, conservative, unserviceable answers.

It is most important to realize that without a hermeneutic circle, in other words, in those instances where the two aforementioned preconditions are not accepted, theology is always a conservative way of thinking and acting. It is so not so much because of its content but because in such a case it lacks any *here-and-now* criteria for judging our real situation. It thus becomes a pretext for approving the existing situation or for disapproving of it because it does not dovetail with guidelines and canons that are even more ancient and outdated.

It is my feeling that the most progressive theology in Latin America is more interested in *being liberative* than in *talking about liberation.* In other words, liberation deals not so much with content as with the method used to theologize in the face of our real-life situation.

In this chapter I shall present four sample attempts at fashioning a hermeneutic circle. But first I think it would be wise for me to reiterate the two preconditions for such a circle. They are: (1) profound and enriching questions and suspicions about our real situation; (2) a new interpretation of the Bible that is equally profound and enriching. These two preconditions mean that there must in turn be four decisive factors in our circle. *Firstly* there is our way of experiencing reality, which leads us to ideological suspicion. *Secondly* there is the application of our ideological suspicion to the whole ideological superstructure in general and to theology in particular. *Thirdly* there comes a new way of experiencing theological reality that leads us to exegetical suspicion, that is, to the suspicion that the prevailing interpretation of the Bible has not taken important pieces of data into account. *Fourthly* we have our new hermeneutic, that is, our new way of interpreting the fountainhead of our faith (i.e., Scripture) with the new elements at our disposal.

The examples chosen in this chapter may or may not be good ones. But if we keep our attention focused on these four factors, I think the examples will be comprehensible and useful. At least that is my hope.

I. FIRST SAMPLE ATTEMPT: COX AND THE SECULAR CITY

As I just indicated, the circle that I described above in theoretical terms begins with a special or particular way of experiencing and evaluating reality in general. It is a critical way of experiencing, almost by its very definition—at least if it is to be the start of a hermeneutic circle. A human being who is content with the world will not have the least interest in unmasking the mechanisms that conceal the authentic reality.

Karl Mannheim writes: "An increasing number of concrete cases makes it evident that (a) every formulation of a problem is made possible only by a *previous actual human experience* which involves such a problem; (b) in selection from the multiplicity of data there is involved an *act of will* on the part of the knower; and (c) forces arising out of living experience are significant in *the direction which the treatment of the problem* follows."[2]

Keeping this in mind about the starting point, let us consider our first sample attempt. Many examples could have been chosen, of course, but I have picked the well-known book by Harvey Cox entitled *The Secular City*. His starting point dovetails with Mannheim's description. It presupposes Cox's own personal experience of his secular society, and it also entails a meaningful selection from the multiplicity of data in that society. Cox is specifically interested in examining the difference between the old way of solving problems and the new way of solving problems that is characteristic of the technopolis. The old way was to appeal to the loftiest human values. The new way is to appeal to the values of technology, to efficiency: in a word, to pragmatic criteria.

One of the subtitles to the book, "A celebration of its liberties and an invitation to its discipline," clearly indicates what Mannheim referred to as "an act of will" on the part of the investigator. Harvey Cox *chooses* to celebrate the liberty of the new pragmatic society and, at the same time, to speak to it of Christianity and its message. Thus, as Mannheim indicated, the author's act of will is significant in determining the way in which the problem will be treated. To be specific, Cox does not accept the way people like Tillich choose to deal with theological problems.

That brings us to the second point in our hermeneutic circle: secularization and urbanization provide an ideological basis for interpreting reality—including theological reality—in a new and presumably more correct way. This is clearly suggested by another subtitle in the book: "Secularization and urbanization in theological perspective." According to Cox, in other words, a "celebration" of the secular city's liberties and an "invitation" to its discipline should provide us with meaningful direction in our attempt to deal with theological problems.

As I indicated, the direction in this case will separate Cox's way of dealing with pragmatism from Tillich's way of dealing with it. Cox says: "We should not be dismayed by the fact that fewer and fewer people are pressing what we have normally called "religious" questions. The fact that urban-secular man is incurably and irreversibly pragmatic, that he is less and less concerned with religious questions, is in no sense a disaster."[3] Cox later says: "We begin by accepting pragmatic man *as he is,* and this means we must part company with Tillich."[4] Why exactly? Because "Tillich's approach has no place for pragmatic man. It is built on the assumption that man by his very nature *must* [Cox's italics too] ask these 'ultimate' or existential questions . . . We must uncover and bring to consciousness this ultimate concern, Tillich argued, for it poses the question for which the Gospel is the answer."[5]

The real challenge posed to the theology of Cox is this: Can the Gospel answer questions that are not even asked by pragmatic man? In other words, can it answer questions in which ultimate concern is not present?

When we see that Cox gives an affirmative answer to these questions, we find ourselves at the third point of our hermeneutic circle. What exactly is the new theological experience that enables us to pose new questions to the Christian sources? Clearly enough the fundamental feature of this experience is the theologian's dialogue with pragmatic man. Dialoguing with him, Cox finds a new light for interpreting many portions of the biblical message. He discovers the possibility for establishing what he himself calls "a viable theology of revolutionary social change."[6] Here we cannot analyze all the rich implications of his new interpretation. The only thing that is of crucial interest to us here is this question: Will this new theology reach pragmatic man?

The answer to this question does not come easily. Cox's pragmatic man picks a new Miss America each year. Now if he looks to the theologian to find out the meaning of this sexual symbol, this is the answer he gets from Cox: "The Protestant objection to the present cult of The Girl must be based on the realization that The Girl is an idol . . . Like every idol she is *ultimately* a creation of our own hands and cannot save us. The values she represents as *ultimate* satisfactions—mechanical comfort, sexual success, unencumbered leisure—have no *ultimacy.*"[7]

What has happened here? Well the fact is that Cox is responding to this particular question in exactly the same way that Tillich would. He is appealing to ultimate values instead of accepting pragmatic man as he is, instead of dropping his concern for those ultimate values. This is clear from the fact that Cox states that pragmatic man erected this idol because "The Girl is . . . the omnipresent icon of consumer society."[8]

Needless to say, Cox never claimed that the word of God has only the

function of approving everything that goes on in connection with pragmatic man. His supposition is that Christianity should constitute a critical
leaven for pragmatic man. But what is to be the basis for this critical
function if at the same time the theologian is supposed to accept pragmatic man as he is? If this point is taken seriously, then pragmatic man as
he is must at the very least accept the *basis* of that criticism. And that basis
cannot be an appeal to ultimate values because that is clearly not a
common basis shared by both the theologian and pragmatic man.

If we are going to take pragmatic man as he is, then there is only one
way we can be critical with regard to the point in question. We would
have to show that the cult of The Girl is not *advantageous* to the interests
of consumer society. But can we use Scripture for an argument of that
sort? Cox does not seem to think so, since he retreats and takes refuge in
arguments like those of Tillich. Those arguments may be valid, but they
leave pragmatic man cold if he truly is pragmatic.

But perhaps it would not be impossible to interpret the Bible and
thereby dialogue with pragmatic man as he is. When all is said and done,
the word of God has always dialogued with human beings preoccupied
with very practical problems. It has dialogued with people facing the
pragmatic necessity of fleeing from bondage in Egypt, with people trying to establish themselves in the promised land, with people facing the
task of returning from exile and restoring the kingdom of David. Jesus
himself dialogued with disciples who were constantly preoccupied with
the notion of trying to make sure that they would get the choice spots in
the coming kingdom. Moreover, many portions of the Bible, including
the Book of Proverbs and many counsels of Jesus, seem to be completely
pragmatic and even downright shrewd. Jesus, for example, advises his
disciples how to sneak up to the best places at a banquet table.

In any case Harvey Cox has no intention of formulating a new—
pragmatic—interpretation of the Bible in order to continue his dialogue
with the man of the secular city. The hermeneutic circle is interrupted
when it seemed at the point of reaching its (provisional) terminus: i.e.,
that of providing a new interpretation of Scripture.

Of course *The Secular City* is much more than an interrupted hermeneutic circle. But the latter is our interest here. We are not interested
in enumerating all the interesting and fecund points in the book.

Now let us ask another question: Exactly why and where is the circle
interrupted? At first glance the latter aspect of the question (where?)
seems easy enough to answer. The circle is interrupted at the third
point, just before it moves to the fourth point (a new interpretation of
the Bible). But if we consider the first part of our question (why?), we
arrive at the curious and interesting conclusion that the circle was

doomed from the very *first* stage. We now know, albeit *a posteriori,* that Cox never really accepted pragmatic man as he is nor the consumer society as it is. He never really committed himself to them. Thus the "act of will" cited by Mannheim as an essential feature of the starting point was never fully present. And this lack of an enthusiastic base, in my opinion, will prevent Harvey Cox from completing his hermeneutic circle and thus revolutionizing theology in some way. This is true, at least, in the case of his book entitled *The Secular City.*

So let me sum up briefly. A hermeneutic circle in theology always presupposes a profound human commitment, a *partiality* that is consciously accepted—not on the basis of theological criteria, of course, but on the basis of human criteria.[9]

The word "partiality" may cause surprise, since the common assumption is that a scholarly science starts out from a state of total impartiality. That is precisely the pretension of academic theology. But it is very important that we do not make the mistake of accepting this claim as valid. Academic theology may well be unaware of its unconscious partiality, but the very fact that it poses as something impartial is a sign of its conservative partiality from the very start. We must realize that there is no such thing as an autonomous, impartial, academic theology floating free above the realm of human options and biases. However academic it may be, theology is intimately bound up with the psychological, social, or political status quo though it may not be consciously aware of that fact.

II. SECOND SAMPLE ATTEMPT: MARX AND HIS CRITIQUE OF RELIGION

Our first example showed us how the hermeneutic circle can be interrupted in the absence of a clearcut and total commitment vis-à-vis some human alternative. As our second example we shall use an author whose partiality and commitment are beyond any shadow of a doubt, whatever one may think of the man or his work. I refer to Karl Marx.

It is not easy to include Marx among the theologians, of course. He himself would be the first to protest such inclusion. At the same time, however, there can be no doubt about his influence on contemporary theology, particularly on the most imaginative and creative brands of it.[10]

The point of departure for Marx's thinking, and specifically for its relationship with religion, is the choice he made between interpreting the world and changing it. As Marx sees it, we must change the world; and we must do this with the proletariat and for the proletariat.

Marx tells us that "the history of all hitherto existing society is the history of class struggles."[11] Then he goes on to say: "Our epoch, the epoch of the bourgeoisie, possesses, however, this distinctive feature: it has simplified the class antagonisms. Society as a whole is more and more splitting up into two great hostile camps, into two great classes directly facing each other—bourgeoisie and proletariat."[12]

Thus thinking that intends to change the world means thinking from within this struggle, and of course thinking that will tip the scales in favor of the proletariat.

Nevertheless it is clear that Marx felt a real need throughout his life to explain, more or less implicitly, why it was that the proletariat—the vast majority of people in all the developed nations—were unable to win immediate victory over the minority forces of the bourgeoisie. In the *Manifesto* cited above, Marx notes the fact that "with the development of industry the proletariat not only increases in number; it becomes concentrated in greater masses, its strength grows, and it feels that strength more."[13] All the more reason then to expect quick victory in such an unequal struggle. Despite countless attempts, however, the revolution did not come and Marx died waiting for it. From the start it would seem that Marx was keenly aware of the delay, felt the need to find some explanation for himself, and sought to find some solid basis for his hopes.

I believe that he found what he was looking for in the notion of *historical materialism.* And with this theory of historical materialism we come to the second stage or point of our hermeneutic circle. We now have a theory that enables us to discover the authentic face of reality in line with our own historical commitment.

For our purposes here we need only say that the theory of historical materialism can be summed up in one sentence from the *Manifesto:* "The ruling ideas of each age have ever been the ideas of its ruling class."[14] This means two things. 1. Even the proletariat itself must change its way of thinking about itself because this way of thinking, which seems *natural,* has been imposed on it by the ruling classes in order to conceal the mechanisms of the existing mode of production against which the proletariat must fight. 2. We must view the ideas of a given age—and that would include philosophical, religious, and political ideas among the rest—as more or less determined by the material mode of production peculiar to that age.

Historical materialism, in other words, teaches us two things. 1. The theoretical and practical superstructure depends unwittingly but in large measure on the economic structure of society. 2. Even though one cannot possibly expect a profound change in the superstructure unless the economic structure is altered, nevertheless ideological changes are not only possible but also decisive if the proletarian class is to become consciously aware of its own true interests and possibilities, if it is to be revolutionary despite its oppressed condition.

Here we cannot discuss at length the well-known problem of determining the exact content of the term "historical materialism" in Marx's mind. First of all, Marx himself never defined the concept in rigorous terms that would serve to designate the relations between the ideological superstructure and the economic structure. He used different words in that connection and qualified them with different adjectives and adverbs to compound the problem. So it is easy to see why there are as many different explanations of historical materialism today as there are commentators on Marx. At times Marx seems to say that the economic structure *determines* the ideologies; at times he seems to say that it *produces* the ideologies; at times he seems to say that it *conditions* them; and sometimes he even seems to say that it *is conditioned* to some extent by them.

If we take Marx's work as a whole, it seems that we can say without fear of error that Marx never failed to include these two conditions in the revolutionary struggle of the proletariat: (1) economic change in the existing mode of production; (2) the theoretical liberation of human consciousness vis-à-vis the ideologies that conceal and sacralize the existing mode of production that is exploiting the proletariat.

Let us cite some passages from Marx that tend to confirm this. In the Prologue to *A Contribution to the Critique of Political Economy,* Marx says: "The mode of production in material life determines the *general* [Segundo: here we have one of those qualifying words that modify a determinist statement] character of the social, political and spiritual processes of life. It is not the consciousness of man that determines their existence, but, on the contrary, their social existence determines their consciousness." A little further on he elaborates: "With the change of the economic foundation the entire immense superstructure is *more or less rapidly* transformed. In considering such transformations the distinction should always be made between the material transformation of the economic condition of production which can be determined with the precision of natural science, and the legal, political, religious, aesthetic or philosophic—in short, ideological forms in which men *become conscious* of this conflict and fight it out."[15]

Now is this distinction designed to tell the proletariat that it should leave aside the *ideological* struggle or rely wholly on the economic process alone? While Marx's work as a whole clearly gives the lie to such an hypothesis, certain passages in his work do seem to point in that direction. In *The German Ideology,* for example, he writes: "Morality, religion, metaphysics, and other ideologies . . . no longer retain . . . their appearance of autonomous existence."[16] He goes on to say: "It does not explain practice from the idea but explains the formation of ideas from material practice, and accordingly comes to the conclusion that all the forms of and products of consciousness can be dissolved, not by intellectual criticism . . . but only by the practical overthrow of the actual social relations . . . that not criticism but revolution is the driving force of history, as well as of religion, philosophy, and all other types of theory."[17]

Now all this may be true, but Marx cannot forget the other side of the revolutionary process: that is, the necessity of creating a revolutionary class. In the same work he admits that "associated with this is the emergence of a class . . . which comprises the majority of the members of society and in which there develops a *consciousness* of the need for a fundamental revolution."[18]

In *Capital,* too, Marx stressed the necessity of using this approach to the study of ideological problems, implying that it represents a new and scientific way of dealing with these problems, particularly the religious ones: "Any history of religion . . . that fails to take account of this material basis, is uncritical. It is, in practice, much easier to discover by analysis the earthly core of the misty creations of religion, than, conversely, *to infer from the actual relations of life at any period the corresponding 'spiritualized' forms of those relations.* But the latter method is the only materialistic, and therefore the only scientific one."[19]

Here Marx is claiming to detach himself from the approach that Darwin uses to disqualify religion, from the easy way out. The difficult but scientific approach to religious problems, the only one that Marx accepts in theory, involves three suppositions: (1) that each and every religious form has a specific place in the ideological superstructure of a given age; (2) that the prevailing religious forms of an age, including those accepted by the oppressed class, derive from the living experience of the dominant classes; and (3) that the process of discovering this connection abets the revolutionary forces of the proletariat.

This at least is what Marx affirms with regard to all the other levels of the social superstructure: legislation, political parties, labor unions, cultural forms, and so forth. So we find ourselves now at the third stage of the hermeneutic circle. When we view religion under the lens of ideological suspicion, it shows up as two things: (a) as a specific interpretation of Scripture imposed by the ruling classes in order to maintain their exploitation—though this intention may never be made explicit; and (b) as an opportunity for the proletariat to convert religion into their own weapon in the class struggle through a new and more faithful interpretation of the Scriptures.

But what happens at this point in the case of Marx? The circle stops because he goes against his own principles. Instead of examining the specific concrete and historical possibilities of religion and theology, he takes the easy way out of disqualifying religion in general insofar as he views it as an autonomous and ahistorical monolith. In the thought of Marx, religion is not viewed as belonging to an ambiguous superstructure. Instead it is viewed as belonging to a purely spiritual plane or, even worse, as being a merely ideal refutation of historical materialism.

At one point Marx writes: "Religious suffering is at the same time an expression of real suffering and *a protest against real suffering.*"[20] Now if that is the case, one would assume that Marx would proceed to infer the exact nature of the concrete spiritualized form of this protest against real suffering in each age. But instead he goes on to say: "Religion . . . is the opium of the people. The *abolition* of religion, as the illusory happiness of men, is a demand for their real happiness."[21] Instead of "abolition," one would expect Marx to have talked about "changing" religion so that it might accentuate and eventually correct the situation being protested against.

Thus the hermeneutic circle of theology is interrupted. To be sure, we could cite various passages from Marx's writings in which his profound intuition spotlights the social influence of such dogmas as that of original sin and individual salvation. Marx, along with Freud and Nietzsche, is regarded by Paul Ricoeur as one of the great masters of "suspicion." But somehow Marx does not seem to have ever entertained the suspicion that ideology could have warped the thinking of the theologians and the interpreters of Scripture so that they ended up unwittingly interpreting it in a sense that served the interests of the ruling classes. Marx does not seem to have shown any interest in trying to find out whether distortion had crept into the Christian message and whether a new interpretation favoring the class struggle of the proletariat might be possible or even necessary.

From our standpoint here, the important thing is to determine at what point the circle was interrupted. At the third point, it might seem. But it might be really interesting and worthwhile to show that it was really interrupted at the second stage, and that Marx's hermeneutic circle was doomed to interruption from there on.

To fully appreciate the significance of the third point or stage in the hermeneutic circle of theology, we must realize that it is a repetition of the first stage in the more restricted area of theology proper. If the first stage assumes a commitment to change the world, the third stage assumes a commitment to change theology. The third stage, in other words, reproduces the three elements that Mannheim spelled out for the

first stage: a concrete evaluational experience of theology, an act of the
will on the part of the theologian with respect to his theology, and a
direction in treating new problems that derives from this act of the will.

Now while Marx made a personal commitment to change the world,
he never had a personal experience of theology as a science tied to
sources. A philosophy of religion cannot perform the same function as
theology, since it does not feel bound to an interpretation of the biblical
sources. Moreover, Marx's act of will to abolish religion is not an act of
will from within theology itself, an act of will that could signify a change
in the way of treating problems theologically. It is rather an abandonment of them.

We know for a fact that during the course of his lifetime Marx's
thinking moved from a basic preoccupation with the problems of the
ideological superstructure towards a deepening interest in the economic
structure. The whole subject of ideology is still present in *Capital,* but
that is due to the need to refute the ideas of the ruling class concerning economics—or, to be more specific, concerning the science of
economics.

One can of course debate, as Althusser has done, the whole question
as to whether there was one Marx or two. That debate makes little sense
to me. But even if it was meaningful, it would have little import for our
discussion here. The important point is that for some reason or another
Marx never managed to carry out the scientific task he had proposed to
do: i.e., to infer the specific, spiritualized forms in the superstructure
that correspond to the material production relationships. To put it a
little better, he never managed to carry out that task at the level of the
complex societies existing in his own day and ours, leaving that task for
present-day Marxism. In *The German Ideology,* for example, we find a
profound and powerful analysis of the relationship between culture and
production in primitive societies. But his analysis becomes ever weaker
and more superficial as it attempts to tackle industrial society—or even
the feudal society of the Middle Ages.

This would seem to suggest, in principle at least, that the more or less
developed social sciences should be able to carry through the analysis
which Marx foresaw and described and set in motion but which he never
carried through on certain decisive levels. In any case Marx's work was
such a stimulus for theology that new methods and profound questions
in present-day theology are an inheritance from him, even though Marx
had rejected theology.

Let me sum up. The purpose of my second example is to make it
clear that a general theory about our perception of reality is called upon
to be incorporated into theological methodology. For insofar as it dis-

covers a deeper or rich layer of reality, it enriches theology with new questions and obliges it to undertake a new interpretation of its own sources. Even if it did just that and nothing else, any general theory capable of providing a methodology for ideological analysis would deserve to be called liberative; for in doing that, it would keep biblical interpretation moving back and forth between its sources and present-day reality. It would thus free academic theology from its atavism and its ivory tower, toppling the naive self-conception it entertains at present: i.e., that it is a simple, eternal, impartial interpretation, or authorized translation, of the word of God.

III. THIRD SAMPLE ATTEMPT:
WEBER ON CALVINISM AND CAPITALISM

For our third example we shall use a thinker who certainly did make the move from the second to the third [22] stage of the hermeneutic circle. I refer to Max Weber.

Like Marx, Weber was not a theologian. But his work obliged him to engage in theological activity to the point where Weber styled himself an "amateur theologian." He was at least that, and a brilliant one. Let us consider a specific work of his.

In one of his most well-known works, Weber's sociological interest led him to study the principal dogmas of Calvinism in connection with the economic attitudes of Western capitalism, using in the process a methodology whose roots can and must be traced back to Marx's historical materialism.

That statement might sound strange to some ears, for Weber has often been dubbed the *Anti-Marx*. Weber's more or less implicit commitment to Western capitalism would seem to place him at the opposite end of the spectrum from Marx and his commitment to the proletariat. But that is not the key reason why Max Weber is dubbed the *Anti-Marx*. The principal reason, in my opinion, is the supposition that Marx's historical materialism is a kind of economic determinism. This supposition is in fact bolstered by official Marxism. But if we recall Engel's famous disclaimer on this point, as well as many texts of Marx himself, then I do not think that one can maintain any radical opposition between the methodology of Weber and that of Marx.[23] It seems clear that Weber's intention was to complement rather than to correct Marx; or at most to correct an excessive emphasis on the economic structure.

In any case, both Marx and Weber base their sociological analysis on the necessary and inevitable relationship between economic and cultural forms, between structure and superstructure. In his analysis Weber concretely tries to point out both the *necessity* and the *possibilities* of carrying forward the analysis of the cultural superstructure of modern society. And in doing this he takes two things for granted: (1) the *relative* independence of the elements of a complex superstructure vis-à-vis the presently existing system of economic production; (2) the *relative* influence of these superstructural forms in adapting people's attitudes to a specific mode of production. I do not think that either of these two presuppositions is opposed to the underlying thought of Marx.

In the first part of the book in question, *The Protestant Ethic and the Spirit of Capitalism,* Weber defines his sociological intention very precisely: "We have no intention whatever of maintaining such a foolish and doctrinaire thesis as that the spirit of capitalism . . . could only have arisen as the result of certain effects of the Reformation, or even that capitalism as an economic system is a creation of the Reformation [Segundo: theses that would be directly opposed to Marx's historical materialism] . . . *On the contrary,* we only wish to ascertain whether and to what extent religious forces have taken part in the qualitative formation and the quantitative expansion of that spirit over the world."[24] In the realm of theory at least, it would be difficult to find a more genuine expression of Marx's thinking about ideological analysis in connection with historical materialism.

Weber's lack of social commitment immediately suggests that he too will fail to complete our hermeneutic circle. But because of what we have just said, we are going to take Weber as our third example here because we have reason to believe that he will make the move from the second to the third step. In other words, it is as if Marx had carried out his proposal to infer the spiritualized forms that correspond to the mode of production at the start of the capitalist era.

It would be futile to try to sum up Weber's detailed exposition of the principal dogmas of the earliest Calvinist era and their later versions among other practicing sects: e.g. pietism, Methodism, and the Baptist sects. Amateur theologian Weber correctly expounds the dogmas in question and establishes their interrelationships in highly intelligent fashion. He also does a very good job of grasping the differences between the thought of Calvin and that of the two other major theologies of the period: i.e., the Lutheran and the Catholic.

An academic theologian might well be put off by Weber's lack of interest in the fonts of theology. Weber certainly pays little attention to the connection between the dogmas he is examining and the internal logic of the Reformation. He is even less interested in some possible distortion of the biblical message—with the exception of two cases which we shall mention further on. His only interest is to find the relationship between really existing ideas, wherever they may come from, and attitudes really existing in the realm of ethical and economic praxis. Weber writes: "We are naturally not concerned with the question of what was theoretically and officially taught in the ethical compendia of the time, however much practical significance this may have had . . . We are interested rather in something entirely different: the influence of those psychological sanctions which, *originating in religious belief* and the practice of religion, gave a direction to practical conduct and held the individual to it."[25]

Despite this pragmatic point of view regarding religious ideas, Max Weber carefully examines the complex structure of Calvin's thought and the reasons which forced his separation from both the Catholic Church and Martin Luther's thinking. He makes an in-depth study of many key doctrines and then compares them with the analogous doctrines in other theological systems. Among the doctrines he examines meticulously are: original sin, the grace of God, predestination to heaven and to damnation, the means for proving the state of grace, the desperate preoccupation with the signs of predestination to heaven, the glory of God as evidenced in natural and historical events, and the quest for some form of certainty outside one's own self.

Thus Max Weber does not take the easy way out of writing off the "earthly core" of religion—as Marx in fact does while censuring that approach. Instead he takes the difficult but scientific path of "inferring the spiritualized forms" that go hand in hand with the real conduct of human beings at that particular point in the process of material production.

To accomplish this, Weber builds a psychological bridge between economic attitudes and religious beliefs. For example, he asserts that it is not just logic that connects the religious superstructure to economic attitudes; many times there is an unexpected psychological connection between the two: "The Calvinistic faith is one of the many examples in the history of religions of the relation between the logical and the *psychological* consequences for the practical religious attitude to be derived from certain religious ideas. Fatalism is, of course, the only logical consequence of predestination. But on account of the idea of proof [Segundo: of predestination], the psychological result was precisely the opposite [Segundo: of fatalism]."[26]

Stressing the psychological relationship between the superstructure and economic attitudes does not mean that Weber is trying to evade the social and political consequences of ideas. On the contrary, psychology enables him to carry out the task that Marx had talked about. In the complex realm of the whole superstructure he is able to infer the "spiritualized forms" which often correspond to economic attitudes.

Psychology, in short, is a decisive feature of any modern ideological analysis of a complex social superstructure.

Now when all is said and done, the reader must not forget that the relationship discovered by Weber between Protestant Calvinism and the spirit of Western capitalism has never been proved by any empirical sociology, much less by statistical studies. Recall Weber's statement of intent: "to ascertain whether and to what extent religious forces have taken part in *the qualitative formation and the quantitative expansion* of that spirit over the world." Well, then, how are we to evaluate the outcome of this twofold intention?

It does not seem probable that the second aspect (the "quantitative" expansion) could ever be proved by a *behaviorist* sociology such as that which prevails at present, nor by any other sociology with objective scientific methods. The part that might have been played by religious forces in the quantitative expansion of the capitalist spirit seems destined to remain a mystery forever. It is hard to explain how Max Weber, in his own day, could have imagined scientific or statistical verification of that sort.

The first aspect (the "qualitative" formation) is not really susceptible of empirical proof either. But if that is true, it is because it basically does not need any such proof. The probative force of Weber's hypothesis lies in a comparison of various concepts. And since it is a qualitative matter, it is hard to see how it could be proved with the quantitative methods of an empirical science. In that sense one can say that Weber's hypothesis is proved, since the conceptual relationship that he establishes by analogy between the two sets of phenomena is clear.

If one wanted to argue with Weber's thesis at all, it would be in connection with the point brought out by Talcott Parsons, the scholar who translated Weber's book into English. He says: "It is the temptation of one who expounds a new and fruitful idea to use it as a key to unlock all doors, and to explain by reference to a single principle phenomena which are, in reality, the result of several converging causes."[27] But it is not our task here to pass judgment on Weber. We are interested only in examining the methodology he uses to move from a general ideology to the specific analysis of theological ideas.

That brings us to the third point of our hermeneutic circle. We must ask ourselves: What is the real experience of Weber himself vis-à-vis the theological reality which he has just discovered, and which he has seen to be linked with all sorts of human vicissitudes and options such as those connected with the course of capitalism? Does he experience that theological life laid hold of in history as a need for judging Calvinism by its fruits? What might its value be in the interpretation of Scripture, once one realizes that this interpretation gives structure to the lives of many human beings in precisely that form?

Strange as it may seem, none of those questions interests Max Weber: "We are here concerned not with the *evaluation,* but the historical significance of the dogma."[28] Even if this particular religious belief were the cause of an atomic war, in other words, Weber would still not be interested in evaluating it. He would simply be interested in considering its historical significance, its bare results. He expresses the same basic intention a bit more precisely elsewhere in the same book: "In such a study, it may at once be definitely stated, no attempt is made to evaluate the ideas of the Reformation in any sense, whether it concerns their *social* or their *religious* worth."[29]

If we can still hear the echo of Marx's passionate voice, we will find it relatively difficult to believe in Weber's impartiality when we read some of his statements. He notes, for example: "The emphasis on the ascetic importance of a fixed calling provided an ethical justification of the modern specialized *division of labor.* In a similar way the providential interpretation of profit-making justified the activities of the businessman."[30] Why? Because "it gave him the comforting assurance that the unequal distribution of the goods of this world was a special dispensation of Divine Providence, which in these differences, as in particular grace, pursued secret ends unknown to men. Calvin himself had made the much-quoted statement that only when the people, i.e. the mass of labourers and craftsmen, were poor did they remain obedient to God."[31]

This description of the ethical attitudes deriving from religious ideas, the unequivocal irony in Weber's tone and the use of certain terms that echo Marx, would seem to suggest a clear-cut partiality, a value judgment, on the author's part. We find the same thing in another similar description: "This consciousness of divine grace of the elect and holy was accompanied by an attitude toward the sin of one's neighbour, not of sympathetic understanding based on consciousness of one's own weakness, but of *hatred* and *contempt* for him as an enemy of God bearing the signs of eternal damnation."[32] To any unprejudiced listener, the attitudes thus described would seem ignoble and inhuman. Yet in Weber's eyes such a description does not constitute a negative judgment on the theological ideas that lend support to those attitudes.

To go even further, Weber is quite capable of "impartially" using descriptive phrases such as "extreme inhumanity." In a central passage of the book, he writes: "In its extreme inhumanity this doctrine must above all have had one consequence for the life of a generation which surrendered to its magnificent consistency. That was a feeling of unprecedented inner loneliness of the single individual. In what was for the man of the age of the Reformation the most important thing in life, his eternal salvation, he was forced to follow his path alone to meet a destiny which had been decreed for him from eternity. No one could help him."[33]

Not even when he uses such qualifying phrases and descriptions as these does Weber admit that he is making a value judgment on Calvinism. And he insists on his impartiality explicitly. One might well wonder whether it is not even more inhuman to perceive and comprehend that whole network of implications without judging it than to have created it in the first place in the belief that it was the only thing that fully and logically dovetailed with the fonts of divine revelation.

At two points Weber does allow himself to challenge the soundness and solidity of Calvin's interpretation of the Bible. But they are only passing observations; they do not represent an evaluational theological commitment. Just before the section cited in the last note, Weber writes this: "The Father in heaven of the New Testament, so human and understanding, who rejoices over the repentance of a sinner as a woman over the lost piece of silver she has found, *is gone.* His place has been taken by a transcendental being, beyond the reach of human understanding."[34] A little later he writes: "It was thus in the last analysis the peculiar, fundamentally ascetic, character of Calvinism itself which made it *select and assimilate those elements of Old Testament religion which suited it best.*"[35]

At first glance such judgments might seem to indicate that Weber is making his first moves from the third to the fourth stage of the hermeneutic circle: in other words, that he is moving towards a new and enriched interpretation of the biblical sources. But that is not the case. Weber is not interested in finding a more authentic and richer theology to liberate people from the anxiety and loneliness which, among other things, are part of the influence of Calvinist theology on their society. For the sake of extending the range of knowledge as far as possible, Weber simply wants to make comparisons between different religious ideas insofar as they exert influence on different economic attitudes. There is no personal commitment involved.

Karl Mannheim, another disciple of Marx, can help to explain this attitude for us. The reader will recall that Mannheim posits an "act of will" on the part of the thinker as a necessary precondition for authentic sociological interpretation. But later on, after he has demonstrated the need for an ideological analysis of all the ideas and molds of a culture, Mannheim seems to forget his point of departure regarding the "act of will." For he concludes with this remark: "That which within a given group is accepted as absolute appears to the outsider conditioned by the group situation and recognized as *partial* . . . This type of knowledge presupposes *a more detached perspective.*"[36] That is precisely the case with Weber.

Right now I think I have made it sufficiently clear to the reader what the last systematic obstacle for any theology committed to human liberation is. It is a certain type of academicism which posits ideological neutrality as the ultimate criterion; which levels down and relativizes all claims to absoluteness and all evaluations of some ideas over others. This is the theological equivalent of another great ideological adversary of liberation: the so-called quest for the *death of ideologies* or their suicide on the altars of scientific and scholarly impartiality.[37]

IV. FOURTH SAMPLE ATTEMPT:
CONE AND BLACK THEOLOGY OF LIBERATION

Let us move on to a fourth example. This time the hermeneutic circle will be completed. Remember that this fact in itself is not a sufficient proof of the truth of the theology in question. The hermeneutic circle itself merely proves that a theology is alive, that it is connected up with the vital fountainhead of historical reality. Without the latter source, the other font of divine revelation would remain dry, not because of anything wrong with it but because of our own opaqueness.

The fourth example is provided by James Cone in his book entitled *A Black Theology of Liberation.* Though the language of the book might seem to be a bit demagogic and shocking—all depending on the color of your skin and your thinking perhaps—Cone's book is a much more serious theological effort than many people might think at first glance. In any case it affords us a chance to see and examine all four points in our hermeneutic circle.

Cone's interpretation begins with personal experience and an act of will on the part of the investigator, as Mannheim posited. Now it is obvious that any "act of will" in the limited range of human possibilities comes down to taking a stand for some individual or community over against other individuals and communities. There is no help for it. Every hermeneutic entails conscious or unconscious partisanship. It is partisan in its viewpoint even when it believes itself to be neutral and tries to act that way.

What is noteworthy and important here is the fact that partiality is not in itself inimical to universality. The possibility of achieving a higher degree of universality through an interpretation of facts does not depend on some sort of impossible *horizontal* partiality, so to speak. It depends on making a good choice insofar as our commitment and our partial point of view is concerned. For the universality in mind here has to do with getting down to the deeper human roots that explain attitudes which are truly universal in their value and influence.

Right from the start of Cone's book, a consciously accepted partiality shows up as a positive and decisive element. For him theology is "a rational study of the being of God in the world in light of the existential situation of an oppressed community, relating the forces of liberation to the essence of the gospel, which is Jesus Christ. This means that *its sole reason for existence* is to put into ordered speech the meaning of God's activity in the world, *so that the community of the oppressed will recognize that their inner thrust for liberation is not only consistent with the gospel but is the gospel of Jesus Christ.*"[38]

Thus Cone, not worrying about causing scandal to academic theology, goes on to establish the usefulness of a particular historical community as the criterion for any subsequent theological investigation: "Black Theology will not spend too much time trying to answer the critics *because it is accountable only to the black community.*"[39] The universality that is renounced on the horizontal level is recovered in spades on a deeper level of the human condition—i.e., where it is revealed to us in an oppressed community that is still in need of liberation. In the process of liberation, the one and only truth is the truth of liberation itself as defined by the oppressed in their struggle: "The revolutionary situation forces Black Theology to shun all abstract principles dealing with what is the 'right' and 'wrong' course of action. There is only one principle which guides the thinking and action of Black Theology: an unqualified commitment to the black community as that community seeks to define its existence in the light of God's liberating work in the world."[40]

Before moving on to the second stage of the hermeneutic circle, a few comments on this point of departure are very much in order. In seminaries and universities we are used to the idea of considering theology as an academic discipline, as a degree program in the liberal arts. The historical fact is that once upon a time theologizing was a very different sort of activity, a dangerous one in fact. It certainly was not a "liberal art" for men like the prophets and Jesus. They died before their time because of their theologizing, because of their specific way of interpreting the word of God and its implications for the liberation of the oppressed.

Perhaps the reader may now understand more readily why only academic theologians can talk about the "death of God." In the concrete struggle for liberation, the danger is not the death of God but the death of the theologian, his interpreter. The theologian may well die in the very name of God, who draws a sharp dividing line between the two opposing positions with regard to liberation.

Faced with these two alternatives (that is, theology as an academic profession versus theology as a revolutionary activity), I must confess that I can understand those who refuse to do theology or to have anything to do with it, because they feel it has no meaning or value for the liberation process, much better than I can understand those who practice it as an academic discipline in the security of some chamber immune to the risks of the liberation struggle. We are fortunate that our God takes a stand in history, and our interpretation of his word must follow the same path. Cone is quite right when he refers to theology as a "passionate language."[41]

Arriving at the second stage in our circle, we must find a theory of some general nature which will enable us to unmask the reality of oppression in general, and specifically its repercussions in theology. For oppression usually does not reveal itself in barefaced fashion; it hides and hallows itself behind ideologies that obscure what is really happening in concrete human reality.

One cannot say that Cone is Marxist in his analysis, for he explicitly diverges from Marx on occasion. For example, he states that the basis of exploitation is not an economic difference which forms different social classes but rather the racial difference which is rooted far more deeply in human psychology. At the same time, however, Cone's divergence here is not as alien to historical materialism as it might seem at first glance. Rather it complements or corrects Marx, pointing up a factor which has been, and continues to be, important in the division of labor. What Mannheim says in a general way might be applied to Cone here. The fact is that many of the elements which Marx used in his ideological analysis of the exploitation of the proletariat have become general features of Western culture—more specifically, of the general methodology of the sociology of knowledge. This means that they can and often are used independently of any Marxist or even Socialist commitment.

Cone is certainly aware of ideological mechanisms and takes them into account in his theologizing. For example, he writes: "This does not mean that Black Theology rejects white theology entirely. Unfortunately, this cannot be done, since oppression always means that the communication skills of an oppressed community are determined to a large degree by the oppressors. That is precisely the meaning of oppression! Since black theologians are trained in white seminaries and white thinkers make decisions about the structure and scope of theology, it is not possible for black religionists to separate themselves *immediately* from white thought."[42]

At the same time, however, Cone does not forget that theology is only *one* of the forms of the total superstructure that go to make up the state. He notes: "Unfortunately, American white theology has not been involved in the struggle for black liberation. It has been basically a theology of the white oppressor, *giving religious sanction* to the genocide of Indians and the enslavement of black people. From the very beginning to the present day, American white theological thought has been 'patriotic,' either by defining the theological task *independently of black suffering* (the liberal northern approach) or by defining Christianity as compatible with white racism (the conservative southern approach). In both cases theology becomes *a servant of the state,* and that can only mean death to black people."[43]

The fine edge of Cone's ideological analysis shows up in the fact that he manages to espy the most potent weapon of the adversary in this ideological conflict. That weapon is an ideology claiming to be *color-blind.* In other words, the oppressor constructs an ideological edifice in which the *cause* of the oppressed people's suffering is not even mentioned, much less studied. In this way law, philosophy, and religion join with the mechanism of oppression and become its witting or unwitting accomplices: "That is why American theology discusses sin in the abstract, debating it in relation to *universal man.* In white theology, sin is *a theoretical idea and not a concrete reality.*"[44] In other words, "there is no place in Black Theology for a colorless God in a society *where people suffer precisely because of their color.*"[45]

Cone therefore calls for a more concrete and realistic sensitivity so that this sort of rationalization will be wiped out in a society where color is a decisive factor: "When blackness is equated with freedom as a symbol both of oppression and of the possibility of man, white people feel left out of things. 'What about the oppression of whites?' they ask. 'Is it not true that the enslaver also enslaves himself, which makes him a member of the community of the oppressed?' There is a danger inherent in these questions. If white intellectuals, religionists, and assorted liberals can convince themselves that the white condition is *analogous* to the black condition, then there is no reason to respond to the demands of the black community. 'After all, we are all oppressed,' they say, *rationalizing* with a single stroke the whole white way of life."[46]

The more a humanism purports to be universal and spiritual, the more danger there is that it will leave concrete liberation aside. Why? Because then the real cause of oppression fades from the mind. As Cone puts it: "White theologians . . . would probably concede that the concept of liberation is essential to the biblical view of God. But it is still impossible for them to translate the biblical emphasis on liberation to the black-white struggle today. Invariably they quibble on this issue, moving from side to side, *always pointing out the dangers of extremism on both sides* . . . They really cannot make a decision, because it has been made already for them. The way in which scholars would analyze God and black people was decided when black slaves were brought to this land, while churchmen sang 'Jesus, Lover of My Soul.' "[47] That final note of ironic spiritualism verifies what we said above: both universality and spirituality are ideological mechanisms of theology.

It should be evident that Cone arrives at the third stage of the hermeneutic circle with a new experience of theology and with an act of will to place it in the service of the Black community. Thus the new direction to be taken by scriptural interpretation will be dictated by the uncovering of the mechanisms of ideology and by the will to root them out of theology.

In doing the latter, the important thing is not so much not to accept the accustomed answers of theology but rather not to shoulder the accustomed questions of theology. As Cone puts it: "It is clear, therefore, that the most important decisions in theology are made at this juncture. The sources and norm are presuppositions that determine *which questions are to be asked,* as well as the answers that are given. Believing that the biblical Christ is the sole criterion for theology, Barth not only asks questions about man that arise from a study of Christology, but he also derives his answers from the man Jesus. Tillich, on the other hand, deals with questions that arise from the cultural situation of man, and endeavors to shape his answers according to that situation. Both approaches are conditioned by their theological perspectives. Because a perspective refers to *the whole of a man's being in the context of a community,* the sources and norm of Black Theology *must be consistent with the perspective of the black community.*"[48] Put another way: "Black theologians must work in such a way as to destroy the corruptive influence of white thought by building theology on the sources and norm that are appropriate to the black community."[49]

If we should ask Cone what he considers "appropriate to the black community," his initial response would be that an oppressed community needs a theology by which to become aware of itself as people "who are in search of new ways of talking about God which will enhance *their understanding of themselves.*"[50] If this particular task is to be properly undertaken by theology (rather than by education or politics, for example), then of course there must be a change in the notion of God and his plans: "It is unthinkable that the oppressors could identify with oppressed existence and thus say something relevant about God's liberation of the oppressed. In order to be Christian theology, white theology must cease being white theology and become Black Theology by denying whiteness as a proper form of human existence and affirming blackness as *God's intention for humanity.*"[51]

From the theological standpoint it is worth noting that Cone, with only one exception, makes these decisive options regarding the pathway that theology is to take before he comes to treat the sources and norm of an authentic theology specifically. At first glance it might seem that theology is being determined by alien criteria. But since theology is part of the superstructure, the ground must be broken by first rooting up the ideological traps. Hence ideological criteria are logically *prior,* but in no way *alien* to theology.

When Cone begins to list the fonts of theology, he begins by listing the experience, the history, and the culture of Black people rather than Scripture. He fully realizes that this will scandalize academic theology, which has a long tradition of proceeding quite differently. But he is not alone in such an approach, and he can cite Tillich in his favor: "I am not unaware of the danger that in this way [the method of relating theology to culture] the substance of the Christian message may be lost. Nevertheless, this danger must be risked, and once one has realized this, one must proceed in this direction. Dangers are not a reason for avoiding a serious demand."[52]

Cone goes on to say: "Though Tillich was not speaking of the black situation, his words are applicable to it. To be sure, as Barth pointed out, God's Word is alien to man and thus comes to him as a 'bolt from the blue,' but one must be careful about which man one is speaking of. For the oppressors, the dehumanizers, the analysis is correct. However, when we speak of God's revelation to the oppressed, the analysis is incorrect. His revelation comes to us in and through the cultural situation of the oppressed. His Word is our word; his existence, our existence."[53]

On the other hand, if Scripture stands as the unique and unbalanced criterion for theology, then one cannot avoid *literalism* and the consequent ideological justification of oppression. As Cone puts it: "Literalism always means the removal of doubt in religion, and thus enables the believer to justify all kinds of political oppression in the name of God and country. During slavery black people were encouraged to be obedient slaves because it was the will of God. After all, Paul did say 'slaves, obey your masters'; and because of the 'curse of Ham,' blacks have been condemned to be inferior to whites. Even today the same kind of literalism is being used by white scholars to encourage black people to be nonviolent, as if nonviolence were the only possible expression of Christian love. It is surprising that it never dawns on these white religionists that oppressors are in no moral position to dictate what a Christian response is. Jesus' exhortations 'turn the other cheek' and 'go the second mile' are no evidence that black people should let white people beat the hell out of them. We cannot use Jesus' behavior in the first century as a literal guide for our actions in the twentieth century . . . Scripture . . . is not a guide which makes our decisions for us."[54]

To avoid the danger signalled by Tillich as well as the danger of literalism, one need only erect his theology on a twofold base or source: "Black people have heard enough about God. What they want to know is what God has to say about the black condition. Or, more importantly, what is he doing about it? What is his relevance in the struggle against the forces of evil which seek to destroy black being? These are the questions which must shape the character of the norm of Black Theology. On the other hand, Black Theology must not overlook the biblical revelation. This means that Black Theology should not devise a norm which ignores the encounter of the black community with the revelation of God. Whatever it says about liberation must be said in the light of the black community's experience of Jesus Christ."[55] In short, "the norm of Black Theology must take seriously two realities, actually two aspects of a single reality: the liberation of black people and the revelation of Jesus Christ."[56]

With this new experience of theological reality, this act of will and its directional impulse, Cone arrives at the fourth stage of the hermeneutic circle: i.e., the new interpretation of Scripture based on new and decisive questions. His hermeneutic orientation might be summed up in these words: "If I read the New Testament correctly, the resurrection of Christ means that he is also present today in the midst of all societies effecting his liberation of the oppressed. He is not confined to the first century, and thus our talk of him in the past is important only insofar as it leads us to an *encounter* with him *now*. As a black theologian, I want to know what God's revelation means right now as the black community participates in the struggle for liberation."[57]

It must be stressed once again that the simultaneous presence of past and present in biblical interpretation is an essential hermeneutic principle. The value of this orientation for achieving a richer interpretation of Scripture lies in the fact that one thereby rediscovers a pedagogical principle that presides over the whole process of divine revelation. The fact is that God shows up in a different light when his people find themselves in different historical situations. That does not simply mean that we must take pains to re-create each specific historical context in the past. For if God continually presents himself in a different light, then the truth about him must be different also. The Israelites moving out of

Egypt and heading for the promised land received the revelation of God's wrath towards their enemies. That particular revelation has little or nothing to do with the image of God which the gospel message conveys when it urges people to "turn the other cheek," or when Paul urges slaves to obey their masters.

When all is said and done, what is one to say about God today to people who are in a situation akin to that of the ancient Israelites? That the latter and later image wipes out the earlier one? Cone gives his answer: "Black Theology then asks not whether love is an essential element of the Christian interpretation of God, but whether the love of God itself can be properly understood without focusing equally on the biblical view of God's righteousness. Is it possible to understand what God's love means for the oppressed without making *wrath* an essential ingredient of that love?"[58] Somewhat further on he says: "The wrath of God is the love of God in regard to the forces against his liberation of the oppressed."[59]

It may well be difficult for us to appreciate the total novelty and freshness of this principle which is introduced into theological interpretation by Cone. For the fact is that from the viewpoint of orthodoxy one of those images of God must necessarily be false at a given moment. Either the old or the new image has to be false at a given point if God is to continue being *universal,* according to the orthodox viewpoint. Cone's logic forces him to reject this search for universality which seems to be the key to the orthodox interpretation of the Bible. He writes: "Some readers will object to the absence of the 'universal note' in the foregoing assertions, asking, 'How can you reconcile the lack of universalism regarding human nature with a universal God?' The first reply is to deny that there is a 'universal God' in the normal understanding of the concept."[60]

What is Cone trying to say here? Unless I am mistaken, he is asserting that orthodoxy possesses no ultimate criterion in itself because being orthodox does not mean possessing the final truth. We only arrive at the latter by orthopraxis. It is the latter that is the ultimate criterion of the former, both in theology and in biblical interpretation. The truth is truth only when it serves as the basis for truly human attitudes. "Doers of the truth" is the formula used by divine revelation to stress the priority of orthopraxis over orthodoxy when it comes to truth and salvation.

Needless to say, there are many hermeneutic dangers in this approach to conceiving and carrying out biblical interpretation, just as there were in the previous stage. But one cannot rule out a particular theological method which is consistent, just because it entails dangers.

Speaking of dangers, for example, one can readily appreciate the fact that the community which Jesus counselled to turn the other cheek could not very well represent the Israelite community that was physically enslaved in Egypt or Babylon. So one should not be too quick to generalize Jesus' advice as if it had been given to humanity for any and all ages, thereby correcting the Old Testament which was also the revelation of God. As it turns out, however, one of the things revealed by God to the exiles in Babylon was the redemptive value of suffering as personified in the Suffering Servant of Yahweh. One might well ask Cone himself why that message to a physically enslaved people is not God's revelation to the Black community of the present day. For Cone claims that it is not: "The black prophet is a rebel with a cause, the cause of over twenty-five million American blacks and all oppressed men everywhere. It is God's cause because he has chosen the blacks as his own. And he has chosen them *not for redemptive suffering but for freedom. Black people are not elected to be Yahweh's suffering people.*"[61]

I certainly hope that they are not so chosen too, even as I cherish the same hope for my country and my continent. But then what about Jesus himself? He, too, was chosen for freedom; and, at the same time, for redemptive suffering. I fully agree with Cone when he says that we cannot accept such decisions about our "election" when they are imposed on us by our oppressors. But if we remain faithful to the Bible, what key enables us to decide which is our real election?[62]

Leaving that issue aside here, I hope that it is quite clear that the Bible is not the discourse of a universal God to a universal man. Partiality is justified because we must find, and designate as the word of God, that *part* of divine revelation which *today,* in the light of our concrete historical situation, is most useful for the liberation to which God summons us. Other passages of that same divine revelation will help us tomorrow to complete and correct our present course towards freedom. God will keep coming back to speak to us from the very same Bible.

Hence I have no intention here of disputing Cone's interpretation of the Scriptures. Sometimes I am in agreement with him, sometimes I am not. Be that as it may, I think that his theological efforts afford us a fine example of the hermeneutic circle.

If we understand and appreciate this circle, then we also will understand and appreciate something that is very important for Latin American theology of liberation. When it is accused of partiality, it can calmly reply that it is partial because it is faithful to Christian tradition rather than to Greek thought. It can also say that those who attack it are even more partisan, though they may not realize it, and tend to muzzle the word of God by trying to make one particular portion of Scripture the word of God not only for certain particular moments and situations but also for all situations and all moments.

NOTES

1. "Interpretation based on faith adds nothing to reality; it simply explicates an element that is overlooked or confused by other interpretations. Thus where there are no signs of mystery in secular life, one would have to say that Christianity and any other religious interpretation would never be anything more than *a superstructure and an ideology*. But that is not the case if one can show that such signs do exist in secular life itself. . . . The only thing that a religious or faith-based interpretation can do is to explicate what is already there in life. . . . The designation 'ideology' cannot be applied to an interpretation which spotlights some aspect of reality itself. For that is simply an explication that gives a name to something that was already there before" (in *La respuesta de los teólogos,* Span. trans., in collaboration with K. Rahner, Congar, Schoonenberg, Metz, and Daniélou, [Buenos Aires: Ed. Carlos Lohlé, 1970], pp. 60–61).

2. Karl Mannheim, *Ideology and Utopia,* Eng. trans. (New York: Harcourt, Brace, Jovanovich, Harvest Book, 1936).

3. Harvey Cox, *The Secular City,* rev. ed. (New York: Macmillan, 1966), p. 60.

4. *Ibid.,* p. 70.

5. *Ibid.,* pp. 68–69.

6. *Ibid.,* p. 95.

7. *Ibid.,* p. 172.

8. *Ibid.,* p. 194. "The Girl symbolizes the values and aspirations of a consumer society" (*ibid.,* p. 171).

9. "This also applies to the realm of theology. The choice of a point of departure is determined and regulated by norms which themselves are based on the theology which should really be the continuation of the first beginning. But in that case there can be no question of a point of departure without prejudice. What is held to be an unprejudiced point of departure turns out to be an 'arbitrary' leap into a certain stream of thought and belief. Sometimes it happens that a person slowly comes to the realization that the stream he has jumped into leads nowhere. Then this experience makes it clear to him that he must get out of this stream; arriving once again at the banks of the stream he must choose a new point of departure and risk another leap . . . Any choice of a point of departure in science, philosophy and theology is an a priori choice of a certain view of the world or life . . . From the very beginning the choice proves that a person has chosen *even before the choice was made*" (W.H. van de Pol, *The End of Conventional Christianity,* Eng. trans. [New York: Newman Press, 1967], p. 191).

10. On the influence of Marxist thought on the creation of a theology of liberation in Latin America, see especially the next two chapters. It must be admitted, however, that there are problems connected with applying the label "Marxist" to a line of thought or a source of influence. First of all, those who identify themselves with Marx and his thinking have a thousand different ways of conceiving and interpreting "Marxist" thought. Aside from that fact, the point is that the great thinkers of history do not replace each other; rather, they complement and enrich each other. Philosophic thought would never be the same after Aristotle as it was before him. In that sense all Westerners who philosophize now are Aristotelians. After Marx, our way of conceiving and posing the problems of society will never be the same again. Whether everything Marx said is accepted or not, and in whatever way one may conceive his "essential" thinking, there can be no doubt that present-day social thought will be "Marxist" to some extent: that is, profoundly indebted to Marx. In that sense Latin American theology is certainly Marxist. I know my remark will be taken out of context, but one cannot go on trying to forestall every partisan or stupid misunderstanding forever.

11. Karl Marx, *Manifesto of the Communist Party,* Eng. trans., Great Books of the Western World 50, (Chicago: Encyclopaedia Britannica, 1952), p. 419.

12. *Ibid.,* pp. 419–20.

13. *Ibid.,* p. 423.

14. *Ibid.,* p. 428.

15. Karl Marx, *A Contribution to the Critique of Political Economy,* Eng. trans. (Chicago: Charles H. Kerr and Co., 1913), pp. 11–12.

16. *Karl Marx: Selected Writings in Sociology and Social Philosophy,* Newly translated and edited by T.B. Bottomore (London: Watts, 1956; New York: McGraw-Hill, 1964), p. 75.

17. *Ibid.,* p. 54.

18. *Ibid.,* pp. 64–65.

19. *Capital I,* in *Selected Writings,* p. 64.

20. *Critique of Hegel's Philosophy of Right,* in *Selected Writings,* p. 26.

21. *Ibid.,* p. 27.

22. The need for a *third* and *fourth* stage in our hermeneutic circle stem from the fact, established at the very start, that we are dealing here with a hermeneutic for *Christian theology.* The fact is that hermeneutics is always necessary vis-à-vis a *tradition,* and in practice it is impossible to have any systematic thought or specific, coherent vision of reality without interpreting that reality. So the first two points of the hermeneutic circle are necessary and adequate to ensure that any tradition whatever may give rise to a richer and more creative line of thought as new situations and problems arise in history. Now tradition is often conveyed in and through specialized methodologies, so that we are led to talk about *theological* tradition, *philosophical* tradition, *sociopolitical* tradition, and so forth. In such specific instances, the one who is tackling the tradition in that concrete form must probe into the *specific* realm involved and concretize his commitment and his overall suspicion there. Only then can there appear a new and richer hermeneutics and subsequently a new and richer reality. Now theol-

ogy, unlike philosophy, does not derive its interpretation of existence from itself but rather from certain written sources. So the hermeneutic circle requires it to propose a new interpretation for those sources if something profound is to change, in line with the basic commitment from which the hermeneutic circle started. One might then ask: Why does the circle have to go specifically through the Bible rather than other existing theological traditions? For that question, see note 55 below.

23. As is well known, from 1890 on Engels had to speak out against a purely "materialistic" or "econometric" version of *historical materialism*. He did so whenever the opportunity arose. This is what he has to say in a letter to Bloch (September 21–22, 1890): "According to the materialistic conception of history, the determining element in history is *ultimately* [Engels' italics too] the production and reproduction in real life. More than this neither Marx nor I have ever asserted. If therefore somebody twists this into the statement that the economic element is the *only* [Engels' italics too] determining one, he transforms it into a meaningless, abstract and absurd phrase. The economic situation is the basis, but the various elements of the superstructure—political forms of the class struggle and its consequences, constitutions established by the victorious class after a successful battle, etc., forms of law, and then even the reflexes of all these actual struggles in the brains of the combatants (political, legal, philosophical theories, *religious ideas and their further development into systems of dogma*)—also exercise their influence upon the course of the historical struggle and *in many cases preponderate in determining their form*" (Marx and Engels, *Selected Correspondence: 1846–1895*, Eng. trans. [New York: International Publishers, 1942], Letter 213, p. 475). See also Engels' letters to K. Schmidt (August 5, and October 27, 1890), and his letter to N.F. Danielson (October 17, 1893).

If one does not accept the "relative independence" of the superstructure, then it becomes difficult to explain many examples gathered by Marx himself and noted in his works. One will find it hard to explain (e.g.) the contrast which Marx points up in *Capital I* between the "unchangeableness of Asiatic societies" and the "never-ceasing changes in dynasty" (Great Books of the Western World 50, *op. cit.*, p. 175). A mechanistic materialism might be able to explain the unchanging societal economy, but it certainly could not explain the countless fluctuations and torments of the superstructure.

24. Max Weber, *The Protestant Ethic and the Spirit of Capitalism*, Eng. trans. (New York: Charles Scribner's Sons, 1958), p. 91.

25. *Ibid.*, p. 97.

26. *Ibid.*, p. 232. This psychological tieup is explored even more fully from a psychoanalytic viewpoint by Erich Fromm in *Escape From Freedom* (New York: Holt, Rinehart, and Winston, 1941), Chapter III.

27. Translator's "Foreword" to *The Protestant Ethic and the Spirit of Capitalism*, *op. cit.*, p. 7.

28. Weber, *The Protestant Ethic*, p. 101.

29. *Ibid.*, p. 90.

30. *Ibid.*, p. 163.

31. *Ibid.*, p. 177.

32. *Ibid.*, p. 122.

33. *Ibid.*, p. 104.

34. *Ibid.*, p. 103.

35. *Ibid.*, p. 123.

36. Mannheim, *Ideology and Utopia,* p. 282.

37. As is well known by now, liberation theology arose as a reaction against the developmentalist theories and models formulated by the United States for Latin America in the decade of the sixties. The developmentalist model was characterized by the fact that it covered over and tried to hide the critical and decisive relationship of dependence versus liberation. Underlying this approach was the vaunted notion that the economic process, without undergoing any substantial modification, could turn the "underdeveloped" countries into modern, prosperous societies once it reached the "takeoff point." From there on it would accelerate cumulatively and come to resemble more and more the process in developed countries. To bolster this ideology, the point was often stressed that this modernization process meant that people would have to accept the "death of ideologies" brought about by a scientific and *neutral* technology common to any and every social model. On this point see Gustavo Gutiérrez, *A Theology of Liberation,* Eng. trans. (Maryknoll, N.Y.: Orbis Books, 1973), Chapter II.

38. James H. Cone, *A Black Theology of Liberation* (Philadelphia: Lippincott, 1970), p. 17.

39. *Ibid.*, p. 33.

40. *Ibid.*

41. *Ibid.*, p. 45.

42. *Ibid.*, p. 117.

43. *Ibid.*, p. 22.

44. *Ibid.*, p. 191.

45. *Ibid.*, p. 120.

46. *Ibid.*, p. 184.

47. *Ibid.*, pp. 122–23.

48. *Ibid.*, pp. 52–53.

49. *Ibid.*, p. 53.

50. *Ibid.*, p. 40.

51. *Ibid.*, pp. 32–33.

52. *Ibid.*, p. 62.

53. *Ibid.*

54. *Ibid.*, p. 68.

55. *Ibid.*, p. 77. In the interdenominational faculties of the United States, and particularly among certain Protestant denominations, I have found that this last stage of the hermeneutic circle, which is hardly ever debated by Latin American theologians, is often questioned. Americans question the necessity of returning to the sources or fonts of *Christian* revelation. They pose such questions as: Why not construct another religious theory closer to our own problems? Or why not have recourse to other "revelations" such as that of Buddhism, for example? Since we find a strong *ideological* influence exerted on and by the Christian tradition, why need we return hermeneutically to its source? Why should we

imagine that God has only revealed himself in the Judeo-Christian tradition?
Cone, for example, cannot ignore the fact that many Blacks in the United States
chose to move on to the Muslim tradition after making the hermeneutic turn
that he himself made. They chose that course over the possibility of returning
with new questions to a source which they felt to be irremediably lost for Black
people. The women's liberation movement has reached a similar conclusion,
deciding to rule out any return to a "revelation" that is totally dominated by the
male element. Now it is certainly true that one need not inevitably move from the
third stage of the hermeneutic circle to the fourth stage we present here. One
can certainly move on to a new theology or a different tradition of "revelation."
What seems odd to me is that any such new theology would continue to call itself
"Christian," as they often do. The designation seems to make sense in such a case
only as an indication of the point of departure. This point will be treated in the
course of the following chapters.

56. *Ibid.*, pp. 79–80.
57. *Ibid.*, p. 64; Cone's italics too.
58. *Ibid.*, p. 130; Cone's italics too.
59. *Ibid.*, p. 133.
60. *Ibid.*, p. 156.
61. *Ibid.*, p. 108.
62. On this point see Chapter IV.

CHAPTER TWO

In Search of Sociology

My long and wordy explication of the avatars of the hermeneutic circle in theology may have discouraged many readers. If the pathway of theology is so technical and tortuous, readers might well feel that it is not worth trying to plod over its trackless wastes.

Perhaps one of the intentions of this chapter, here at the beginning anyway, is to dispel any such feelings. Despite its curious terminology and its scientific apparatus, the previous chapter was trying to describe the return of theology from the rarefied atmosphere of academia to the world of common sense. Needless to say, however, the "common sense" in question here has little or nothing to do with the prepackaged "common sense" that is handed out to us over the communications media or in the commonplaces of an oppressive, consumer society.

Complicated as the last chapter may have seemed to the reader, I hope it did make a few points clear:

1. That a theology worthy of the attention of a whole human being is not the outcome of abstract scientific or academic interest. It stems from a pretheological human commitment to change and improve the world.

2. That we must understand and appreciate the ideological mechanisms of established society if theology is to take the word of God and convert it from a vague outline to a clearly worked out message. Otherwise theology will become and remain the unwitting spokesman of the experiences and ideas of the ruling factions and classes.

3. That without a keen sensitivity and a determination to turn theology into a serviceable tool for orthopraxis, for a social praxis that is liberative, a false and quasi-magical concept of orthodoxy will dissolve theology into universal, ahistorical concepts.

4. That we must salvage the sovereign liberty of the word of God if we are to be able to say something that is really creative and liberative in any given situation.

And perhaps one more thing has been brought out clearly to the reader, something that is of the utmost importance. It is the fact that the one and only thing that can maintain the liberative character of any theology is not its content but its methodology. It is the latter that guarantees the continuing bite of theology, whatever terminology may be used and however much the existing system tries to reabsorb it into itself. It is the methodology that ensures that the existing system will continue to look like an oppressor on the horizon of theology itself; that offers the best hope for the future of theology.

I. THE IDEOLOGICAL INFILTRATION OF DOGMA

As I noted, the seemingly abstract and overly scientific cast of my discussion of theology and the hermeneutic circle in the last chapter may have caused difficulty to the reader. Perhaps it would be wise to take a couple of practical examples a little closer to home, using them to demonstrate how the average intelligent Christian, who is aware of the need for liberation, has already covered at least half of the hermeneutic circle on his own.

We must not underestimate Christian common sense as it has been applied to certain ambiguous things in the Church,[1]—to the *sacraments,* for example. It is quite obvious to most people that Masses, baptisms, and weddings—in short, the basic parish activities—consume most of the time, money, energy, and personnel of the Catholic Church. Now in the last chapter we came to see that a liberative theology must of necessity be an historical theology grounded on the questions that well up from the present. It cannot simply drag out metaphysical or universal questions that have been handed down from generation to generation by long tradition. Thus simple logic tells us that only a Christian community that is keenly sensitive to history can provide the basis for such a liberative theology. Attention to the signs of the time is the theological criterion which sets off a theology of liberation from a conservative, academic theology.

But the fact is that the concept of "sacrament" which filters through the concrete praxis of the Church is the image (or better, the idol) of an *ahistorical* sacred efficacy. Everyone is perfectly aware that in most ordinary cases Sunday Mass is the only bond relating the average Christian to God. This Mass is characterized by unvarying liturgical elements, pre-established readings, an unchanging Eucharistic service, and the eternal return of the same feasts on the yearly liturgical calendar. In short, it constitutes the polar opposite of a religion based on historical sensitivity. Except in minor details, the Sunday Mass remains the same before and after a general disaster, an international crisis, and a thoroughgoing revolution.

What does that mean? To the majority of Christians it undoubtedly means that God is more interested in nontemporal things than in solutions for the historical problems that are cropping up. And it is too much to ask the average Christian, who is subjected to such strong theoretical and practical pressure, to detach his scale of values from what seems to be the religious realm *par excellence* in order to associate it with another type of activity in the name of Christianity itself.

This situation is heightened by the desperate pleas of the Church for unity—for *sacramental* unity of course. However, the average Christian is well aware that the people gathered to receive a given sacrament share nothing with each other except their need to receive it. Wherein lies the decisive importance of receiving that sacrament, then, if those people will continue to be divided on the most important decisions of their lives? The only logical response is that the decisive importance lies in the vertical and ahistorical—but absolute—importance of the sacrament itself. Needless to say, these remarks about the sacraments could easily be applied to many equally ahistorical features in the Catholic Church and in other Christian denominations: cultic worship, conversion, eschatology, and so forth. Despite theological disagreements about the nature and essence of the sacraments themselves, the use of the sacraments in many Christian churches represents a substitute for the security that should come from our committed efforts to transform and liberate history.

Is it by chance, then, that this conception and practice of the sacraments dovetails perfectly with the interests of the ruling classes and is one of the most powerful ideological factors in maintaining the status quo? Would it be too much to admit the fact that sacramental *theology* has been influenced more by unconscious social pressures than by the gospel message itself?

Irreverent and improbable as the hypothesis may seem, we must realize that at some point in theological tradition an alien element must have been injected into it. Why? Because the Christian sources do not present us with any concept of a religious efficacy that is vertical and ahistorical. In the Letter to the Hebrews, for example, we read: "He thus annuls the former to establish the latter. And it is by the will of God that we have been consecrated, through the offering of the body of Jesus Christ *once and for all*. . . .For by one offering he has perfected *for all time* those who are thus consecrated" (Heb. 10:9–10, 14).

If someone were to read those lines without knowing the later history of the Church, could he possibly think that the Church would now have religious ceremonies so that human beings might obtain the divine grace they need? Is it not only too clear that if the Christian community is still getting together every week, it certainly is not to fulfill the function that was performed once and for all by Jesus Christ? From the pages of the New Testament itself it is clear that religious efficacy is ruled out for any and every ritual or cultic assembly precisely insofar as the latter is based on the assumption that the grace of God was not given once and for all but must be won over and over again in and through such rites.

Ruling out any attempt to take gradual possession of divine grace, Christ freed his Church once and for all so that it could devote itself to its commitment and function in history. But when we note that the overall panorama of the Church presents us with a very different picture, we suddenly realize that someone must hit us over the head with strange-sounding hypotheses so that we may be able to read and interpret even the most clear-cut passages of the Gospels and the New Testament. We must be told that at a certain moment in history the Church stopped listening to the voice of Christ and began to listen to the voice of the ruling classes and their selfish interests. We need these seemingly harmful hypotheses to wake us from our ideological slumber.

It should be obvious to the reader that we have just completed a hermeneutic circle with these remarks on the sacraments. It is a relatively simple thing to do when one is operating out of a commitment to liberation, for one readily suspects that commonly held notions are not as neutral as they are made out to be. Of course the last stage, the new interpretation of Scripture, can call for more than average knowledge of the Scriptures. And one might well debate whether the average Christian should or should not put more effort and energy into learning about the fonts of his faith than into activities that are laden with ideology. Be that as it may, a Church composed of Christians sensitive to reality and Christians more fully acquainted with the sources can and should join together to carry out the task more fully described in the final chapter of this book.

A second example may help us to appreciate this critical task a little more fully. This one has to do with the question of *unity,* to which I have already alluded. The unity in question here is that within a given Christian church on the one hand, and that among all Christian churches on the other. In the latter case we talk about ecumenism.

As Cone made clear in his book, the internal unity of a Christian church can be attained or maintained today only by minimizing and playing down the radical historical oppositions that divide its members. In other words, one must pass over in silence such matters as color, social class, political ideology, the national situation, and the place of the country in the international market. At the same time one must stress the values that are presumably shared by all the members of the Church in question. In short, the Church must pay a high price for unity. It must say that the issues of suffering, violence, injustice, famine, and death are less critical and decisive than religious formulas and rites.

At this point someone might complain, with some reason, that I am erring by going to the opposite extreme; that I am wrong in placing only *religious rites and formulas* over against things that are historically decisive. After all, one might object, don't the shared features go beyond mere formulas and rites? Don't they include a deep faith and general conceptions about God and the importance of eternal life?

If I do not place these latter issues in the balance scale, it is precisely because they are *not* shared in common. Faith in God, for example, is not something shared in common by all. One person pictures a God who allows dehumanization whereas another person rejects such a God and believes only in a God who unceasingly fights against such things. Now those two gods cannot be the same one. So a common faith does not exist within the Church. The only thing shared in common is the formula used to express that faith. And since the formula does not really identify anything, are we not justified in calling it a *hollow* formula vis-à-vis the decisive options of history?

It would seem that the Church cannot arrogate to itself the divine right of choosing between the oppressors and the oppressed precisely because of this overvaluation of Christian unity. For example, on numerous occasions the bishops of Chile have denounced the inhuman consequences of capitalism for the vast majority of Chileans. But when a conflict arose between the capitalist system and a socialist system, they came out and said that the Church could not choose.[2] Why? Because the Church, according to them, belongs to all the people of Chile; to choose one specific option in the name of justice, human rights, or the liberative plan of God, would have excluded some portion of the people from the Church—and therefore from the best opportunities for salvation.

But of course not choosing at certain critical junctures in history is really choosing anyway. If a person or group refuses to choose because they have *higher* values to defend, then they are downgrading the values that are at stake in a given specific situation. They are saying that the latter values are dangerous, inferior, or at the very least secondary. Whether they realize it or not, whether they want to or not, they are thereby helping to perpetuate the existing situation.

Unfortunately this very approach has often been used in efforts to promote unity between different Christian churches. Ecumenism is exalted at the expense of human values. Richard Hofstadter has this pertinent observation on the Catholics of the United States: "It seems a melancholy irony that a union which the common bonds of Christian fraternity could not achieve has been forged by the ecumenism of

hatred . . . After more than a century of persecution, it must feel luxuri-
ous for Catholics to find their Americanism at last unquestioned, and to
be able to join with their former persecutors in common pursuit of a new
international, conspiratorial, un-American enemy with a basically
foreign allegiance—this time not in Rome but in Moscow."[3]

The Church responds to such criticisms, of course, alluding to fundamental biblical principles. It points to the "service of reconciliation"
that Christians are supposed to perform, according to Paul (2 Cor. 5:18
ff.); it also points to the universal reconciliation that is supposed to come
about from Christ's work (Col. 1:20). But in the very process of alluding
to these things it forgets that the final eschatological reconciliation mentioned in those very texts is supposed to come to pass in and through the
liberation of human beings; that it is not the result of any pious blindness
towards existing oppression today and the means to combat it. And one
of those means, if not the principal one, is to separate those suffering
oppression from those who are its fomentors or accomplices. If such is
not the case, then one might ask when did Christ reconcile himself with
the Pharisees, or when did Paul reconcile himself with the Judaizers?

The real problem of Christian unity, in my opinion, comes down to
this: When will we manage to break that conservative, oppressive, undif-
ferentiated unity of Christians in order to establish an open dialogue
with all those, be they Christians or not, who are committed to the
historical liberation that should serve as the basis for the "service of
reconciliation" in and through real justice?[4]

Once again, we have made a tiny hermeneutic circle by starting out
from common Christian attitudes that are not highly speculative. And it
has enabled us to unmask an ideological interpretation of Scripture.

A third and final example is offered us by the notion of *God* which
underpins the Church's exaggerated valuation of the sacraments and
church unity. If the value of the latter things derives from God, what
kind of God are we dealing with? He certainly seems to have a strange
conception of human attitudes, and he seems to value them all the more
highly when they are separated from any historical commitment.

Before going deeply into this question, we would do well to begin by
mistrusting the classical formulation of theology. To the extent that
academic theology accepts our question at all, it formulates it in the
terms we first used at the start of the previous paragraph. It asks: What
notion or *concept* of God underpins those ecclesial attitudes? But it does
not go on to our second formulation of the question: *What kind of God* lies
behind such attitudes?

Classical theology would say that the second formulation is poetic
and evocative, but certainly not scientific or in line with the industrial

and technological mentality of the Western world today. If we wanted it to stand literally, then we would have to go back to the bygone ages of *polytheism* and idolatry. In that rejection of our question we might well perceive a note of unconscious alarm, and with good reason.

When all is said and done, can we really say that polytheism and idolatry have been uprooted from Western culture? Is that true in strictly scientific terms? Was the victory over polytheism in the West anything more than a linguistic victory? We do not mention or allude to different gods by different names any more. Instead we simply use the one word "God" to refer to any and every type of religious experience, even to experiences that are quite contrary to one another.

Let me put that in more practical and down-to-earth terms. For centuries human beings struggled with the anxiety of not knowing whether their religious rites and prayers and practices were being addressed to a good god, a malevolent god, or to nothing at all. These doubts and anxieties faded quickly, perhaps too quickly, when Christianity began to exert a strong influence on cultural patterns. "God" became the one and only sacred name, and there was no longer any need to add other titles to the messages addressed to him. The name "God" was enough to avoid all confusion in our mailings to heaven.

Sociologically speaking, we can easily see that the solution was just a little bit too simple. If different and even opposing religious experiences make use of the same word, the only sensible conclusion is that people are using the same word to allude to different things or even different beings. Using the same name does not mean that one is talking about the same person, especially when the descriptions contain very different traits.

I think that Barth would be in agreement on this crucial question for theology. With his profound concern to rely solely and exclusively on divine revelation and to rule out divine constructs fashioned by human thought, his general approach is akin to our approach here. In any case it is clear that he was more sensitive to the dangers of idolatry stemming from philosophy than to the dangers stemming from the ideologies that are inevitably bound up with the socio-political struggle.

Vatican II moves in the same direction when it says: "Believers can have more than a little to do with the birth of atheism. To the extent that they neglect their own training in the faith, or teach erroneous doctrine, or are deficient in their religious, moral, or social life, they must be said to conceal rather than reveal the authentic face of God and religion."[5] Unless I am mistaken, two conclusions can be drawn from that statement. Firstly, the only logical explanation for certain moral or social attitudes is a false concept of God: i.e., faith in a false, nonexistent god.

The conciliar document is suggesting that atheism stems in part from a logical rejection of the false, nonexistent god that underlies and justifies those attitudes. Secondly, when believers hide the authentic face of God and religion and when they teach false doctrines about him, they are actually believing in a false god, a nonexistent god. How else could believers hide what they clearly possess?

Now if we accept these two conclusions, and I think we must, we can proceed with our investigation and ask why classical theology presents God as immutable, impassible, eternally self-sufficient and self-satisfied with his own perfection—to the point where the fate of human beings for good or ill cannot alter this eternal, self-sufficient existence.

The first and all too facile response is to allude to the influence of Greek thought on Judeo-Christian thought. There is no doubt that the picture of God in the Bible is a very different one, presenting us with a passionate God who suffers along with his people, who empties himself to assume our human condition and accept even death, and who is overjoyed at the repentance of a single sinner.

But it is not enough to attribute the classic image of God to the influence of Greek philosophy. That does not explain the phenomenon, for one would assume that the biblical image would have rooted out the other image once the fact had been brought to light. Yet even now, when Greek philosophy is a museum piece, that old notion of God continues to dominate not only certain strains of popular thought but also scholarly theological tracts.

Thus there is good reason to assume that there is another explanation somewhere, and there is no absence of significant data to back up that assumption. First of all, the innermost tendencies and desires of man tend to crystallize almost of themselves around God. At the same time man is not an isolated being outside of time. He is a social being in time. So the social and historical tendencies through which he is living also tend to crystallize in his concept or idea of God. In short, man fashions God out of the materials which go to make up his own experienced or imagined socio-historical triumph. His human victories are projected onto God.

Now in the societies that we inhabit, economic and social competition is a precondition for survival and hence for victory. How are we to picture this triumph except as impassibility and self-satisfaction, given the fact that my victory is based on the suffering of another? Moreover, the satisfaction must find its unquenchable source in myself and not be at the mercy of or under the influence of anyone else. In other words, my perfection must be safe and secure from the vicissitudes caused by others outside of myself. Gradually and systematically my ideal is transformed into an imagined state, the latter into a concept, and then the latter begins to undermine the data of revelation even in the work of theology itself.

When the work of generations was completed, Christianity found itself with two gods. One was the authentic god of revelation, the other was a nonexistent god which gave rise to atheism and was erroneously attributed to the impact of Greek philosophy. Can we honestly attribute the erection of this idol in the popular mind to a philosophy which only a few learned people really know, rather than to a powerful social tendency that has been pinpointed in all existing societies?

Having reached this point, I think we would do well to ponder two things. The first is that formal orthodoxy is not a sufficient guarantee against idolatry. One can recite all the creeds of theological history and still believe in an idol. And that fact should not surprise us. Jesus himself accused the most monotheistic people in history of idolatry, as did Paul. The "adulterous generation" to which Jesus refers bitterly is the biblical image of an idolatrous people, a people who leave their true spouse and go out to worship false gods. It is worth noting that Jesus directs this accusation against a group that demands a sign from heaven (Matt. 16:1–4). They fail to realize that the real-life liberation being effected by Jesus is a sufficient sign of God. Here we have a religious attitude which, without departing from orthodoxy, can only be viewed as idolatry as far as Jesus is concerned; in his eyes it is the worship of a nonexistent god.

The second point, and this leads us into the next section, is that the hermeneutic circle which we have just completed here summons us to a task in which we cannot prescind from sociology, that is, to a study of the human attitudes that are bound up with social structures. It is true of the third stage of our circle as it is of the preceding stages.

II. THE RETREAT OF SOCIOLOGY

From the preceding chapter it should be clear that a liberation methodology, such as that proper to a completed hermeneutic circle, presupposes that for certain reasons of convenience the mechanisms of social reality normally remain hidden from human awareness even though they are operative and determinative. And among those mechanisms we naturally find those which, gradually and unbeknownst to us, go on shaping our theology so as to uproot it from its base in divine revelation and place it in the service of social interests.

If that is not evident from what was said in Chapter I, it should be clear from the examples we discussed in the previous section. At the same time, however, the simple and obvious nature of the examples might have led some people to the erroneous conclusion that one does not need any special training in sociology in order to perceive such facts and find a probable explanation. That conclusion might be reinforced by the fact that a certain veneer of sociology is now part and parcel of our culture and our educational process. But it would be wrong to assume that it is easy to formulate such working hypotheses concerning theology and then to go about the task of verifying their validity or falseness, thereby eventually creating or inventing theological hypotheses that will significantly contribute to a liberative change in society.

It is with good reason that various interdisciplinary attempts have been made in Latin America to link up theology with sociology, but the results have been of varying merit. And in general it must be said that some of the most common features of sociological work pose serious problems to any such collaborative effort, however logical and important the effort itself might seem. The sociology that prevails in Latin America, and probably in the whole realm of intellectual effort, is what is called positivist or behaviorist sociology. In a word, it is *United States* sociology.

Here we would do well to follow the general lines of a presentation offered by an Argentinian sociologist named Eliseo Verón. Taking Marx's *The German Ideology* as the backdrop for his discussion, and as the foundation stone of modern sociology, he goes on to describe how present-day sociology is retreating from realms of human social life that are of increasing importance and simply refusing to deal with them. For our purposes here the important point is that they are the very realms which are most important in any collaborative effort between sociology and theology, if that effort is to be meaningful in its range and scope.

Verón describes seven shifts in emphasis that indicate that present-day sociology has retreated from the ground that Marx had claimed in his *The German Ideology*. We shall consider them here.[6]

1. *Shift from a broad field of facts to fragmented specialties.* The plethora of detail and the lack of meaningful content in many present-day sociological works is too well-known to require any special comment. But as Verón points out, the very fact that sociology has been divided up into specialized fields within the context of an overall culture constitutes a rejection of earlier sociological tradition; for that tradition claimed and sought to study society as a whole. It is easy enough to see that the possibility of making an ideological analysis of a given culture disappears once that culture is neatly divided up into distinct and separate fields. As Verón puts it: "The sociology of law, the sociology of art, and the sociology of religion are specialized disciplines in which the notion of ideology, linked up with an overall model of culture, is not utilized systematically."

What happens to theology as such, especially insofar as it seeks to be liberative by making an ideological analysis of its own content? In such a state of affairs it can only feel that its main problems have been left out of account. For it is not interested in the least in a sociology of religion. It is interested in a comprehensive sociology where religion plays an ideological role and is analyzed from that standpoint. Overly specialized sociology leaves theology in the lurch, forced to formulate its own hypotheses in a field that is not its own.

Thus one loses sight of many fruitful problems that are important not only for theology but also for liberation. A nonsociologist, Richard Hofstadter, makes the following pointed observation: "One reason why the political intelligence of our time is so incredulous and uncomprehending in the presence of the right-wing mind is that it does not reckon fully with the *essentially theological concern* that underlies right-wing views of the world."[7] If that is true, and Hofstadter makes out a good case that it is, then a sociology that dissociates the political realm from the theological realm will never be able to offer us guidance in the attempt to elucidate such problems.

In this connection it ought to be pointed out that it is extremely hazardous to let some religious sociology determine the "results" of a given pastoral approach. But that is precisely what is happening. In general one can say that the pastors of the Church are constantly searching for better, more effective pastoral approaches and tools. But how are they to be evaluated? How are we to analyze the results? Usually it is done by purely quantitative means that are provided by some sort of religious sociology. Restricted to its own field, this sociology knows how many people go to Mass, but it cannot know how this Mass attendance is translated into political attitudes and other things of that sort. That is why pastoral activity often seems to be a desperate search for goals of which it really has no clear picture.

2. *Shift from theoretical abstraction to everyday happenings.* In this instance Verón is referring to the growing refusal of contemporary sociology to tackle problems regarding values that could give meaning to the whole life of humankind. In day-to-day life the average human being can have a host of opinions about countless things and yet lead a meaningless life. Yet the only truly common field where sociology and serious theology might meet in collaboration would be precisely this neglected field of values that give meaning to life.

Verón writes: "Those investigating ideologies seem to have descended from the heights of metaphysics and philosophical abstraction to the familiar ground of humdrum everyday life. They have moved from the study of works that have something significant to say about the ideas or culture of a given historical epoch to the opinions of the average person about things existing in their immediate context." This new type of sociology might pay lip service to sociologists like Weber, Veblen, and C. Wright Mills, but it refuses to discuss theories as complex as the ones treated by those figures. In particular it refuses to discuss the relationship between certain religious beliefs on the one hand and the formation of a political consensus on the other. Max Weber, for example, had to deal with highly abstract theological works such as those of Luther and Calvin on such issues as grace, divine wisdom, and predestination. For that very reason no one today feels competent to decide whether he did it successfully or not. If we could reach some sort of certainty on that point, or if we could have done that some fifty years ago, theology might have been able to engage in a great venture. It could have tried to determine what sort of dogmas would serve as the proper vehicle for a social consensus supportive of socialism and then decide whether or not those dogmas were more in accordance with the fonts of Christian revelation. It thus might have been able to alter the human—or inhuman—face of many existing socialisms today. Such a venture would at least have enriched politics and theology far more than the commonplaces that are now mouthed by theology about socialism and by socialism about theology.

Unfortunately present-day sociology studies Weber as one might study Plato—as a classic figure who must be read if one is to be regarded as a scholar in his field. But no one has the slightest idea how we might prove or disprove his type of theory, though we all can readily find out what the ordinary person thinks about the Watergate affair or the Arab-Israeli situation. The problems that would be most relevant for a liberation-oriented theology are left unanswered. Indeed they are not even treated in any systematic way because they are regarded as unscientific problems.

3. *Shift from global ideas to specific opinions.* Comparing this particular shift with the two previous ones, we can easily see what is involved here. As opposed to the first point mentioned above, the fragmentation alluded to here is not the division of sociology into different fields (philosophy, art, religion, and so forth). It is the division of sociology into a host of different facts and events that lack broad referential scope. As opposed to the second point mentioned above, sociology now treats opinions that are not systematically related whereas the early sociologists treated ideas and opinions as "*systems* comprising a general interpretation of social reality," whatever the degree of abstraction that might have been involved.

Today, for example, no social system—be it capitalist or socialist

—can reasonably function without deciding scientifically what degree of liberty and democracy really exists within the system. Even such pragmatic considerations as the nature and role of economic incentives depend upon some sort of scientific answer being given to that issue. But to find an answer to that question, it is not enough to go around sampling people's individual opinions on the issue. It is not enough, in other words, to go around asking individuals whether they feel free to think, to work, to exercise political influence, to change jobs, and so forth.

If we gather those individual opinions and run them through the computer, we can come up with a portrait of the average citizen that is absolutely false. In a given situation, for example, the average citizen does not realize that the opportunity to choose between two political parties that are essentially alike has nothing to do with the possibility of exercising decisive political influence and really choosing the political system under which one wants to live. In such a situation the citizen can vote from now till doomsday and yet never get the system he wants. The possibility of effective political expression depends more and more on being a master manipulator of the mass media or a major shareholder in companies that can exert political muscle. Otherwise freedom of expression comes down to being able to talk to one's wife or husband and children. Freedom to work seems evident to many people until they realize that economic factors determine salaries, raises, work hours, the number of workers, the required qualifications, and perhaps even the political affiliation of the worker. And the same holds true in every other area of liberty or democracy.

Now if specific opinions in these areas are not to be trusted, what are we to say about specific, individual *religious* opinions? Clearly the same thing holds true. They will not help us very much to find out the exact place held by religion and theological beliefs in the overall functioning of the social system.

To take the United States as an example, here is a statement by former president Eisenhower during his 1952 campaign: "Our government makes no sense, unless it is founded in *a deeply felt religious faith*—and *I don't care what it is.*"[8] What are we confronted with here? Is it an indication of a profound religious influence on the total structure of United States society or rather an unwitting indication of an even more profound atheism? If we recall what was said above about the intimate relationship between certain religious forms and idolatry—the latter often giving rise to atheism if it is not atheism itself—then I think we would not be surprised to find that the latter alternative is the correct answer. But the fact that we can easily enough come to that conclusion does not mean that we have a sociology capable of pointing up the fact in a scientific manner. We might well suspect that the inscription on the dollar bill, "In God we trust," is an expression or source of atheism when we have taken due account of the overall ideological context. But such an affirmation would be regarded as a purely political stance, since sociology as a science *in principle* is supposed to take away our doubts without adopting any political stance.

It should be evident enough that we Latin Americans have plenty of examples of our own to show that theology can use the help of sociology. For example, there is the intriguing fact that religious symbols are systematically used to underpin anti-Christian values whereas atheistic symbols are used to propagate Christian values. Sociology could help us to explain that fact, but it would have to abandon its concentration on specific opinions and get back to global ideologies.

4. *Shift from cognitive categories to evaluative dimensions.* Verón points out that in *The German Ideology* Marx laid down the general lines for a "sociology of knowledge," i.e., for a scientific study of the social mechanisms that govern the formation of ideas and concepts. In present-day empirical sociology, on the other hand, "refinement of technique has been accompanied by a change in the focus of interest; most of the tools measure adhesion, degree of acceptance or rejection."

Now even in the most developed country, the ascertainment of acceptance or adhesion leads to very dangerous conclusions. To take just one example, here is what the Catholic bishops of the Philippines had to say in a pastoral letter dated July 4, 1973. The statement is a typical one, by the way. "The religious fervor of the Philippine people is a rich treasure. *Even though the underlying motivations are not always clear,* (religious) practice suggests that our people are open to God."[9] Now why do I say that jumping to such a conclusion is dangerous? Because there is no serious sociological relationship between being open to God and any line of practice, be it religious or not, when one does not know the underlying motivations. And also because that conclusion, however unfounded, will be decisive in judging the function of the Church in a given country.

The absence of the alleged sociological relationship is explained very well by a nonsociologist, Erich Fromm. He writes: "It is important to consider how our culture fosters this tendency to conform . . . Education too often results in the elimination of spontaneity and in the substitution of original psychic acts by superimposed feelings, thoughts, and wishes." Later he adds: "What education may not have accomplished is usually done by social pressure in later life." And he concludes with a comment that might well be pondered by the Philippine bishops and others who take the same tack: "Who am I? What proof have I for my own identity other than the continuation of my physical self? . . . I have no identity, there is no self excepting the one which is the reflex of what others expect me to be: I am 'as you desire me.' "[10]

If that is the case, and it clearly is in most instances, neither theology nor pastoral work will be helped greatly by a mere description or quantification of those imposed religious feelings and sentiments. What is needed is a sociology that would get below societal impositions and find out that which spontaneously relates the individual in any society to Christianity. But that is precisely what sociology does not explore, because it is interested in measuring degrees of religious acceptance whatever the source may be.

A more profound sociology would be deeply interested in ascertaining and verifying the existence of imposed feelings, thoughts, and desires in the area of religion and in every other area of culture. For that would be essential if it were to study a subject of the utmost importance to theology: i.e., the religious mechanisms that help to impose cultural traits on the one hand, and the possible deformation of religion resulting from cultural adaptation on the other hand.

Here we have one of the big gaps in the "death of God" theology. It is based on "evaluative dimensions" that fail to reveal the social mechanisms that adapt people to the prevailing social system. And Latin America is far from immune to the dangers of such an approach. It tends to consider the problem of secularization, one of its most serious and important theological problems, on the narrow basis of religious adhesion and the means used to attain it among the indifferent or Christian masses.

5. *Shift from "systems of ideas" to isolated opinions.* At first glance Verón's point here might seem to be identical to his third point above, the one in which he talks about a shift from "global ideas" to "specific opinions." But here he seems to be alluding to the dynamic character of early sociology, which enabled it to "analyze the intrinsic properties of idea systems: their coherence, their way of deriving some ideas from others, and so forth." There are "many efforts" in that direction in present-day sociology but the "laws of organization" that derive from those efforts tend to have features which shy away from ideological investigation in any real sense.

It is important to realize that any and every ideology is some sort of internal contradiction. It is a misrepresented reality, a justification that claims not to be such. In his *Affluent Society,* for example, John Galbraith describes what has taken place in the United States over a period of time. Up to a certain point in time it was a society professing and practicing economic liberalism. Gradually, however, it came to accept and even

demand economic measures that were logically inconsistent with liberal
economics. Thus its ideological dynamics revealed an inner contradiction. Like it or not, it had to reconcile respect for the virtues of the liberal
past (free competition, survival of the fittest, and so forth) with the more
up-to-date demands for social security and a more equalitarian
economic policy. The equilibrium of United States society depends on,
and has been forged by, this ideology. Yet the latter can be detected and
studied only by procedures which are not employed for the most part
today.

If we move from this "secular" example to theology, and in particular
to theology as it is translated into pastoral action, we find a similar
contradiction at work in the heart of every pastoral approach. On the
one hand Christianity shows up as the most sublime, difficult, and heroic
life-style possible; on the other hand it shows up as the life-style that God
has determined for the mass of human beings in order to save them. We
have a whole system of Christian praxis based on the first conception,
with its own institutions, practices, demands, and theologies. And alongside that we have another comprehensive system of Christian praxis
which makes no mention of those difficulties or ideals but rather lays
down a minimum code designed to keep as many people as possible
within the system. Needless to say, the latter system also has its own
institutions, practices, and theologies.

Take Christ's commandment that we should love others, even going
so far as to give up our lives for those we love and to show love for our
enemies. What does that mean? In the context of the second system just
described, this commandment is more or less a rarefied ideal which
people might practice a couple of times in their lives and which might
possibly forestall physical aggression at some point. But the average
Christian need not be too concerned about it, since it will never be
concretely enforced as an ecclesiastical or social law. What is more, trying
to turn this ideal into a societal law in this world would be tantamount to
putting "a positive premium on being bad," as Freud so sensibly pointed
out.[11]

In the context of the first system just described, however, this commandment of Christ is such an essential element of Christianity that one
cannot even claim to be a Christian unless he is giving his life for others
and broadening the range of his love beyond the narrow circle of those
who are almost automatically loved and who pay back this love in kind.
Moreover, one cannot be a Christian unless one fights imaginatively and
resolutely to make sure that socio-political structures reflect and permit
an ever more generous and gratuitous love among the citizenry. Of
course this effort is not a naive one. It agrees with Freud that the adven-

ture of gratuitous love must be grounded on greater justice if it is not to put a direct premium on being bad. But the two aspects of this struggle, the emphasis on justice and the summons to gratuitous love operating in a carefully balanced way, presuppose such a radical change in our existing societies that they turn the Christian into a revolutionary vanguard. They expose the Christian to all sorts of danger and demand the most heroic sort of virtue. And they do this in the name of an ideal which, in this case, is regarded as the *basic minimum* for being a Christian.

Any sociology that tackles this problem from the standpoint of isolated opinions will be inclined to commit the sociological blunder of viewing this internal contradiction as merely a matter of different degrees of adhesion to the gospel nucleus.[12] It will fail to note the existence of two different, incompatible theologies. It will also fail to note that the two theologies are professed simultaneously by the same people, depending on the issue involved or on the particular level that a problem is treated. The documents of the Medellín Conference, for example, could provide the basis for a very interesting and profitable sociological analysis, if it were not for the fact that sociology is preoccupied with isolated opinions rather than with systems of ideas.

6. *Shift from the unconscious level to the conscious level.* This is the most obvious shift, and the one most fraught with consequences. Authentic ideological analysis is an analysis of the collective unconscious. To put it in more orthodox Freudian terms, it is an analysis of that portion of the superego which is internalized to the point where it is identified with the unconscious level of primary instincts and operates in an instinctive way.

Morality is very important for the ruling classes when and if they wish to justify their domination. But in most cases it also prevents them from collaborating in a conscious way in the task of giving ideological formation to the collective unconscious and thus disguising and sacralizing their domination. They contribute to the process in an unconscious way: they believe their own ideology.

In other words, what goes on with the sexual instinct also goes on with the whole process of domination. Just as some sort of *censorship* usually prevents people from satisfying their sexual instinct in its crudest form, so some sort of *censorship* prevents people from openly formulating the ideal and methodology of domination in their crudest forms. These latter are accepted only when they are disguised in nobler forms, as also happens with the sexual instinct. Verón puts it this way: "The ideological system determines the representations of the social realm entertained by those active in it, but the organizing laws underlying it do not strike their consciousness in their true light." Unfortunately for both sociology and theology, "a large number of investigations simply register the opinions of the respondents which reflect the way in which they perceive different aspects of reality on the *conscious* level."

What this means for society is fairly evident. What does it mean for theology? It means, of course, that theologians and aficionados of theology must learn to recognize the most obvious mechanisms of sociological work if they are to make use of them. After all, theologians are actors with a certain role assigned by society for its own proper ends. Why not? But they perform this role, according to Verón, without being aware of the organizational laws that structure their role. And those laws certainly have a great deal to do with the very content of their theological work even though they may ingenuously believe—as Schillebeeckx does—that this content is dictated to them directly by divine revelation.

Theology deals with the ultimate values of human life, with the various images of the destiny reserved for the individual and humanity in history, with the most elevated ideals and symbols of what is going on above and beyond human experience. It does not take much imagination to realize that it is most unlikely that those dealing with issues of that sort would not be tainted by the concrete suffering and ideals of the society within which they are performing their work.

Unfortunately academic theology lacks that modicum of imagination. It operates on the assumption that the theologian is unaffected by the surrounding society. A truly liberative theology must start from the opposite assumption. But how can it if sociology itself gives up that ground and abandons it to unverifiable hypotheses? The influence of unconscious social factors on the elaboration of Christian eschatology is one of the key points for any liberation theology. But here again the theologian looks for help which is not forthcoming.

7. *Shift from sociology to psychology.* This might seem to contradict what was just said in the previous section: namely, that sociology has given up the study of the collective unconscious in the ideological realm. What is Verón referring to here? He is referring to the transformation of sociology into a particular kind of psychology or social engineering. It does try to go beyond the content of consciousness, but it is only interested in measuring—and perhaps procuring—the adaptation of individuals to their appropriate social roles.

Hofstadter paints a picture of religion in nineteenth-century America which dovetails in significant ways with our present-day situation in Latin America: "Since there need be only a shadow of confessional unity in the [Segundo: Protestant] denominations, the rational discussion of theological issues—in the past a great source of intellectual discipline in the churches—came to be regarded as a distraction, as a *divisive force.* Therefore, although it was not abandoned, it was subordinated to practical objectives which were conceived to be far more important . . . The denominations were trying to win to church allegiance a public which, *for whatever reason*, had not been held by the traditional sanctions of religion."[13]

The same ecclesiastical tendency is clearly present today. And there is a brand of sociology around that promises church authorities that even though it may not be able to determine the reasons why people are alienated, it can provide concrete means for winning back those people—again, *for whatever reason*. And what is even more important, perhaps, it can do this without having to resort to theological debates that are divisive because they oblige people to take a stand.

III. THE OVERSIMPLIFICATION OF MARXIST SOCIOLOGY

It is up to sociologists to discuss and decide whether the picture presented by Verón is accurate or not. From where I stand, however, the only way to prove his points false would be for sociology and theology to effectively collaborate on the problems he points up and many others that are shown to be decisive by theological experience.

Some of the points brought up by Verón in his description of present-day sociology seem indisputable. It clearly tends to take advantage of the new technological elements placed at its disposal by other disciplines. Fundamentally that comes down to the elements provided by applied mathematics in the last analysis. This means that greater stress is put on the quantitative aspect of hypotheses and verifications, which of course removes present-day sociology further and further from the problematic frame of the early sociologists and from the whole realm of ideology.

This evolution, or involution, of sociology would seem to be bound up with the technology that now prevails in both the capitalist and socialist societies of the developed world. And the tie-up gives us reason to suspect that our problems will not get any help from the sociology which claims to be descended from Marx and his *German Ideology* either. Moreover, we have already noted the fact that Marx himself did not really tackle this particular form of ideology. So any application of his sociological analysis to religion or theology would necessarily represent an *extrapolation*, however logical it might be.

In other words, it is very unlikely that a Marxist sociology, to the extent that it does exist and does differ from the sociology described above, can get us out of our hole. We would do well to focus on this point for a moment because one often comes across self-styled "Marxist" sociologists in Latin America. I do not use the word "self-styled" in a pejorative sense. I simply mean that in this case, as opposed to the situation described above, it is not a matter of describing a basic method and then including specific sociologists under that frame of reference. Instead the first step is to declare a Marxist affiliation, and one moves from there to determine whether there really is an investigative methodology shared by those so affiliated.

The issue that concerns us here is the possibility of collaboration between Marxist sociology and liberation theology. From that frame of reference we can pinpoint two negative traits which, for the moment, would seem to hinder any such collaboration. The first point relates more to Marx himself, the second to his successors.

1. *Marxist sociology is not consistent in its application of the concept of ideology to religious phenomena.* In the thinking of Marx himself it is difficult to determine whether religion and its theoretical formulation (i.e., theology) is a superstructure just like the others that he cites whenever he feels some inclination to list them in more or less detail. For example, he will list religion, art, politics, philosophy, law, and so forth.

But what is to be the fate of all these ideological forms in the final stage of the socialist revolution, with the advent of *communism* in the strict sense?[14] Some, such as art, will survive whereas others, such as the state and religion, will end up being destroyed by the revolutionary process.

I confess that I find it difficult to comprehend, within the single framework of historical materialism itself, how there can be different fates for different forms of the ideological superstructure. But even if we bypass that possible inconsistency, we might well be struck by the fact that Marx has a different treatment in store for the state and religion, two of the superstructural forms that are destined to disappear in the final stage. The coercive power of the state seems to be useful and even necessary during the first stage of the revolution—the socialist stage—because the holdovers and the resistance of the earlier capitalist society will still be strong; but the state's reason for being will gradually disappear along with the forced division of labor. It should be noted in passing that Marx always attributes every phenomenon of a given ideological superstructure to the division of labor—or at least to a division of labor that is *a priori* with respect to human potentialities, capacities, and callings.

There is some reason to doubt that Marx could picture the final Communist period without any socio-political laws whatever. If that doubt is well founded, then we would have to study the relationship between whatever laws did continue to exist and spontaneity. But even more surprising is the difference between the fate of the state and that of religion.

At times Marx assigns one sort of role to religion. *Corrected and im-*

proved, just as the state would be, religion would seem to have a role compatible with the revolutionary process—at least with its early stages. As the reader may recall, Marx tells us that religion is both an expression of real suffering and a protest against real suffering. Thus it would seem that religion would gradually disappear along with the forced division of labor, the root source of that suffering. That is at least a logical conclusion from Marx's line of thought.

But Marx seems to have a very different conception of religion. Instead of viewing it as a specific sector of the culture, and disregarding the variety, richness, and universality of its forms, Marx seems to view it as *nothing but* an error. In Marx's view, philosophy can *make* errors and undoubtedly has made them many times; but religion *is* an error, a unique and universal illusion, a barrier to any and all significant social change.

In the context of historical materialism it is very difficult to explain how such an ideological and superstructural form could ever have arisen from the division of labor. For this particular form seems to be almost wholly independent. Unlike other superstructural forms, it does not possess the ambiguous two-sided characteristics that typify such forms and help to explain their useful functions.

Be that as it may, the fact is that when Marx pursues the logic of this particular interpretation of religion he makes its abolition a *precondition* for the revolution rather than an *effect* of the revolution. Such is not the case with the other ideological forms. In his *Critique of Hegel's Philosophy of Right* Marx writes: "The true happiness of the people calls for the suppression of religion, since the latter provides only an illusory happiness. Calling for the renunciation of illusions relating to our specific situation means calling for the rejection of a situation that requires such illusions. Criticism of religion dis-illusions man so that he can think, act, and determine his own reality as a human being who has reached the age of reason."[15]

Contrary as this latter view may be with the rest of his thought, it is the interpretation that has been officially adopted by the first established socialist societies. Unlike philosophy, art, and politics, religion is not to be brought in line with the revolution—which course would pose a difficult but creative task to the Church. Instead it is to be destroyed, not by the revolution but by science.

Insofar as it is based on an academic theology and a corresponding praxis, religion itself has contributed a great deal to this brand of Manicheism that is quite foreign to historical materialism. For us and our purposes, the end result is the same in any case. A sociology based on that particular trend in Marx's thought cannot be of any help to theology if and when the latter is trying to divest itself of its ideological content and become an effective weapon in the social struggle of the oppressed.

2. *Marxist sociology has not accepted the relative autonomy of the superstructural levels in its methodology.* As everyone knows, Marx enunciated as a basic law the proposition that the economic structure (or infrastructure) determines the ideological superstructure. To put it another way, the economy or the production relationships determine the ideological forms of people's thinking. And this dependent relationship—not the simple negation of the spirit or of spiritual values—was given the name "materialism." To be more precise, it was given the name "historical materialism."

As we have just seen, the thinking of Marx himself is not clear-cut on this *determination.* It seems to range from mere conditioning to outright determinism. Now if we were to take such terms as "determination" and "materialism" literally and outside of any context, then sociology could not do anything more than offer a statistical verification of the concrete state of this determination at any given moment. It could only spell out statistically the concrete way in which the superstructure is being determined by production relationships.

But aside from the fact that Marx's texts on this precise point are few and ambiguous, there is also the fact that Engels reacted sharply against any mechanistic economic view. Refuting the "economicists," he stressed that neither he nor Marx had ever spoken in terms of purely economic determinism; that they had referred to the economic element as *ultimately* the determining factor, but not as the *only* determining factor on the superstructure.[16]

What does that mean in concrete terms? It means that the various structures operate with a range of possibilities that are framed by the existing production relationships; that in one way or another they take a stand—authentic or disguised—vis-à-vis those production relationships; but that they also enjoy real if not only relative autonomy with respect to their own proper mechanisms, so that the economic infrastructure is determining only in an ultimate sense.

There is nothing in that view that would be unacceptable from the standpoint of the ideological criticism we are trying to bring to bear with respect to theology. Indeed if sociology were to accept that formulation, then it would also have to accept the notion that *all* the superstructures, including religion, can play a determining role in furthering or retarding any possible social change within the existing economic framework. In other words, it would have to accept the fact that whether or not we leave the superstructures at the mercy of the ideological forces that are presently infiltrating and directing them is a matter of the utmost importance. Any sociology that undertook the task of determining those mechanisms and roles would clearly have to purify its methods in many respects.

And here we encounter the great paradox. Official Marxist sociology, born in a country where economics truly was determining only *ultimately,* persistently and profusely propagates a variety of sociological analyses in which economics and those things directly associated with it play the role of the *one and only* determining factor. And so those analyses have little or nothing to tell us about the greater or lesser potential of the superstructures to abet the process of liberation. The current Marxist analyses of society and its cultural structures are clearly tinged with "idealistic voluntarism."[17] They stress only the ever-growing internal contradictions of capitalist economics and the equally growing awareness of the exploited masses about those contradictions. Such a sociology hardly seems to be a science. Instead it often seems to be a practical and pedagogical tool to make the exploited masses aware of the simple fact that "the ruling ideas of each age have ever been the ideas of its ruling classes."

When this particular brand of sociology does dip into the superstructure, it does so only to associate some particular kind of art or philosophy or law with some particular place in the class struggle. Given the notion of religion just described, it rarely considers that phenomenon at all. In the Introduction to his book, *Critique de la raison dialectique,* Sartre pointedly criticizes such sociology. He notes, for example, its handling of the French writer Gustave Flaubert. Present-day Marxist sociology, he says, looks at Flaubert and concludes that he was one of the *petit-bourgeoisie,* politically speaking. And that is all it has to say. But, says Sartre, many French writers of the same period were *petit-bourgeois;* yet none of them exerted the socio-cultural influence that Flaubert did. And the latter point is crucial to any real ideological—and revolutionary—analysis. But Marxist sociology and analysis stops at that point and leaves aside the rest of the economic process at work in the French society of that era.[18]

There are obvious exceptions to this general picture. We have figures like Lúkacs, Schaff, and Althusser. We have independent Marxists like Sartre, Goldman, Lefebvre, and others. We have other similar figures in Europe and Latin America.[19] But such exceptions do not constitute the day-to-day operation of a science, and here we are envisioning and calling for an ongoing collaboration between sociology on the one hand, and a theology equally concerned about liberation on the other hand.

My two observations about Marxist sociology, when combined with

Verón's description of United States sociology, present liberation theology with a serious problem. It is a problem which has not been satisfactorily resolved as yet, and the consequences of that fact will be spelled out more clearly in the next chapter. But our search for a sociology that will suit liberation theology cannot end with this summary review of foiled expectations.

IV. ON THE NEED FOR VERIFICATION

In all likelihood we have been chasing a mirage in trying to find support for our humanistic and theological suspicions in scientific types of verification that would come from sociology. Perhaps we were dazzled for the moment by Weber's grand attempt and saw it as our golden highway, only to be brought up sharply by the realization that there was no empirical proof of its truth.

Of course it was not all in vain. Suppose it has been demonstrated to us, even if only in negative terms, that one cannot impute to early Calvinism any connection with the inhumane consequences which Weber describes and does impute to it. (That is not a value judgment in his eyes, but it is in ours.) Suppose we must admit that science has absolutely nothing to say about some possible influence of Calvinism on attitudes conducive to, say, socialism. If those suppositions are correct, then any possibility of nurturing theological suspicion and posing new questions to Scripture falls apart also. Theology for us becomes more and more scientific and atemporal. Scripture becomes a book growing older and older every day. And that is that!

But wait a minute! Perhaps we have jumped to conclusions. We have seen that it is impossible to obtain any sort of *quantitative* verification. Must we therefore conclude that no *rational* verification is possible? (Whether that *rational* verification would be scientific or not would, of course, depend on the relationship we entertained between science and quantitative verification.)

Let us consider two scholarly scientists and the possibility of verifying their theories. I refer to Teilhard de Chardin and Weber.

The theory of universal evolution, associated very closely with Teilhard de Chardin in recent years, is based on a type of verification that is not easy to determine. Teilhard de Chardin himself devoted more than a little attention to the question.

On the animal level, for example, we can prove empirically that the most successful results of the tendency to adapt to the surrounding milieu, and to complex and changing milieus, presuppose complex syntheses of energy—or, what comes down to the same thing, complex distributions of energy. We can also prove experientially that the degree of complexity of such syntheses is accompanied by a corresponding degree of growing effort. And at a certain level of animal life, this effort can be meausred empirically and directly.

Now if it is to be consistent, the theory of universal evolution must operate on the following presupposition. It must assume that the elements distinctive of a given level are found in greater proportions and in more perceptible ways on higher levels, and in lesser proportions and less perceptible forms on lower levels. In Teilhard de Chardin's view, nothing could show up as a decisive feature at one level of evolution which did not already belong to all the prior levels, even though on the prior levels it might be very disguised and practically imperceptible.[20]

So we are faced with this difficulty, among others: on the level of physicochemical matter we do not seem to find the least trace of spirited effort. We do find matter arranged in more or less rich and complex molecules; and as we approach the level of living molecules this richness and complexity becomes notably greater. But where exactly can there be spirited effort? Teilhard de Chardin points to two "signs" or "indications" of such effort on the lower levels.

Firstly, he notes the spirited effort that physicists and chemists must expend in their laboratories to obtain the same type of molecule, insofar as its complexity approaches the level of life. They are "difficult" molecules, at least in terms of experimental procedures and calculations. Secondly, he notes the scarcity of such molecules as compared with the astounding plethora of inorganic matter on the most simple level.

Obviously there is no empirical, quantitative proof that material energy "makes a spirited effort" to create richer and more complex molecules. Taking the term in its strict sense, what we "experience" on the animal level is something we cannot "experience" equally on the physicochemical level. But signs of an undeniable *analogy* do exist. From the theory itself we already know that we are not going to find *the same thing in smaller quantities* on the lower levels. We know that the essential features of life must be present on the level of pre-life, but in a disguised, less perceptible, analogous form.

It is obvious, then, that only our perception of such analogies between all the elements and levels of the *cosmos* can open up our thinking and get us to elaborate hypotheses which could never be proved or verified in quantitative terms. Why couldn't they be verified in those terms? Because they attempt to explain things existing on different levels of reality which are the subject matter of sciences whose quantification procedures depend on different instruments and deal with different parameters.

Teilhard de Chardin is fully aware of the fact that it is senseless to elaborate hypotheses which can never be verified. He firmly believes that the possibility of verification does exist, given the unity and convergence of everything existing in the universe. It is the unity of human thinking that must overcome the compartmentalization which not only obstructs the verification of the most critical hypotheses but also prevents the creation of the natural and human techniques that would be most important to the convergence process. This leads him to turn *analogy* into *the parameter,* that is, the common measure of all things.

This is what he has to say in *The Phenomenon of Man:*

> The apparent restriction of the phenomenon of consciousness to the higher forms of life has long served science as an excuse for eliminating it from its models of the universe. A queer exception, an aberrant function, an epiphenomenon—thought was classed under one or other of these heads in order to get rid of it. But what would have happened to modern physics if radium had been classified as an "abnormal substance" without further ado? Clearly, the activity of radium had not been neglected, and could not be neglected, because, being measurable, it forced its way into the external web of matter—whereas consciousness, in order to be integrated into a world-system, necessitates consideration of the existence of a new aspect or dimension in the stuff of the universe. We shrink from the attempt, but which of us does not constantly see identical problems facing research workers, which have to be solved by the same method, namely, *to discover the universal hidden beneath the exceptional?* "[21]

He goes on to say: "Latterly we have experienced it too often to admit of any further doubt: an irregularity in nature is only the sharp exacerbation, to the point of perceptible disclosure, of a property of things diffused throughout the universe, in a state which eludes our recognition of its presence. Properly observed, even if only in one aspect, a phenomenon necessarily has an omnipresent value and roots by reason of *the fundamental unity of the world.*"[22]

Thus, although it may not be of much help to us right at the moment, we can say that it is only a matter of time before epistemology will refine the criteria for a different kind of verification. This verification is real. It will be applied and recognized as valid, even though it is only used in a vague and confused way at present and has not yet reached the level of human activity and social behavior patterns.

Now if we turn to Max Weber's famous thesis on the relationship between Protestantism and the spirit of capitalism, we can see that here too some sort of *analogy* is at work between different measuring rods peculiar to different disciplines. In this case the two disciplines in question are theology on the one hand and economics on the other. And just as we could not quantitatively discover an exact equivalent between spirited effort on the animal level and spirited effort on the physico-chemical level, so we cannot work up any statistical proof that most of the people who found economic success in the early capitalist period of the United States had a corresponding attachment to the ceremonies and beliefs of Calvinism.

If quantitative proof means that we must tear down the barriers existing between the standards of measurement in different scientific disciplines, then we can conclude that such quantitative proof will never be forthcoming. But suppose that we find analogies between the quanti-tative element at one level and the quantitative element at another level. Then, in my opinion, we can and should talk about scientific proof even though we cannot be talking about *quantitative* proof in the strict sense. For even though science has not yet worked out a clear, operational theory about that kind of verification, it has been leading humanity to a fuller realization of the basic point underlying any such proof: i.e., the fundamental unity of the universe.

It is no accident that Max Weber's hypothesis has exerted a deep fascination on sociologists. We can, and I think, must say that the reason for this fascination lies in a kind of verification which is certainly not quantitative in any direct sense but which is indirectly bound up with the quantity of observations made possible by the hypothesis.

We can say that Max Weber's theory has been verified in three re-spects. Firstly, if we accept his theory, we can perceive an evident inter-nal analogy between certain demonstrable economic attitudes and cer-tain equally demonstrable religious beliefs. Secondly, his hypothesis is surprisingly fruitful in helping us to explain, in whole or in part, other psychological and sociological facts on other levels or at other periods of history. It should also be remembered that Weber himself investigated more or less similar possibilities for the start of capitalism in very differ-ent nations, such as the United States and China for example, and in relation to the prevailing religions of the nations in question. Thirdly, there is another point which should not be overlooked. In the fields with which we are dealing, an hypothesis can also be verified through its opposite. To take one small example, we might consider the influence of the Catholic doctrine of grace on economic attitudes such as those which prevailed at the start of capitalism. Even before hearing of Weber and his hypothesis, I think one would promptly reject the notion that there was any real operative influence between the two.

Needless to say, this summary and cursory presentation of proofs that Teilhard de Chardin and Weber might adduce in favor of their respective hypotheses merely serves to point us in a certain direction. I have certainly not solved the problem of the proper relationship and the possibility of collaboration between sociology and theology.

We must leave the question open, as in fact it is. There is no valid reason why we must resign ourselves to an irrational separation of the two disciplines, even in the framework of the most up-to-date scientific canons. But neither can we twist history to our purposes and allege a cooperation that is not there in fact.

Right now theologians, except in exceptional cases, must perform the task of introducing the most fruitful elements of the social sciences into their own everyday work of theologizing. That this is a large and frightening order on the personal level can hardly be denied. But the most important consequences for theology are those which we shall examine in the next chapter. They can be summed up in one word, which is more or less taboo: *politics.*

NOTES

1. On the three examples presented here, see my paper presented at the El Escorial theological meeting (1972). It and the other papers of that meeting are collected in *Fe cristiana y cambio social en América Latina* (Salamanca: Sígueme, 1973), pp. 203–12.

2. "The Church *does not choose* between different human groups. In and with Jesus Christ, the Church decides in favor of those whom Jesus decided in favor of: in favor of all the people of Chile" (*Evangelio, política y socialismos,* working draft issued by the Chilean bishops, Santiago, May 27, 1971. Reproduced in *Documentos del episcopado: Chile 1970–1973* [Santiago: Mundo, 1974], No. 13, p. 65). For more comments on this rather odd appeal to Jesus Christ to adopt an attitude exactly the opposite of the one which he adopted towards his own people, see Chapter V in this book and note 2 of that chapter.

3. Richard Hofstadter, *Anti-Intellectualism. in American Life* (New York: Knopf, 1963), p. 141.

4. See my article, "Reconciliación y conflicto," in *Perspectivas de diálogo* (Montevideo), September 1974, pp. 172–78.

5. Vatican II, *Gaudium et spes,* n. 19; Eng. trans., *The Documents of Vatican II,* edited by Walter M. Abbot, S.J., (New York: Guild-America-Association), 1966.

6. Eliseo Verón, "Ideología y comunicación de masas: la semantización de la violencia política," in collaboration with Prieto, Ekman, Friesen, Sluzki, and Masotta: *Lenguaje y comunicación social,* (Buenos Aires: Nueva Visión, 1971). The following citations all come from the same article.

7. Hofstadter, *Anti-Intellectualism,* p. 134.

8. Cited by Hofstadter, *ibid.,* p. 84.

9. Pastoral Letter, "On Evangelization and Development."

10. Erich Fromm, *Escape from Freedom* (New York: Holt, Rinehart, and Winston, 1941), pp. 241–43, 254.

11. Sigmund Freud, *Civilization and Its Discontents,* Eng. trans. (New York: W.W. Norton, 1962), p. 58.

12. See further on in this book, Chapter VII, section 2.

13. Hofstadter, *Anti-Intellectualism,* pp. 83–84.

14. In *The German Ideology* Marx paints his famous portrait of the ultimate Communist society: "As soon as the distribution of labour comes into being, each man has a particular, exclusive sphere of activity, which is forced upon him and from which he cannot escape. He is a hunter, a fisherman, a shepherd, or a critical critic, and must remain so if he does not want to lose his means of livelihood; while in communist society, where nobody has one exclusive sphere of activity but each can become accomplished in any branch he wishes, society regulates the general production and thus makes it possible for me to do one thing today and another tomorrow, to hunt in the morning, fish in the afternoon, rear cattle in the evening, criticise after dinner, just as I have a mind, without ever becoming hunter, fisherman, shepherd or critic" (*The German Ideology: Part One,* ed. C.J. Arthur [London: Lawrence & Wishart, 1970], p. 53). Intermittent though it may be, the "critical" activity clearly presupposes the existence of art, literature, or philosophy at that stage. On the survival of the superstructure and ideologies in the final stage, see the pointed arguments of Louis Althusser in *For Marx,* Eng. trans. (New York: Vintage, 1970), Part Seven.

15. Cited by Jean-Yves Calvez, *La pensée de Karl Marx* (Paris: Ed. du Seuil, 1956), p. 92.

16. In arguing against the "economicists," Lenin sharply stresses this point, particularly in *What Is To Be Done?* There he attacks those who see the "spontaneity" of the proletariat as the determining element on the economic situation—"determining" in the strongest sense of the term. After citing K. Kautsky on the correct interpretation of Marx, Lenin proceeds: "The phrase employed by the authors of the 'Economic' letter in *Iskra,* No. 12, about the efforts of the most inspired ideologies not being able to divert the labour movement from the path that is determined by the interaction of the material elements and the material environment *is tantamount to the abandonment of socialism*" (Lenin's italics too; *What Is To Be Done?,* Eng. trans. [New York: International Publishers, 1929], p. 41).

17. The phrase comes from Lúkacs. It is cited by J.P. Sartre in his *Critique de la raison dialectique* (Paris: N.R.F., 1960), I, p. 28.

18. Sartre is perhaps excessively ironic in his treatment of present-day Marxist sociology: "They cannot step out of themselves. They *reject* the enemy phrase (out of fear or hatred or laziness) at the very moment they are pretending to open up to it. This contradiction blocks them up. They literally do not understand a word they are reading. And I am not attacking this incomprehension in

the name of any bourgeois objective but rather in the name of Marxism itself. Their rejections and condemnations will be all the fiercer, their refutations all the more successful, the more they really know what they are refuting and condemning" (*Critique,* p. 35).

That is often the impression that a theologian gets. And a comment of Engels to K. Schmidt would seem to show that the impression is not entirely off-base: "In general the word 'materialistic' serves many of the younger writers in Germany as a mere phrase with which anything and everything is labelled *without further study;* they stick on this label and then think the question disposed of. But our conception of history is above all a guide to study, not a lever for construction after the manner of the Hegelians. All history must be studied äfresh, the conditions of existence of the different formations of society must be individually examined before the attempt is made to deduce from them the political, civil-legal, aesthetic, philosophic, religious, etc., notions corresponding to them" (*Marx and Engels: Selected Correspondence,* Eng. trans. [New York; International Publishers, 1942], p. 473).

19. On the theoretical level see, for example, Frank Hinkelammert's book, *Ideologías del desarrollo y dialéctica de la historia.* On a more practical level one can cite various works of Latin American Marxist sociology dealing with the ideological content-materials conveyed through the mass communications media. See, for example: Armand Mattelart, *La comunicación masiva en el proceso de liberación* (Buenos Aires: Siglo XXI, 1973); Armand Mattelart, Carmen Castillo, and Leonardo Castillo, *La ideología de la dominacíon en una sociedad dependiente* (Buenos Aires: Signos, 1970); Ariel Dorfman, *Superman y sus amigos del alma* (Buenos Aires: Galerna, 1974); Ariel Dorfman and Armand Mattelart, *Para leer al Pato Donald* (Valparaiso: Universitarias, Valparaiso Catholic University, 1971).

20. If Teilhard de Chardin manages at all to sum up the point of *The Human Phenomenon,* it is when he writes: "We are back at the refrain that runs all the way through this book. *In the world, nothing could ever burst forth as final across the different thresholds successively traversed by evolution (however critical they be) which has not already existed in an obscure and primordial way"* (Pierre Teilhard de Chardin, *The Phenomenon of Man,* Eng. trans. [New York: Harper Torchback Edition, 1961], p. 71: author's italics too).

21. *Ibid.,* pp. 55–56; author's italics too.

22. *Ibid.*

CHAPTER THREE

The Political Option

If we start with the assumption that any authentic interpretation of Scripture must keep going through a full hermeneutic circle, and if we further assume that this entails a commitment to change the world in accordance with our ever fresh analysis of the real world concealed under the mechanisms and instruments of ideology, then we cannot help but go out in search of sociology. Changing the world presupposes an assurance that our projected new image of it is better than the one operating at present, and that it is also feasible. In trying to discover the mechanisms that obscure and at the same time shore up the present situation, we must engage in ideological analysis and eventually verify our hypotheses in a scientific manner.

But consider where these presuppositions lead us, given the existing situation of sociological science as described in the previous chapter. Two choices seem open to us: either we must deny theology any possibility of directing us towards liberative hypotheses and options, thereby restricting it to its hoary abstract certitudes; or else we must move forward without sufficiently scientific certitudes of a sociological nature, with the result that theology plunges headlong into politics.

It is curious that our everyday speech contradicts one of the most clear-cut facts of etymology. It makes a clear-cut distinction between sociology and politics, when in fact the Latin word *societas* was a direct translation of the Greek word *polis*. But everyday speech ignores etymology and sticks to customary usage. And customary usage has found that there are two different kinds of people at work here. On the one hand there are the scientific professionals known as sociologists, who never present an opinion without backing it up with proof. On the other hand there are the people called politicians, whose talent and function is precisely to make critical decisions without any scientific proof as a backup.

Now if our remarks in the previous chapter are correct, no decisive stand can be taken without taking into account ideological mechanisms; and no ideological analysis can indulge in the luxury of looking to soci-

ology for scientific support. Politics is caught between the devil and the
deep blue sea. On the one hand it must take the risk of making some
choice, with all that entails, but it cannot appeal to any scientific basis as
the justification for its decision.

That may explain the subtle mixture of respect and mistrust that the
politician inspires. The pejorative overtones of the word "politics" are
played down when it comes to people whose vocation is politics, insofar
as the latter is a necessity. But those overtones are stressed and may even
turn into outright repugnance when the adjective "political" is added to
disciplines that are supposed to stay clear of those kinds of problems.
Such seems to be the case with theology, for example.

Roger Vekemans, a Jesuit, is one of the most forceful and outspoken
opponents of liberation theology in Latin America. The English title of
one of his books is *Caesar and God*.[1] By "Caesar" he means "politics" of
course; by "God" he means religion and theology. And in stressing the
supposed distinction between the two realms, a distinction that he attributes to Jesus himself, Vekemans is attacking what he regards as the
confusion between the two realms introduced and promulgated by liberation theology. This confusion, says Vekemans, is clearly evident in
the lives of many priests and ministers in Latin America. They fail to
realize that there is an unbridgeable gap between the two realms.

The curious thing here is that this affirmation comes from a priest
who is most deeply and conspicuously involved in Latin American politics. Moreover, Vekemans is well educated in the European tradition, as
the numerous footnotes in his book attest; and he is not unaware of the
fact that a very respectable and scientific "political theology" does presently exist in Europe. This would lead a theologian to suspect that the
alleged gap between the two realms might not exist in fact at all. One
might also expect that someone who took such a stand would explain
certain facts of dogmatic tradition, such as the political interventions and
wars of the popes; and also such *theological* facts as the canonization of
Joan of Arc, whose divine vocation was *exclusively* political. Did the
Church sanction *her* politics by canonizing her? Did it at least sanction
her conception of the union between religion and a very debatable
brand of politics, without necessarily passing judgment on the latter?

Faced with such historical facts, one is inclined to suspect that something else underlies the recent taboo against mixing theology and politics
that has been imposed by Vekemans and many others who share a
definite place on the political spectrum. Are there other than purely
theological mechanisms at work here? Or, at the very least, does the
taboo stem from a theology whose underlying roots are very hazy and
obscure, however academic they might seem?

I. THEOLOGICAL RESERVATIONS ABOUT THE POLITICAL REALM

Let us start with several highly significant facts. And here we can assume that Gustavo Gutiérrez has paved the way for our discussion by his remarks in his important book (*A Theology of Liberation*). He notes: "Theology is reflection, a critical attitude. Theology *follows*; is the second step. What Hegel used to say about philosophy can likewise be applied to theology; it rises only at sundown."[2] As we go on it will become clear that here we have a basic principle for dealing with the whole question of the relationship between theology and politics.

But first let us ask another question: What is the first step, the one that precedes theology? Gutierrez answers: "It is—at least ought to be—real charity, action, and commitment to the service of men."[3] What, then, is the relationship between this *first step*—after which comes the second step known as theology—and politics? Gutiérrez puts it this way: "Human reason has become political reason. For the contemporary historical consciousness, things political are not only those which one attends to during the free time afforded by his private life; nor are they even a well-defined area of human existence. . . . It is the sphere for the exercise of a critical freedom which is won through history. It is the universal determinant and the collective arena for human fulfillment. . . . Nothing lies outside the political sphere understood in this way. Everything has a political color. . . . Personal relationships themselves acquire an ever-increasing political dimension. Men enter into relationships among themselves through political means."[4]

Whatever one may think about the political stance or the political neutrality of Jesus himself,[5] it seems evident that his commandment of love and his countless examples and admonitions concerning it in the Gospels must be translated to an era in which real-life love has taken on political forms. To say that machines have nothing to do with the gospel message because it says nothing about machines is to fail to understand that message. To suggest that almsgiving should continue to be the Christian response to the whole problem of wealth and its relationship to love is also to seriously distort the gospel message (see Vatican II, *Gaudium et spes*, n. 30). And the same thing applies to any attempt to inculcate an apolitical love today—presuming that love can be apolitical at all in a world where politics is the fundamental human dimension. And once we discover that liberation theology can and must engage in ideological analysis, and that it cannot look to sociology for fully scientific proof or support, then some relationship between theology and politics becomes necessary and in fact decisive.

Taking due account of all that, we should not be surprised to find that the more recent documents emanating from the Vatican on social matters are in fact *political*. From *Mater et Magistra* to *Octogesima adveniens* all the encyclicals purportedly dealing with what used to be called the "social doctrine" of the Church have concentrated on what is really the "political doctrine" of the Church. Only the general appellation has remained the same, for whatever reasons. The fact is that those recent documents have not focused as much on such issues as social classes, wages, and work conditions as they have on national and international political structures. Yet curiously enough, except for a few strong reactions against *Populorum progressio* (in one instance labelled "warmed-over Marxism"), the popes have not been accused of mixing religion and politics.

An example of a quite different sort might help to explain this fact. A year before the Medellín Conference, a group of fifteen bishops from the Third World wrote a letter which had international repercussions. In it they wrote, among other things: "Insofar as the Church maintains her essential and perduring ties, i.e., her fidelity to Christ and communion with him in the gospel, she is never bound up with any given social, political, or economic system. *When a system ceases to promote the common good and favors special interests,* the Church must not only denounce injustice but also break with the evil system. *She must be prepared to work with another system that is juster and more suited to the needs of the day"* (n. 8).[6]

So far the statement of the bishops would seem to be quite similar to statements in the general social doctrine of the Church. No strong reaction would be expected. But even here we can bring up a critical point that must engage our attention. With what means or scientific instruments can the Church determine when a system has ceased—once and for all, presumably—to promote the common good? And how can it be scientifically sure of the existence of another system that is more just before coming up with such proof?

The fact is that the reaction will come when the bishops, taking their own general statement seriously, move into the realm of real facts and happenings and take a stand vis-à-vis them. This is the novel and scandalous element in the magisterium of the Church. The general principles were tolerable enough so long as it was left up to each believer to take up the task of reaching a concrete decision on the basis of those principles. But now the bishops say: "Taking account of the necessary preconditions for material progress in some areas, the Church in the last hundred years has tolerated capitalism, its loans at a legitimate interest rate, and its other mechanisms that are hardly in conformity with the moral code of the prophets and the gospel. But *she cannot help but rejoice over the appearance of another social system that is less at variance with this moral code....* Christians must show that 'authentic socialism is Christianity lived to the full, in basic equality and with a fair distribution of goods' (Maximos IV Saigh).'"[7]

Here we run head-on into the political taboo in all its force. Clearly enunciating abstract principles about politics is very different from *entering into* politics, and the Third World bishops cited above took the latter course. They not only enunciated political principles but also made a political choice. They chose one of the two existing positions, not just as a moral position[8] but also as a political position. And then they imposed it as such on the faithful in the name of the gospel message.

Clearly we are faced with something that is not familiar to us, at least in that particular form. Are the bishops really politicking? If they are, what is to be our *theological* judgment about that, prescinding from purely emotional reactions?

To answer these questions, we might well make use of an important and indicative statement from Karl Rahner that Vekemans cites in his book. Rahner is referring specifically to pronouncements of the church magisterium about matters which are so practical and concrete that they fall within the bounds of sociological and political knowledge and expertise. Here is Rahner's statement: "This is the point at which the problem suddenly becomes awesome: how can the Church know the context of her action since this kind of knowledge obviously *cannot be entirely deduced from revelation?* . . . Willingly or not, she is consequently dependent upon sources and methods of knowledge which are partially beyond her control . . . We are faced with a problem to which, if I may say so, ecclesiological epistemology has not yet paid enough attention . . . How can [the Church] make obligatory pronouncements [on such matters]? In this context, how can the Church avoid the danger either of stating obvious things which are better expressed elsewhere, or else of risking statements that can be refuted by specialists in sociological analysis?"[9]

It is easy enough to see the implications of these questions for liberation theology. If it is shown or proved that the most acute human problems, all of them, come under this head, then the implication seems to be that theology should keep its mouth shut so as not to be refuted by scientific or scholarly specialists.

An obvious case of the problem is that of the Third World bishops just cited. For the vast majority of Latin Americans, choosing between the capitalist system and the socialist system is clearly one of the possible and critical options open to them, although no one imagines that that will end all problems. But how can the Church decide between these two alternatives if it can be proved wrong in the future and if it does not possess scientific means to foresee that future?

Of course the bishops in question are not totally defenceless against such objections. They write: "History shows us that certain revolutions were necessary, and that they have produced good effects after their temporary flirtation with antireligious sentiments. There is no better proof of this than the fact that the French Revolution of 1789 allowed people to proclaim the rights of man" (n. 3).[10]

Nevertheless theologians apparently tend to reject this sort of recourse to history for two different and even opposing reasons. The first reason derives from the field of sociology, although it is phrased in theological terms. The French Revolution, it says, is a singular event and proves nothing—unless one opts for historical determinism and claims that every revolution is necessarily a good one. One cannot claim to make a scientific evaluation of the socialist revolution based on the good effects of the long past French Revolution. History is not the eternal return of the exact same thing.

The second and more theological reason for objecting to the bishop's argument takes just the opposite turn. Since history seems to have a clear tendency to repeat itself over and over again, one can make human forecasts and provisions about its future development. But the more scientific and well founded those provisions are, the more purely human they are and hence the less room they leave for the eschatological future and the hand of God. That is the kind of argument Gaston Fessard, for example, used against the "New Theology" of the forties in France. He accused it of having decided what the exact relationship between theology and communism should be, on the basis of the French Revolution of 1789. The "New Theology," in other words, was trying to plan out future history with the sole aid of human foresight and hindsight.[11]

What Fessard does not say, and does not even seem to perceive, is that there is not one whit less human foresight involved in reforming the present situation or leaving it alone than there is in trying to adapt to historical change by planning for the future. Not choosing something because it is human is just as human a choice as the one that is supposedly being avoided.

Let us close this first section, then, by summing up three basic points which I take to be established by what has been said so far. We can then use them to continue our analysis of the relationship between theology and politics:

1. Every theology is political, even one that does not speak or think in political terms. The influence of politics on theology and every other cultural sphere cannot be evaded any more than the influence of theology on politics and other spheres of human thinking. The worst politics of all would be to let theology perform this function unconsciously, for that brand of politics is always bound up with the status quo.

2. Liberation theology consciously and explicitly accepts its relationship with politics. First of all, it incorporates into its own methodology the task of ideological analysis that is situated on the boundary line between sociology and politics. And insofar as direct politics is concerned, it is more concerned about avoiding the (false) impartiality of academic theology than it is about taking sides and consequently giving ammunition to those who accuse it of partisanship.

3. When academic theology accuses liberation theology of being political and engaging in politics, thus ignoring its own tie-up with the political status quo it is really looking for a scapegoat to squelch its own guilt complex.

II. THEOLOGY IS THE SECOND STEP

If we keep those three points in mind, perhaps we can formulate the whole problem of political options in theology in a more profound and realistic way. Two analyses, one phenomenological and the other exegetical, can help in our reformulation.

The first analysis has to do with the order in which the questions are posed. One need only contemplate that order to detect something odd about the classical formulation embodied in Rahner's text cited above. Recall the essential question: How can the Church *know the context of her action* since obviously this type of knowledge *cannot be deduced entirely from revelation*?

If one pays close heed to that question, one cannot help but note the amazingly and thoroughly inhuman cast of the formulation. What is more, there is no doubt that the passage was cited by Vekemans precisely because if Rahner's question makes sense, the problem can never be solved. *Quod erat demonstrandum.* The assumption seems to be that the first thing known by the Church, or any group, or any human being is specifically "the context of their actions." And because they know and accept the challenges posed by that context, they move on to ask themselves what they should do in that context. Rahner seems to believe that the Church knows what it is supposed to do but does not know the context. How can that be? The final words of the remark quoted above offer us the key. As Rahner sees it, we can deduce certain knowledge about what is to be done by resorting to divine revelation independent of any and every context. Revelation presumably provides us with deductive conclusions about that which is eternally Christian in human conduct. But since real-life conduct depends *in part* on knowledge and appreciation of the context which cannot be deduced from the divine revelation, the problem comes down to whether we should take the risk of giving up total certainties for partial certainties. In other words, is it sensible for theology to abandon the realm in which it possesses answers and move on to a realm where it can be refuted, at least with respect to those things that appertain more diectly to knowledge of history and its context than to revelation?

Now the plain fact is that the general human situation, the situation that holds true for all human beings including theologians, is exactly the opposite of what Rahner pictures it to be. Just to make the point clearer and more obvious, let us assume that in the theology of the Church human beings do possess a corpus of atemporal scientific certitudes akin to those of mathematics. Even in that forced and hypothetical instance, human options depend upon an understanding and appreciation of the surrounding context and must be taken before the scientific certitudes of theology have anything to say.

The fact is that the major problems of man are definitely not tackled on a plane of certain knowledge, after which we must decide whether they are also to be framed in terms of some specific historical context. The real situation is just the opposite. We live and struggle in the midst of decisive contextual conflicts without science being able to provide any ready-made option in advance. Once a human being has made some general option, science or scholarship can point out some set of instruments that would dovetail with his option. The most we can say about it is that our option depends on science indirectly insofar as no one wants to opt for unrealizable fantasies and hence everyone tries to be informed ahead of time about the *factual* possibility of carrying out one's ideal. But even in that case scientific certitude is at best instrumental in nature and it does not say anything about the decisive value of what we are doing.

Is theology an exception to this universal law? It definitely is not. First of all, man's acceptance of theology, and of divine revelation itself, supposes a prior option that can only be viewed as the challenge posed by a specific, well-known context. Only on the basis of this contextual option does theology begin to have any meaning at all; and it retains meaning only insofar as it remains in touch with the real-life context. In other words, theology is not chosen for theological reasons. Quite the contrary is the case. The only real problem is trying to decide whether it puts a person in a better position to make a choice and to change the world politically.

Clearly, then, the alleged problem of deciding whether we should or should not remain on the level of theological certitudes deduced from revelation is really no problem at all and hence can never be resolved. That is what Gustavo Gutiérrez had in mind when he said that "theology comes after."

One might well wonder how and why such an obvious point should come to constitute a decisive issue in liberation theology. The only possible explanation is that unreality has taken over the methods of academic theology to such an extent that it is hard to find a theologian, even a highly intelligent theologian such as Karl Rahner, who does not turn the real order of issues and problems upside down.

In addition to this phenomenological analysis of human behavior and the impact of scientific knowledge on it, an exegetical analysis might be useful and decisive here.

If we look at the Gospels, we will note an interesting difference between the theological methodology of Jesus and that of the Pharisees. Scholarly exegesis usually points up the difference in the content of their theology, and that is evident too. But it tends to bypass the whole matter of the method used by Jesus in *theologizing* vis-à-vis the context that he shares with the Pharisees.

In the Synoptic Gospels it is clear that the Pharisees, when faced with Jesus' actions, pose the same question that Rahner posed above: How can the synagogue understand and pass judgment on the historical context before it, a context that includes Jesus, when the fact is that a true evaluative understanding of that context cannot be deduced wholly from past revelation?

That is precisely the theological formulation of the Pharisees, as is evident from their countless attempts to trap Jesus into attitudes or remarks in which he must confront the whole body of past revelation and nothing else but that. Moreover, we must start out with the assumption that the Pharisees were acting in good faith when they started out on this theological search. After all, they had been formed and trained in that theological tradition. Their aim is to divest the concrete phenomenon before them of anything and everything that cannot be wholly deduced from divine revelation, so that they won't run the risk of making a mistake or being refuted by specialists in other fields.

Consider the following passage in Mark's Gospel: "On another occasion when he went to a synagogue, there was a man in the congregation who had a withered arm; and they were watching to see whether Jesus would cure him on the Sabbath, so that they could bring a charge against him. He said to the man with the withered arm, 'Come and stand out here.' Then he turned to them: 'Is it permitted to do good or to do evil on the Sabbath, to save life or to kill?' They had nothing to say; and, looking round at them with anger and sorrow at their obstinate stupidity, he said to the man, 'Stretch out your arm' " (Mark 3:1–5).

The theological methodology of the Pharisees is all too clear. They do not know how to apply their theological certitudes to the phenomenon of Jesus because he does not fit into "theological" categories. He is something new about which past revelation has nothing specific to say;

from it nothing certain can be deduced about him. Thus any theological judgment about Jesus runs the risk of being refuted by all those who have a solid acquaintance with the phenomenon that he represents. The occasion cited by Mark is therefore unique, because Jesus has placed himself in a situation where God's revealed law will enable the Pharisees to render a direct and irrefutable judgment. For the context here is that of the Sabbath, one in which theology can pass theological judgment on Jesus without having to leave its own proper field of knowledge and certitude.

To their surprise, however, Jesus rejects the possibility of forming any concrete judgment on the initial basis of theology or its realm of competence. One cannot begin with certitudes deduced from revelation: that is his response to them, embodied in the question for which they had no answer. It seems to be a purely human question in which the Sabbath is no different from any other day of the week: "Is it permitted *to do good* or *to do evil* on the Sabbath?" The Pharisees were prepared to answer a different question—an abstract, formal question of classic theology which took account of only the Sabbath itself, not human beings: "Is it permitted to do *anything at all* on the Sabbath? Faced with Jesus' question, they have no theological criterion whatever and so they have nothing to say at all. Jesus' question points up a level that is prior to any and all theological questions, a level where human beings make their most critical and decisive options: i.e., the heart. And since the theology of the Pharisees has bypassed the human entirely, as if it were insignificant by comparison with loftier criteria and certitudes, Jesus is saddened and angered by their silence. To paraphrase Gutiérrez once again, theology is the second step in the methodology of Jesus and the first step in the methodology of the Pharisees.

In the same chapter of Mark's Gospel we read this: "The doctors of the law, too, who had come down from Jerusalem, said, 'He is possessed by Beelzebub', and, 'He drives out devils by the prince of devils'. So he called them to come forward, and spoke to them in parables: 'How can Satan drive out Satan? If a kingdom is divided against itself, that kingdom cannot stand; if a household is divided against itself, that house will never stand; and if Satan is in rebellion against himself, he is divided and cannot stand; and that is the end of him' " (Mark 3:22–26).

Here again the Pharisees try to apply purely theological criteria to Jesus. Jesus is curing sick people; in terms of their theology, that means that he is driving out demons. But they still have one theological certitude, one theological loophole, which cannot be disproved theologically—or so they hope at least. They can entertain and spread doubt about the power that Jesus is using over the demons. If no positive judgment about Jesus is possible, then at least a very important negative judgment is not out of the question: no one can really know whether or not Jesus might be expelling demons because he himself possesses demonic power. Once again, however, Jesus reformulates the question or the problem on the only level where it can find a positive answer: in terms of what is good for people. For all practical purposes, his response can be paraphrased as follows: it really doesn't matter who liberates them so long as they are really and effectively liberated. Why? Because it is God who is directly or indirectly behind any and all liberation. The question posed from the vantage point of theology makes no sense and hence has no answer. Any and every theological question begins with the human situation. Theology is "the second step." The ultimate criterion in Jesus' theology is the remedy brought to some sort of human suffering, however temporary and provisional that remedy may be.

We could go into a host of examples of this sort. But I think it would be well to conclude this discussion by citing a third example which points up a concept that has become decisive for liberation theology. It is the notion of "the signs of the times." It is in Mark's Gospel once again that we find the following passage: "Then the Pharisees came out and engaged him in discussion. To test him they asked him for a sign from heaven. He sighed deeply to himself and said, 'Why does this generation ask for a sign? I tell you this: no sign shall be given to this generation' " (Mark 8:11–12).

In his Gospel Luke points up an important feature of the context in which people were asking for such signs: "He was driving out a devil which was dumb; and when the devil had come out, the dumb man began to speak. The people were astonished, but some of them said, 'It is by Beelzebub, prince of devils, that he drives the devils out.' Others, by way of a test, demanded of him a sign from heaven" (Luke 11:14–16). Both Luke and Matthew spell out the reason cited by Jesus for his refusal to give a sign. Here is what Matthew reports, according to some texts of the Gospel: "His answer was, 'In the evening you say, 'It will be fine weather, for the sky is red,' and in the morning you say, 'It will be stormy today; the sky is red and lowering.' You know how to interpret the appearance of the sky; can you not interpret the signs of the times?' " (Matt. 16:2–3).

This last example shows exactly the same framework as the preceding two examples. First there is an attempt by the Pharisees to confront Jesus with purely theological criteria: they ask for a sign from *heaven*. Secondly, they again try to close off theology from any criterion stemming from the relative realm of history: a sign of the times, such as the liberation of a deaf mute, is not satisfactory. Thirdly, Jesus again refuses to go along with such theological maneuvering. He tries to show them that they must leave room and openness in their theology for the relative, provisional, uncertain nature of criteria that human beings actually use to direct their lives in history when they are open to what is going on around them.

But Jesus goes even further here and accuses them of being *hypocrites*. Today we would not dare to go so far. At most we might accuse theology of being too academic. But Jesus goes one step further, and that further step is typically *political*. If the Pharisees do in fact know very well how to find historical direction within a context of uncertainty, their quest for some theological authority is not prompted by any overwhelming anxiety in the face of events. It is prompted by their intention to impose on other people a kind of authority from which there is no appeal. That authority ranges from the realm of religion itself to the whole socio-political structure of Israel, which is determined far more by them than it is by the Romans (see Matt. 23:4–7).

The other very different possibility, which might seem more logical but in fact is much more difficult in such matters, would be to place theology and its certitudes in the service of human beings who are scanning the complex signs of the times and trying to use them to find out how to love more and more, how to love better and better, and how to make a commitment to that sort of love. In other words, one could let theology be "the second step," as it obviously is in Jesus' own methodology. As Luke recounts the story, Jesus ends his remarks by saying to the Pharisees that they should not look for signs from heaven but rather decide for themselves what is right.

We can assume, I think, that the Pharisees would have felt that they needed greater certainty. That is what they would have said to Jesus and his advice, if they answered him at all. But Jesus' theology says something very different. It suggests that when people stop at theological certitudes, those certitudes fall apart in their hands. For they are not designed to take the place of an upright human heart as the primary source of any and every historical judgment.

Now remember what Gutiérrez proved rather convincingly in his book. He showed that today uprightness and openness of heart must be sought in and through the political dimension—a dimension, by the way, which clearly was not absent from the theology of Jesus himself. Thus no truly liberative theology can seriously entertain the question as to whether it should or should not *descend* from its own proper certitudes to the shaky terrain of concrete history, sociology, and politics. Why? Because that is precisely the kind of approach that is ruled out by Jesus.

The only real problem is how will theology open itself up to the human realm in all its dimensions, and formulate questions for revelation on the basis of options taken in that realm.

There is no unbridgeable gap between the Church and politics, as Pharisaical theology claims. There is an intimate tie-up between the realm of human sensitivity and political commitment on the one hand, and theological reflection on the other hand. Recognition of that tie-up is an essential precondition for any theological methodology that purports to imitate the liberating creativity of Jesus' own methodology. And this point has been stressed more than once in recent statements of the Latin American hierarchy.[12]

III. COMMITMENT IS THE FIRST STEP

If our remarks so far are correct, then the liberation theology of Latin America has rediscovered an essential feature of Christian theology and is in a position to engage in serious criticism of academic theology on that point. What is more, the political theology which has come to the fore in Europe recently does not have a great deal in common with our formulation of the issue since it derives politics from theological sources whereas the theology of Jesus derives theology from the openness of the human heart to man's most urgent problems. Indeed Jesus seems to go so far as to suggest that one cannot recognize Christ, and therefore come to know God, unless he or she is willing to start with a personal commitment to the oppressed. That comes down to saying that if Jesus had been recognized by some sort of sign from heaven, then neither he or God would have been truly recognized at all.

But that brings us to a new problem. We started by justifying theology's engagement in politics. We said that theology could opt for one or another sort of political system without having any verifiable scientific basis to justify the option. But our line of argument took hold of us and carried us much further. For if our remarks so far are correct, then we must ask the same question that has been asked by various Latin American theologians in recent days: Is it possible to know and recognize the liberation message of the Gospel at all without a prior commitment to liberation? As is evident, this is merely a new version of the hermeneutic circle discussed in the first chapter. But whereas there we seemed to be talking about a theoretical condition, here the condition shows up in all its concrete importance.

Let us begin our considerations by noting a rather odd contrast pointed up in the Gospel texts. It is a contrast which *perhaps* is to be generalized. The fewer theological certitudes entertained by a contemporary of Jesus, the easier it was for that person to recognize God in his teaching and his deeds. In other words, prior theological certitudes seemed to close people's minds and hearts to Jesus, preventing them from giving full and absolute value to the *signs* that revealed Jesus for the person he truly was.

It is an historical fact that the people who were *best informed about God's revelation in the Old Testament* let Jesus pass by and failed to see in him the new and definitive divine revelation. The Christian message has come down to us through the *amaretz* of Israel, that is, the people who were less knowledgeable about the law and its interpretation.

Does this contrast, which is an historical fact, remain valid for our own day? In itself the question might seem rather theoretical and abstract. But liberation theology in Latin America has been obliged to confront it in very concrete terms, in the light of real happenings which have been quite obvious and decisive in the history of the Latin American continent. The whole problem can be posed in three stages:

1. Do Christians have a specific contribution of their own to make to the process of liberating our continent? If the answer is "no," then it is not worth being a Christian at all according to Jesus' own understanding of theology.

2. Assuming that Christians do have a specific contribution of their own to make, are we to say that they should generally refuse to figure out what that contribution is supposed to be unless and until they commit themselves concretely to the problems involved in historical liberation? After all, the Pharisees could very well have worked up some prefabricated "theology of liberation" from the Mosaic law itself. But even then the assumption would have to be that such a theology, when confronted with other, more human criteria, would not have enabled them to recognize Jesus either—precisely because it constituted a criterion prior to concrete historical data and human facts.

3. Does that mean that the less human beings know about Christianity, the more guarantee there is that they will get involved in an authentic liberation process and therein come to discover the authentic message of the gospel? If we want an authentic Christian education, in other words, must we be willing at first to substitute an authentic commitment to liberation for it, so that we can then look for a key to this message within the liberation process and work up a nondistorted version of it?

Speaking in general terms, we can say that there would seem to be three lines of argument that would prompt us to answer the above questions in the affirmative. Let us consider them in detail.

1. The first line of argument comes from the very same biblical theology that concerned us in the previous section. In one way or another,

to a greater or lesser degree, the general lines of our exegetical analysis would seem to be confirmed and validated.

Needless to say, one might very well come across a very ingenuous kind of liberation theology which assumed that it could *deduce* its content for any given situation from the gospel message itself. At one point in his book, Gustavo Gutiérrez makes the following statement: "From the viewpoint of faith, the motive which in the last instance moves Christians to participate in the liberation of oppressed peoples and exploited social classes is the conviction of *the radical incompatibility of evangelical demands with an unjust and alienating society.*"[13] Isolated from the context of the whole book, this remark might seem to be a perfect example of a fundamental theology of liberation. For it seems to assume that the straightforward words of the gospel message by themselves are enough to convince the Christian that the maintenance of existing social structures is incompatible with his or her faith. But that is far from evident, and millions of Christians hear the words of the gospel message without drawing any such conclusion.

But one can only interpret the author's remark in those terms by isolating it from the rest of his book. At another point the first edition of Gutiérrez's book contained this sentence by itself: "The annunciation of the Gospel thus has a conscienticizing function, or in other words, a politicizing function." In the final version, the following clarifying remarks were added after that sentence: *"But this is made real and meaningful only by living and announcing the Gospel from within a commitment to liberation, only in concrete, effective solidarity with people and exploited social classes. Only by participating in their struggles can we understand the implications of the Gospel message and make it have an impact on history."*[14]

The circle is complete, and its central importance in the mind of the author is brought out clearly by his paper at the El Escorial theological meeting in 1972.[15]

This same inversion of the classical approach can be found in at least two sections of the Medellín documents. In their "Message to the Peoples of Latin America" the bishops state: "In the light of the faith that we profess as believers, we have undertaken to *discover the plan of God in the 'signs of the times.'* We interpret the aspirations and clamors of Latin America as signs that reveal the direction of the divine plan."[16] The text is clear and straightforward.

In addition to this text, the bishops are even more explicit in their general "Introduction to the Final Documents": "The Latin American Church . . . has in no way 'detoured from,' but has actually 'returned to' man, aware that 'in order to know God, it is necessary to know man.'. . . . Just as Israel of old, the first People (of God), felt the saving presence of God when He delivered them from the oppression of Egypt by the passage through the sea and led them to the promised land, so we also, the new People of God, cannot cease to feel his saving passage in view of 'true development, which is the passage for each and all, from conditions of life that are less human, to those that are more human.' "[17]

We can also cite a passage in the bishops' document on "Education" where they allude to Paul's Letter to the Romans: "Therefore, all 'growth in humanity' brings us closer to 'reproducing the image of the Son so that He will be the firstborn among many brothers.' "[18] Now "reproducing the image of the Son" would clearly entail knowing that image better. Therefore "growth in humanity" becomes a preliminary condition for any authentic understanding of Christ and his message. Once again we have the full circle of the hermeneutic process.

The aforementioned official pronouncements by the bishops of Latin America make it clear that (political) commitment is necessary for any and all authentic knowledge of the gospel message and its demands. Quite clearly and logically they imply that any hermeneutic is insufficiently critical and therefore inadequate if it presumes to attain that knowledge in an abstract scientific way without going through the prior step of making a commitment to liberation on every plane—particularly if it discards that step as improper.

In other words, the bishops give priority to something else over scholarly dialogue concerning the possible contribution of Christians to the political struggle or to revolution. In the passages just cited, they indicate that one cannot possibly know the nature of that contribution solely by having recourse to the gospel message, because one's interpretation of the gospel will vary depending on whether it is carried out from within or outside a political commitment to liberation. If Gutiérrez is right when he says that theology comes "after," then any preliminary consideration of the possible nature of some specifically Christian contribution to liberation—a process in which people of many different beliefs and ideologies participate—is senseless and hence unanswerable.

2. Curious and shocking as it may seem, then, various Latin American theologians have come to the conclusion that it is impossible to know what a specifically Christian contribution to liberation might be, prior to a personal commitment to liberation. Here, for example, is what J.P. Richard has to say: "It is not what are called 'evangelical values' that give meaning to social praxis. Quite the opposite is the case. Social praxis gives meaning to the former. Only this approach will enable theology to get beyond the subject-object distortion that characterizes the present ideological character of Christianity. The latter prevents Christianity

from shouldering the social praxis of liberation. Christians should not redefine social praxis by starting with the gospel message. They should do just the opposite. They should seek out the historical import of the gospel by starting with social praxis."[19]

That is easy enough to say, but it clashes with the awesome reality of ecclesiastical praxis. Long before a Christian decides to swell the ranks of a liberation group, he or she has been bombarded on all sides with a specific image of Christ and his message. If liberation theology has become a live issue for many Christian groups in Latin America, one can certainly say it is because at some point in their Christian education priests and catechists began to draw new, unheard-of conclusions from the same gospel message. In other words, the pastoral success of the theology of liberation has been a process of moving from the gospel message to liberation, not from the liberation process to the gospel message.

But the force of the arguments does lead us towards the second alternative as the correct one. Two types of argument in particular point us in that direction.

The first is more theoretical in nature. It has been developed fairly completely by European theology, even though that theology has been timid about drawing the ultimate conclusions. The timidity may be due to the fact that those consequences seem to be merely destructive if one does not already possess and espouse a liberation perspective.

First Protestant and then Catholic exegesis in Europe discovered over the last hundred years or so that it was impossible to get back to any certain picture of the *historical* Jesus. (I am using "historical" here in the modern, scientific sense of the term.) It was found that the Gospels were not so much witnesses to who Jesus really was and what he really said and did as they were witnesses to the postpaschal faith of the primitive Christian community and how it saw and interpreted Jesus. Our own faith in Jesus, therefore, has to proceed by way of at least one theological interpretation: the theological interpretation of the Gospels themselves. For the Gospels present the interpretation (or interpretations) of a specific concrete community which had to face specific historical problems that bear little resemblance to our own problems.

Now of course that does not mean that Jesus is a myth or that the interpretation of the early Christian community is unworthy of belief insofar as it talks about Jesus. But it would certainly be incredible if that concrete historical community, in recalling Jesus, had not injected into the process many elements peculiar to its own situation in history. We have proof, for example, that certain parables of Jesus show up in the Gospels as parables directed to the attention of church authorities, when in fact they must originally have been addressed to the religious authorities of Israel.[20]

We can go even further and say, with Bultmann, that the primitive Christian community saw Jesus suspended over the whole methodological backdrop of its age. It presented him in terms of such things as heaven and hell, miraculous interventions of God in history, voices from heaven, resurrection from the dead, and so forth.

Now Latin American theology—and praxis—is particularly suspicious of the *ideological* elements that must certainly have influenced the first Christian community, the community that sought to interpret Jesus and gave us its version in the Gospels. As James Cone noted in the passages we quoted in Chapter I, it is not at all certain that Jesus would have altered the Old Testament view and advised us to turn the other cheek if he had been confronted with the whole issue of Israelite slavery in Egypt.

How is it, then, that his words about turning the other cheek seem to sum up his thinking and his message in the Gospels? The most logical answer to that question is that the community to which Jesus addressed those remarks was living in a situation very different from that of the ancient Israelites in Egypt. Or, at the very least, the situation of the first Christians was very different.

Now if we pursue this argument further, we come to the conclusion that the real problem is not whether Jesus did or did not speak those exact words in that particular context. For Jesus, too, belonged to a specific historical context, and he spoke and acted accordingly. So even if we had an authentic tape recording of his words, that would not absolve us from the task of trying to find out what elements in his message should be attributed to the surrounding circumstances. Cone, then, is perfectly right when he says that any and every sort of liberalism—be it fundamentalist, scholarly, or Marxist—is essentially conservative.

Now if we begin to work on the Gospels with a suspicion that ideology is involved somewhere, where will we stop? The problem might seem highly theoretical, but it touches upon the very nucleus of our religious certitudes and can lead to psychological panic. Nevertheless there is only one logical answer. It must be admitted that the more we divest our minds of ideological trappings, the more we will free the message of Jesus from its ideological wrappings and get closer to its deeper, perduring truth. Jesus is not an historical monument. If he were alive and active today, he would say many things that would differ greatly from what he said twenty centuries ago. Without him, but not

without his Spirit, we must find out what he would say to free us if he
were alive today.

In the last analysis, the task of de-ideologizing our minds in order to
really pay heed to the gospel message is not a merely intellectual one. In
Jesus' day, the people free from the snares of ideology were those who
were not fettered by theology in such a way that they could not recognize
human need and human oppression around them. The same holds true
for us today. A real, effective option on behalf of the oppressed can
de-ideologize our minds and free our thinking for the gospel message.
Theology is the second step. We should not begin by asking what is the
specifically Christian contribution to the historical process of liberation.

3. But as I hinted above, there is another approach that has led Latin
American theologians to the same conclusion. It is the approach of concrete historical experience.

As we have seen, the Church shows up, and perceives itself, as a
privileged level of certitudes that have been derived or deduced from
divine revelation. Only with great caution does it make an effort to
descend from those certitudes to the thorny, uncertain ground of terres-
trial certitudes; for it fully realizes that if a particular option is debatable
on scientific or scholarly grounds, it cannot be imposed on the whole
Church. Instead of being accepted as the word of God, such an option
would only divide Christians on matters that God did not deign to
reveal—undoubtedly because he did not think them really important.

The first step towards correcting this situation is taken when one
realizes the point made by someone like Moltmann, for example: "When
and if Christians do take a stand in the political struggle, will they not be
setting aside God's universal love for human beings? That is the fundamental question. I think the answer is 'no.' The goal of Christian universalism can only be won through the dialectical process of opting for the
oppressed."[21] It is not easy for the Church to accept Moltmann's view
because it operates with an ecclesiology which we shall have occasion to
describe in a later chapter. But the impact of liberation theology has
certainly been to give more value to a real option for liberation than to
an inoperative brand of Christian unity that has no liberative thrust at
all.

But that leads us right away into a second question: What does opting
for the oppressed mean *in the concrete*? Obviously it means doing everything we can for them. But what is "everything we can"? We are forced
to confront the whole issue of *means*. Ordinarily a Christian and a Marxist do not share the same idea of what doing "all we can" entails.

The reader probably will think of the problem of violence at once, but I do not think it is the main problem. As should become apparent in the course of this book, I think the critical dividing line in connection with means is whether or not we must manipulate human masses and turn them into tools before we can raise their consciousness.

Right now, in any case, the most important point is not trying to determine where encounter and conflict will arise. The important point is that in any discussion of means Christians think they know from the very start what sort of means are permitted or prohibited by their faith. Let me give you an example of the problem here.

At the Salzburg dialogue between Marxists and Christians, Dominique Dubarle spelled out the following ideal of coexistence: "To free the state of all suspicion . . . it is not enough to inscribe the principle of individual freedom of opinion and religion in the Constitution. It is also necessary: (1) to grant the various confessional communities reasonable opportunities for internal organization, expression, and political exercise—opportunities that everyone must grant if they claim to respect the personality and freedom of others—in short, *civil tolerance;* (2) to neutralize the administrative functioning of the state vis-à-vis the ideological or religious preferences of those in power . . . so that no administrative organs of the state give preferential treatment to one particular kind of conviction or ideology or simply serve the interests of the people or parties in power—in short, *political impartiality.*"[22]

Now it gets somewhat interesting when we realize that this sort of ideal, which is certainly somewhat utopian, is reserved for a dialogue with Marxists. It is not spelled out in the same form, or with the same vigor and clarity, when it is a matter of other governments in the West—be they Christian or not—such as that with which Dubarle is familiar in his own country. The government of his own country, for example, certainly does not respect either of the two conditions laid down. When a Christian talks like that, one cannot help but contrast his words and the underlying ideal with the violent suppression and outlawing of Marxist parties and ideologies in most of the nations that call themselves Christian.

But let us follow Dubarle a bit further: "As to the concrete political forms which Marxism has taken up to now, a religious person cannot be content to tolerate the form in which he is obliged to live out his conviction and his community life." There is no doubt, in my opinion, that Dubarle is alluding to real facts that are visible to all. It is possible that Dubarle might sing a different tune if he were to probe deeper and explore the real conception and the resultant political influence of such religious communities in nations where the state considers itself Marxist.

But the fact still remains that even Christians inspired by revolutionary and liberative ideals, for one reason or another, do feel restricted in the public and political expression of their faith.

Let us move on to the principal point, the conclusion that Dubarle draws after his comparison between the real-life situation and his ideal: "Thus, so long as the political problem surrounding his convictions has not found a more satisfactory political arrangement, the determination of the Christian is to fight against any new establishment of Marxist states, because *in this respect* the existing non-Marxist states appear to be less unsatisfactory."[23]

This curious mental process shows up quite frequently. Note that it leads to critical and radical decisions based on *one particular aspect* of the overall process, an aspect that allows for different standards of measurement in the different systems. If we want to explain how such a line of thinking works, I think we must appreciate three factors involved:

1. The whole reasoning process is worked out prior to, and outside of, the historical process. The very definition of the ideal (which becomes the critical condition for praxis) reveals that the definer himself is not a politician faced with concrete problems. It would seem clear enough that any overall evaluation of a process must give due weight and value to the new human being who supposedly can and should arise through it. All the partial aspects, precisely because they are such, are relativized (not eliminated) by the overall process. They cannot be turned into *conditions* for entering into it in the first place.

2. Ordinarily a religious—and Christian—evaluation made prior to, and outside of, an historical process presupposes that a reading and understanding of the gospel message provides one with *absolute* certainties. Thus, instead of relativizing the religious aspect of the process, one relativizes the process in the name of a gospel message that one supposedly has come to know and interpret correctly. No attempt is made, for example, to balance such things as people's suffering, humiliation, and death against the results—limited and human of course—that can be hoped for from the process.

3. Since some ideal is taken from the gospel message prior to, and outside of, the historical process, and since this ideal is declared to be absolute, *minority* aspects (e.g., freedom of thought, freedom of religion, freedom for Christian political action) seem to be systematically overvalued in comparison with factors that are more revolutionary because they affect great human *masses* at one extreme of the process: e.g., in conditions of dire poverty, ignorance, disease, and death. Thus insofar as an estabished regime grants more and more opportunities for free-

dom to minorities, it will systematically be given preference over any revolutionary movement of the masses by this type of theology.

IV. THE PROBLEM OF A SPECIFICALLY CHRISTIAN CONTRIBUTION

Having reached this point, let us go one step further and consider the concrete political consequences connected with the whole problem of a specifically Christian contribution to the liberation process.

In one of his articles, Hugo Assmann acknowledges that the use of Christian labels for leftist political movements can have "temporary and tactical value" insofar as it undermines "the use of Christianity by the political right."[24] Aside from this temporary, tactical use, however, Assmann thinks it is evident that the normal involvement of the Christian with the political left should not be viewed as an involvement between "Christian revolutionaries" on the one hand and "other revolutionaries" on the other hand. There is no "Christian ally," with a distinctive nature and contribution of his own, who can be isolated from the other revolutionaries in this way.

Of course Assmann cannot rest content with that assertion. For if it is true that Christians have no distinctive contribution of their own to make to liberation, why be a Christian at all?

So Assmann starts over again and tries to explain himself more clearly: "That does not at all deprive the expression 'Christian contribution' of valid content. It simply moves us beyond *the traditional way* of posing the problem, which entailed picturing the 'Christian contribution' as some alienating and restraining contribution of a specific sort . . . as some sort of doctrinal *a priori* set above and over against revolutionary facts and deeds."

So far there are two elements in this treatment that deserve consideration. The first is that Christians, even before they come in contact with the revolution and commit themselves to it, feel they possess certain Christian principles that are decisive for it. The second is that revolutionary events give the lie to any such principles.

Now let us continue with Assmann's line of thought: "The view of a specifically Christian contribution as some sort of ideological 'advance payment,' as something defined 'before' and 'outside of' the concrete revolutionary process, is finished. Such a view is an idealistic one dangerously opposed to the inescapable mediation of unitary praxis in the unique revolutionary process. It was the classic source of all the familiar 'third ways' (*tercerismos*) and the parallel but distinct Christian approaches which have been so fatally expropriated and used as tools by the forces of reaction."[25]

Two more noteworthy points can be found in this passage, and we must add them to the two mentioned above. The third point, then, is that Christians ordinarily do not experience the Christian doctrine of revolution and find its means in real life; instead they deduce it directly from divine revelation. The fourth point is that when the pragmatic rules of the revolutionary process reject the idealistic Christian exigencies, the Christian contribution tends to go off on its own and to look for some third or middle road between the status quo and the revolution; the fatal end result is that it is reabsorbed by the status quo. In other words, Christians start out in sympathy with the revolution but impose "evangelical" conditions on it; and so, in the name of the gospel message, they end up opposing the revolution and fight on the antirevolutionary side.

I think that the whole phenomenon of adopting "third ways" presents a profound methodological challenge to liberation and represents the ultimate consequence of an erroneous way of formulating the whole problem of the relationship between theology and politics. Perhaps the clearest concrete example of the process in Latin America can be found in the origin and later development of the Christian Democratic political party in Chile.

Some decades ago, a group of younger Christians split off from the Conservative Party and established a political movement that was originally known as the "Falange." That in itself is significant. First of all, it shows that up until relatively recent times the "normal" political stance of the Christian was membership in some conservative political party. This fact itself poses an interesting theological problem. Secondly, the fact that the splintering was done in the name of Christian exigencies raises the whole hermeneutic question of a political interpretation of Christianity being derived from the gospel message itself.

As it turned out, the Falange, which later came to be known as the Christian Democratic movement (and its members as Christian Democrats), found its interpretation of the gospel message in what is called the "social doctrine of the Church." Now as everyone knows, the latter doctrine represented an attempt by the Catholic hierarchy to determine and spell out the "specifically Christian contribution" to the process of bettering and improving the existing real-life situation. It was concerned more particularly with the situation existing in Europe. Its norms were either deduced from divine revelation or else grounded on some alleged natural right—the latter, in turn, being based on some eternal natural law governing things.[26]

In reality the "social doctrine of the Church" started out by trying to guide Christians to lead a societal life more in conformity with the gospel within the existing capitalist structures. When *Rerum novarum,* the first great social encyclical, made its appearance, socialism was only a hazy ideal. The concrete world to which the encyclical was addressed, and within which a more consistently Christian line of conduct was envisioned, was completely dominated by the principle of private ownership of the means of production. Socialism was condemned as an abstract ideal opposed to the natural right of all human beings to own private property.

It is worth noting in passing that the imagined picture of a society without private ownership of the means of production, the picture that served as the basis for the Church's argument, was quite unreal. The assumption was that in any attempt to realize the socialist ideal people would lose any and all possibility of real self-fulfillment. More recent encyclicals dealing with the same theme have felt obliged to maintain the condemnation on the one hand, but also to admit that the situation of the average employee in bureaucratic Western society is similar in almost every respect to that which would hold true in a society where there was no private ownership of the means of production. Yet that does not seem to entail any impossibility of living a truly human life.

But our main concern here is to trace the progress of the Christian Democratic movement in Chile. One can say that it came into being and developed under the aegis of a very unrealistic condition: supposedly it would alter an economic system through a process of moral preaching, without changing the prevailing rules of the game.

This being the case, it was only natural that the Christian Democratic Party would occupy the center spot on the political spectrum, operating as a third possibility between the socialist parties on the one hand and the conservative parties on the other. Thus it could and did attract a growing number of members from the middle class, who were afraid of both extremes.

The most interesting thing of all, however, is the fact that the Christian Democrats were brought closer and closer to the sources of real power, not by virtue of their own intrinsic political doctrine but by virtue of something extrinsic to their own position: i.e., the failures of the parties on the left and the right. The extrinsic nature of this thrust was evident to the Christian Democrats themselves; for the fact is that as they came closer to the reins of power, they felt a more pressing need to work out a political platform of their own and to leave behind the incredible doctrinal discussions that bore witness to their early split-off from the Conservative Party.

In other words, it became clearer and clearer that the "social doctrine of the Church" could not pass for a political program—either in the eyes of the electorate or in the eyes of those Christian Democrats who might eventually win power. Realistically speaking, a sermon on socio-economic morality could not take the place of a consistent and effective political policy. If the Christian Democracy movement was to differentiate itself politically from the extreme right and the extreme left, it would have to do something more than preach a sermon. It would have to introduce some clear and consistent modification into the law of supply and demand.

All this time, however, the "social doctrine of the Church" had also been evolving, and its "third way" cast had become even more clear-cut. For a time its moral pronouncements against specific evils of capitalism combined with its total condemnation of socialism had concealed its third-way character. Since it never attacked the basic principle of the capitalistic system—i.e., private ownership of the means of production and the law of supply and demand as the basic rule of the economic game—the Church's social doctrine had been viewed as capitalistic itself. But a gradual evolution was taking place in the doctrine. It began to call for an ever-increasing "socialization" of the means of production—deliberately avoiding the use of the word "socialism." And it also began to condemn capitalism in clear-cut terms because it was a system based on the pursuit of individual, private profit.

In this general setting the Christian Democratic Party of Chile arrived at a crucial set of elections under the banner of two slogans. It proposed "communitarian ownership" and a "revolution in liberty." Both slogans pointed to what was clearly and unmistakably a Christian ideal. Whether they were feasible or not was of course another question. The call for "communitarian ownership" clearly represented a middle road between the alleged evils of private ownership on the one hand and of dehumanizing state ownership on the other hand. In a more subtle way, the call for a "revolution in liberty" was also a third-way out, standing between the revolutionless exercise of power by the conservative parties on the one hand and the dictatorship of the proletariat that socialism proclaimed as the necessary way to bring about any radical change in the economic and political system.

It is worth asking why no one had thought of this panacea before. The point is important, and there seems to be only one answer—an obvious one at that. It simply must be admitted that here again we are dealing with an "evangelical" ideal. Both the possibility of establishing "communitarian ownership" and the possibility of effecting a "revolution in liberty" would depend on the possibility of *converting the hearts* of the people who would be affected by the changes. This became very clear when Allende eventually did try to carry out this "revolution in liberty."

When the Christian Democracy movement did gain power through the electoral process, it became very obvious that it did indeed represent some third-way approach of its own. Faced with real-life historical difficulties both internally and externally, it refused to transfer ownership to the community or to revolutionize the capitalistic economic system. One solid proof of this is the fact that its program of agrarian reform, the only clear-cut accomplishment of its tenure, not only did not seem incompatible with the capitalist system but actually seemed to be demanded by that system.

Paradoxically enough, the failure of the Christian Democratic Party on those two fronts really did convert people's hearts to socialism. The latter was relatively victorious in a later set of elections, thanks to a coalition of political parties under the leadership of Salvador Allende. But perhaps it would be more accurate to say that Allende's victory was due to the splintering of the middle class. Members of that class lost confidence in the Christian Democratic Party because the presidential campaign of its candidate, Radomiro Tomic, was remarkably similar to that of Allende. For a brief moment, in other words, the third-way cast of the Christian Democratic Party faded into the background. It seemed to be moving sharply towards the left.

That this was only a temporary phenomenon, perhaps due to the bad policy of Tomic himself, was clearly demonstrated by subsequent events. Mathematically speaking, the third-way cast of the Christian Democratic movement became crystal-clear during Allende's presidency. It systematically allied itself with the right, forming decisive majorities against the policies of the left. It also became clear that its talk about "community ownership" and a "revolution in liberty" was only its way of saying it was not with the left—not even when the left was trying to put through those very objectives. Finally, through direct dealings with other groups and indirect acts that paralyzed the country, the Christian Democrats handed over the reins of government to the military junta.

It is hard to find, in the historical annals of a "Christian" party, a more convincing confirmation of Assmann's basic hypothesis: i.e., that "evangelical" conditions imposed on the revolutionary process in *a priori* terms eventually turn into third-way stands; and that they also turn into counterrevolutionary forces when and if the revolution becomes feasible.

And so we come to the end of this chapter with a question still unanswered. We started out considering what a political option taken in the name of Christian theology might be, and we ended up with the conclusion that there is no such thing as Christian theology or a Christian interpretation of the gospel message in the absence of a prior political commitment. Only the latter makes the former possible at all. The unanswered question still before us on the practical level is this: Does that mean that we must hold back, hoping that some political option will be possible, and that it will be a favorable one, before we can begin to understand and appreciate and make use of the gospel message?

NOTES

1. That at least is the title of the English-language version, the only one that I could check: *Caesar and God* (Maryknoll, N.Y.: Orbis Books, 1972). Vekemans systematically combats Latin American liberation theology in every issue of his periodical *Tierra Nueva* (Bogotá). An assiduous co-worker on that periodical is Bishop Alfonso López Trujillo, secretary general of CELAM (the Latin American Episcopal Conference).

2. Gustavo Gutiérrez, *A Theology of Liberation*, Eng. trans. (Maryknoll, N.Y.: Orbis Books, 1973), p. 11; author's italics too.

3. *Ibid.*

4. *Ibid.*, p. 47.

5. If we agree with Gutiérrez that the realm of politics is the most prevalent and pervasive factor in present-day human life, it is anachronistic to ask what Jesus' attitude might have been towards this *present-day* situation of ours. The discovery of the pervasive influence of politics is our contemporary discovery, not his. Hence Jesus' stance vis-à-vis the Roman Empire or the Zealots, as a political stance, is also relatively beside the point. The fact is that the concrete, systematic oppression that Jesus confronted in his day did not appear to him as "political" in our sense of the term; it showed up to him as "religious" oppression. More than officials of the Roman Empire, it was the religious authority of the Scribes and Sadducees and Pharisees that determined the socio-political structure of Israel. In real life this authority was political, and Jesus really did tear it apart. This is evident from the fact that the concern to get rid of Jesus physically—because he threatened the status quo—was primarily displayed by the supposedly "religious" authorities rather than by the representatives of the Roman Empire.

6. "A Letter to the Peoples of the Third World," in *Between Honesty and Hope: Documents from and about the Church in Latin America,* Eng. trans., (Maryknoll, N.Y.: Maryknoll Publications, 1970), p. 5.

7. *Ibid.*, p. 7, quoting from an address made at Vatican II by Patriarch Maximos IV Saigh, September 28, 1965.

8. The cited passage is clearly talking about the choice of a social or political or economic system, which we tend to subsume under the cover term "political."

9. Cited in Vekemans, *Caesar and God,* pp. 29–30. I have not been able to check the original context of Rahner's statement, so my remarks here are based

on the use Vekemans makes of it rather than on Rahner's specific statement in its original context.

10. "A Letter to the Peoples of the Third World," in *Between Honesty and Hope*, p. 4.

11. See Gaston Fessard, *De l'actualité historique* (Paris: Desclée, 1959), II, 63–65. See my criticism of Fessard's position in *Evolution and Guilt*, A Theology for Artisans of a New Humanity, Volume 5, Eng. trans. (Maryknoll, N.Y., Orbis Books, 1974), Chapter III, Clarification II, pp. 65–67.

12. More than one statement by the bishops of Latin America and other church groups has insisted that the Church must intervene in politics. See the many documents in the anthology *Between Honesty and Hope*.

13. Gutiérrez, *A Theology of Liberation*, p. 145.

14. *Ibid.*, p. 269.

15. See "Evangelio y praxis de liberación," in *Fe cristiana y cambio social en América Latina* (Salamanca: Sígueme, 1973), pp. 231–45; especially pp. 241–44.

16. Documents of the Medellín Conference, *The Church in the Present-Day Transformation of Latin America in the Light of the Council*, Eng. trans. (Washington D.C., Latin American Division, United States Catholic Conference, 1970), Vol II, Conclusions, p. 38.

17. No. 1 and 6, *ibid.*, p. 47 and 49.

18. No. 9, *ibid.*, p. 101.

19. The article cited is probably "Racionalidad socialista y verificación histórica del cristianismo," which appeared in *Cuadernos de la realidad nacional* (Santiago de Chile), April 1972. It is cited without a reference by Adolfo Ham, "Introduction to the Theology of Liberation," in *Communio viatorum* (Prague), Summer 1973.

20. This has been shown by people like Joachim Jeremias, for example; see his *Parables of Jesus*, rev. ed. (New York: Scribner's, 1971).

21. "Dieu dans la révolution," in *Discussion sur 'la théologie de la révolution'*, by J. Moltmann, Dom Helder Camara, D.A. Seeber, M. Lotz, H. Gollwitzer, R. Weth, A. Rich, W. Dirks, H. Assmann, A. Bezerra de Melo, French trans. (Paris: Cerf-Mame, 1972), pp. 70–71.

22. "L'avenir humain et la permanence du fait religieux," in *Marxistes et Chrétiens: Entretiens de Salzbourg* (1965), French trans. (Paris: Mame, 1968), pp. 115–16.

23. *Ibid.*

24. "Prologue" to *Habla Fidel Castro sobre los cristianos revolucionarios* (Montevideo: Tierra Nueva, 1972).

25. *Ibid.*, pp. 22–24.

26. See, in *Rerum novarum*, the argument from natural law in section 7 and from divine revelation (based on the curse of original sin) in section 12.

CHAPTER FOUR

Ideologies and Faith

From what has been said so far it should be evident that liberation theology is struggling with dangerous issues and problems. At the very least they are dangerous from the standpoint of church authorities and church structures. For if our remarks are indeed a logical conclusion from theology accepted at the Medellín Conference, then we must have a new kind of authority in the Church, a new ecclesial structure, a new kind of faith and pastoral effort, and a new role for the laity in the very process of defining what authentic Christian faith is. At the very least we can readily understand two evident facts: (1) the alarm of Latin American church authorities at the unexpected consequences of the doctrines they formulated at Medellín as an accurate reflection of Vatican II; (2) the perturbation of significant groups of Christian lay people with a magisterium that seems to be in steady retreat ever since Medellín.

But something very curious happens when we examine the ultimate conclusions that follow from Assmann's line of argument. They seem to go far beyond the premises. It seems we must accept the fact—and indeed our hermeneutic circle is based on the same fact—that a political option in favor of liberative change is an intrinsic element of faith and helps to de-ideologize the latter. We can only have an authentic faith, in other words, when we have committed ourselves to an authentic struggle that opens our eyes to the new possibilities and meanings of God's word.

Now does it logically follow that the less we know beforehand about that divine word, the more authentic will be our commitment and hence our first reading of the word of God? My feeling is that the whole matter is more complicated; that if this is the correct interpretation of Assmann's view, it stands in need of correction. In any case our argument here would certainly hold true if there is to be a *continuing* hermeneutic circle. For as the reader may remember from Chapter I, our supposition is that our hermeneutic keeps moving on towards an ever more authentic truth that is to be translated into ever more liberative praxis.

The specific point under discussion here, then, is *the very beginning* of the process—what classical theology called the *initium fidei,* the "beginning of faith."

I. IDEOLOGIES PRIOR TO COMMITMENT

The first point to be discussed here closely resembles a point in Bultmann's hermeneutic circle. To understand the word of God addressed to human beings, Bultmann feels one must begin by understanding one's own existence. Why? Because God speaks to us through that existence. If the word of God did not allude in some way to real human experience, then his message to us would be formulated in a foreign language, as it were.

It is a complicated problem, however, because the average human being has a very superficial and unauthentic conception of his or her own existence and so he fails to note or grasp a large portion of God's message. To introduce a different example here, we can consider a work of art. Even though it may speak the same language as the viewer, the latter must have as profound a grasp of that language as the artist who painted the picture. The profundity of our comprehension is bound up with the profundity of our own real-life experience, and the latter is also bound up with the words of our language.

In order to attain the existential authenticity and profundity required to gain an ever deeper understanding of the word of God, Bultmann proposed to base his methodology on the existential analysis of Heidegger.[1] The latter becomes a prerequisite for any interpretation of the Scriptures.

Of course this proposal has given rise to a fierce controversy. Others ask Bultmann what right he has to set up *one* methodology among many possible ones as a prerequisite for understanding the word of God in all its freedom.

The same question could be posed to Assmann, for he ties the authenticity of one's real experience to a specific political option. The notion of a "specifically Christian contribution" is rejected because he views it as a "doctrinal *a priori*" opposed to "revolutionary facts and deeds." This would imply that there are *revolutionary happenings* which can be recognized independently of any *doctrine* that one might hold regarding revolution.

This supposition shows up quite frequently in Assmann's remarks. He uses the definite article and the singular in talking about "the concrete revolutionary process," and he poses personal commitment to that process as a prerequisite for understanding the gospel message. Presumably the revolutionary process, independent of any understanding of the gospel message or of any doctrine at all, can be recognized for what it is and summon us to a concrete personal commitment. Finally, in words that hearken back to Bultmann, Assmann talks about "the necessary mediation of *unitary* praxis in the *one and only* revolutionary process." Here the prerequisite is quite clear. There do exist a revolutionary process and a revolutionary praxis which speak for themselves and call for our personal commitment.

Thus the same question can be posed to Assmann that has been proposed to Bultmann: Why should one show favor to one specific political option as a necessary precondition for understanding God's message in the Scriptures?

Assmann's answer, presumably, would run along the lines of Bultmann's own answer. The latter would admit that Heidegger's methodology in itself offers no sure or eternal guarantee of being the most appropriate one for leading human beings to a deeper understanding of their own existence or the word of God. But *for the moment* it is the best we've got. If a better one were to come along, then we should latch onto it.

That, I think, is the line that Assmann's response would take. One must make a philosophical judgment among the existing philosophical methodologies in order to get an authentic and liberative understanding of human existence. In like manner, one must make a political judgment on the political processes and movements around, choosing the one that lends itself best to ensuring liberative authenticity on the part of the one who makes the commitment. But there is no magical, eternal guarantee in the revolutionary process as such.

In terms of the concrete situation in Latin America, the argument would go something like this. In every Latin American country one can find groups of people who are keenly aware of the oppression suffered by our people and who are determined to use the effective means required to change that situation. All these groups can be regarded as part of a unique revolutionary process, even though they may differ in their tactics from place to place. Thus, instead of consulting the gospel message to see how they should put through a revolution or what means they should use, Christians should join those groups and then reexamine the gospel message from within the revolutionary struggle. Instead they often try to haggle over their participation in the struggle, making that dependent on a prior reading and interpretation of the gospel.

Though this criticism may seem to be logical and acceptable, I believe it greatly oversimplifies the reality of the revolutionary process. A very realistic distinction made by Mannheim can help us to appreciate the point here.

Let us assume that the existing socio-political structures of Latin America do indeed constitute a "sinful situation" as the Medellín Conference indicated. Using the terminological distinction made by Mannheim, we can say that the praxis of Christians should be "utopian" rather than "ideological." This is how Mannheim explains the distinction: "A state of mind is utopian when it is incongruous with the state of reality within which it occurs."[2] He goes on to say: "Only those orientations transcending reality will be referred to by us as utopian which, when they pass over into conduct, tend to shatter, either partially or wholly, the order of things prevailing at the time."[3] On the other hand "ideologies are the situationally transcendent ideas which *never succeed de facto* in the realization of their projected contents . . . The idea of Christian brotherly love, for instance, in a society founded on serfdom remains an unrealizable and, in this sense, ideological idea, even when the intended meaning is, in good faith, a motive in the conduct of the individual."[4]

Now I think there is something critical and important to be kept in mind as we look at the political situation in Latin America as it presents itself to various groups committed to liberation. We must keep in mind the fact that the revolutionary character of a given option does not lie in its content but rather in its real capacity to break up the existing structure rather than to be reabsorbed by the latter. It is precisely in this respect that the political scene in Latin America poses a great challenge to us—even in clear-cut situations such as that which existed in Chile during the rule of Allende. If they are truly honest, all the liberation groups—including those with the most revolutionary political platform—must admit that they cannot at all be sure that they are not serving and helping to reinforce the existing system, even if only against their will. The situation in Chile speaks volumes in this respect. If one considers the regimes which preceded and then followed Allende, there can be no doubt that Allende's government unwittingly but objectively gave to the system the instruments, pretexts, and mechanisms which it needed to acquire an immense increase in power.

Of course the problem is not a simple one. One might say that the risk has to be taken in any case, that the long-term results might well prove that the existing system was profoundly undermined even though that might not seem to be the case, and so forth. Such comments are in order and must be given serious consideration. I have no intention of treating them here, however. My only purpose is to point up the real-life difficulties entailed in any political analysis which purports to say that one or another specific option represents the one and only possible revolutionary process.

The fact is that dozens of groups, movements, and parties claim to possess the one key that will open the door to real revolution. No one can *decide* that his or her praxis is included in the unitary praxis of the one and only revolutionary process without first basing his stand on his ideology or his faith. And deciding on that basis is nothing more than what Lúkacs calls "voluntary idealism."

My purpose here is certainly not to discredit the revolutionary good faith of any group or movement. Nor is it to claim that real revolution is impossible, although it certainly is a far more difficult process that any revolutionary handbook might suggest. What I want to make clear is that one is suggesting the impossible when one says that the *first step* is to join the ranks of the one and only revolutionary process, that this is the first and necessary precondition for authentic praxis, that only then can one move on to search for hermeneutic authenticity. The fact is that personal commitment to revolution is preceded by some ideology or other, whether it comes from Marx, or Mao's sayings, or the gospel message. Further on we shall consider whether that ideology should be called "faith" or not. Right here it is enough to realize that there are an infinite number of more or less revolutionary processes in real-life praxis and that choosing between them presupposes personal motivations and a conception of the overall process that stem from prior conditionings in the mind.

In other words, Assmann may certainly demand or prefer that someone come to the revolutionary process with a Marxist faith rather than a Christian faith. But he cannot entertain the thought that it is better to begin simply with being a revolutionary, for such a revolutionary cannot possibly exist.

That means we should take a look at the beginning of the whole process. We must consider the whole matter of the *initial* faith or ideology.

II. THE COMMON ORIGIN OF FAITH AND IDEOLOGIES

It seems to follow from Assmann's line of argument that the danger of imposing unreal conditions on reality stems from the Christian faith precisely insofar as it is *faith,* that is, insofar as it looks to some source other than *historical* reality for possible solutions.

If my concluding remarks in the last section were correct, however, no one can enter into the revolutionary process without forming some idea for himself of the goal of the process and the proper means to be used to achieve it. To keep our explanation clear and simple here, I shall label the latter process as *ideology*. Note that here the term does not have the pejorative connotations that it had in Chapter I. By "ideology" here I am simply referring to the system of goals and means that serves as the necessary backdrop for any human option or line of action. We need not label the ideology any further, or fit it into a neat little pigeonhole. It could be a classic ideology such as capitalism or Marxism, or it could be an eclectic improvisation stemming from the mind of a sick person. The only thing I am maintaining here is that "entering into the one and only revolutionary process" does presuppose that one already possesses some preliminary ideology that enables one to recognize the revolutionary process.

Now if we phrase the problem in terms of the notions of faith and ideology as just defined, we see that the difficulty noted by Assmann stems from "faith," not from "ideologies." His point is that the Christian does not make a distinction between his faith and his ideology, or that he demands ideologies from his faith. Authentic ideologies would not demand any sort of *a priori* advance payments from the revolution; they would adapt to historical demands and necessities in and through a process of slow maturation. When an ideology is unwittingly based on faith, on the other hand, it takes on absolutist features and tries to impose conditions on everything else, forcing history to dance to its tune.

Needless to say, I am not trying to solve profound problems with merely verbal definitions. But one must admit that there is something to the point just made. The Christian faith makes us run back over the course of history to find the fonts of divine revelation, and then we come back to the present with answers from the past that boast of an absolute guarantee. So as not to lose this guarantee, we feel obliged to apply the answers as faithfully and as literally as possible to the real situation we are facing today. And so liberation theology is confronted with a difficult methodological problem. *What is the relationship between faith and ideology?*

Our everyday experience with language indicates that this is indeed a real problem for Latin American theology. "Faith is not an ideology": that is a frequent statement from the hierarchy when it launches an attack on liberation theology. "Faith is not an ideology—and what we need now is an ideology": that is the frequent complaint of younger Christians, who are told to go back to the gospel message but who do not find in it sufficient direction for making a sound political commitment vis-à-vis liberation. "Faith is not an ideology: That is why we hold

a Christian faith but a Marxist ideology": that is the attitude of growing numbers of Christians who have moved or been pushed towards the
margins of Latin American life.

Such are the attitudes and remarks one hears frequently. And there
is a pervading suspicion that any faith adopted prior to an ideology, the
latter being necessary for any sound historical commitment, will of
necessity exert a conservative influence on the ideology. Hence we are
forced to go back to the beginning and ask ourselves where both faith
and ideologies come from.

In this connection we might do well to consider the phenomenological analysis that underlies one of Albert Camus' plays entitled
Caligula. The thesis underlying that play is that most human beings are
never satisfied in life because they do not manage to attain the ideal they
had set for themselves. They are always caught in the painful process of
striving for their ideal, but they never manage to reach it; hence they
never feel real satisfaction in life, and death comes upon them in that
state. But why don't they attain their goal or ideal? The answer is not
that life is too short. It is that human beings are never consistent in
pursuing the ideal they have set up for themselves. Pushed and pulled
by a thousand different feelings and emotions, they allow themselves to
be distracted in countless ways. By the end of their lives, they have
dedicated only a few days, or weeks, or months to the effective pursuit of
their goal. So it is not surprising that they never experience the satisfaction that life could provide if it were lived in a logical fashion.

As emperor of Rome, Caligula is in a fine position to undertake this
adventure and show other human beings how they can attain real freedom and happiness, how they can carry out what they will to do. Caligula
has come to realize that the *distractions* which divert people from their
goal derive from the physical and emotional bonds that fetter human
freedom. He can reduce the physical bonds to a minimum because he is
almost omnipotent. That leaves only the emotional bonds. To overcome
them, Caligula takes the hard way. He chooses to root out all the emotional and affective ties that encumber man (e.g., love, friendship, moral
sentiments). But when he does succeed in doing that, it turns out that no
ideal really interests him any longer. And his inhuman quest for freedom draws death down upon him.

The "parable" is clear, at least insofar as it relates to our analysis
here: *no human being can experience in advance whether life is worth the trouble,
of being lived and in what way it might be worthwhile.* No human being can
take an exploratory trip first, find out how to realize an ideal and
whether it is worth the effort, and then go back and start out on the road

that leads to it. Real life for a human being presupposes a nonempirical choice of some ideal that one presumes will be satisfying. It is this ideal, chosen ahead of time by nonempirical standards, that organizes and gives direction to the means and ends used to attain it. Those means and ends are what we have been calling ideology here.

So the chief problem remains: How are human beings to choose their ideals when there is no empirical possibility of determining whether those ideals are worthwhile and will bring real satisfaction? In reality, the sociological response is simple. It comes down to choosing some model of life with the human elements available, to opting for some image of life that seems both feasible and satisfying.

What this common-sense answer does not tell us is that this process begins very early in the life of a human being, at a time when the tools and elements available to our imagination are quite limited. We are not really faced with a great task of construction based on imaginative thinking; we are faced with a problem of faith, of human faith rather than theological faith. We begin by having faith in the real persons closest to us. We regard them as omniscient and are satisfied with the values that they show us.

Be they Christians or not, all human beings begin to build up a set of values by trusting *in other human beings.* In the case of little children, the trustworthy values are incarnated in the people with whom they have the closest affective and effective ties of dependency, usually their parents. When there is some conflict in this area, the ties may link them to a favorite teacher, an older brother, a protecting friend, or someone else.

Take the case of a child who is *considered a Christian.* If a theologian tries to find in that child the features that are described as essential to faith in theological manuals, he will be sadly disappointed. A relationship to Christ is distant at best, and the child is even less likely to consider Christ as a revelation from God. The authority of a revealing God probably means nothing to the child. The fact is that this *Christian* child has faith in his mother or father or both, and that is all. If he considers himself a Christian at all, he does so because that is the label his parents give to the value system they hold. If they were to change the label and describe their system as "Buddhism" or "atheism," the child would do the same without encountering any great problems. At this point concern for "orthodoxy" is psychological in nature. For the child "orthodoxy" comes down to identifying himself with the values of his parents, for in reality it is in them that he has "faith."

It is worth noting that at this stage one cannot see any real distinction between "faith" and "ideologies." If we compare a Christian child and a Marxist child at this stage, we will find that both are motivated by a *faith,* a human faith; and that the result is an *ideology,* a logical system of interconnected values.

Adolescence brings new problems and a basic crisis, transforming the faith or ideology of childhood. Adolescents discover their own personalities and become fascinated with other figures and heroes outside the family circle. There is a rapid decline in their faith in their parents as the bearers of perfect or even adequate values and satisfactions.

That does not mean, however, that there is any less need for some human image in whom one may trust to find guidance and orientation for life and its growing complexity. Freedom of action in choosing those images is now much broader in scope, but the adolescent still must rely on living persons in order to fashion a credible and trustworthy image of some sort of feasible happiness.

Let us assume that the adolescent selects Christ or Che Guevara for that image. What happens now with faith and ideology? Our answer must be that as yet nothing significant happens at all. The Christ of the adolescent may possess more traits directly stemming from the gospel message, but as yet he is not the authentic revealer of a revealing God. The Che Guevara of the adolescent may possess more characteristically Marxist traits, but as yet he is not the orthodox disciple of Marx. Once again, in other words, *faith and ideology* are inextricably intermingled. The adolescent adopts the Marxist ideology of Che Guevara because he has *faith* that this human being did not lie in demonstrating that a life based on those values would be the most satisfactory possible. The Christian adolescent believes in Christ because his whole life appears to be structured—*ideology*—so perfectly that even his passion and death seem to be the most satisfying way to lead a human life.

This little phenomenological analysis, which presents faith and ideology as inextricably linked together, is most important for several reasons. Why? Firstly, because it is in adolescence that people make their basic option either in favor of liberation or against it. Secondly, because the vast majority of Christians and Marxists never get beyond this level for the rest of their lives. Only a few mature people conscientiously live out their faith or ideology right down to its ultimate consequences.[5] Above all, this analysis is important because it introduces a major distinction into the whole problem posed by Assmann. In his presentation, the notion of a "specifically Christian contribution" existing prior to personal commitment seemed to lead to pernicious third-way approaches and ultimately to antirevolutionary attitudes. Our question here is: Is Assmann talking about a *Christian* contribution that clearly distinguishes between faith and ideology, or is he talking about a *Christian* contribution that does not distinguish between the two? Only the former instance is a truly theological problem, one that deals with the *Christian faith.* The latter is a sociological issue, for it has to do with cultural elements linked up with Christianity.

Two important conclusions can be drawn from our distinction insofar as we are dealing with the many Christians who do not distinguish faith and ideology and the many Marxists who do not distinguish between faith in an historical figure and Marxist analysis (or ideology). 1. Sociologically speaking, we can be sure of one thing in the case of any brand of Christianity that does not reach the level of mature faith, that does not manage to differentiate the historical figure of Christ from the historical context in which he preached his message. Such a brand of Christianity will always be conservative, or at least conservative within the process of revolution. Manipulating "Christian" masses in a revolutionary sense can be a dangerous mistake, for the historical figure of Christ lends itself to use within a revolutionary process only if the historical context of that figure is relativized; and only a mature faith can relativize Christ's historical context. We shall return to this problem a bit later. 2. Even though it is not exactly the same, a similar difficulty faces any revolutionary process in which revolutionary ideology is still lived out as a faith. To take Marxists as our example here, we can say that their revolutionary process is bound to end in failure if they do not manage to relativize the context within which their ideological sources conceived the revolutionary process. In other words, third-way approaches are not the only enemy of revolution. It has internal enemies of its own. The revolutionary process is not a unique process. On the level we are considering here, people who opt for that process may come to it with all the absolutism characteristic of faith; they may be quite incapable of analyzing historical situations in a creative way and of relativizing their ideological fonts. That this is a critical and decisive element for any revolution is proved by *all* the revolutionary efforts that have taken place in Latin America over the past hundred years.

Hence we must get to the level where faith and ideology are clearly distinguished, whatever we may decide about their mutual relationship.

III. FAITH WITHOUT IDEOLOGIES: DEAD FAITH

An important and perhaps decisive element in our distinction between faith and ideology is the stress laid on the absolute nature or on the relative nature of our existential systems.

We recognize an ideology in the fact that it has no *pretensions* about representing any *objectively* absolute value. An ideology is worth as much as the reasons or arguments that support it. This feature differentiates the founders of ideologies from the founders of religions. The former try to convince people with arguments, the latter appeal to the fact that they are in possession of some absolute value. Needless to say, however, the fact that an ideology is grounded on arguments whose value is relative does not alter the fact that a person lives it *subjectively* as an absolute value. But in the mind of a mature person there is a tacit acceptance of the fact that even though he may give up his life for his ideology, it is not worth more than the arguments in its favor; that if the latter lose their force, then his ideology would also lose its force.

By contrast, we recognize a faith in the fact that it claims to possess an *objectively* absolute value. In his faith a person supposedly comes in contact with an objective font of total truth. By the same token, a person may accept this encounter on many varying levels of subjective certainty. Thus a Marxist may die for his ideology while a Christian may deny his faith. But we should not confuse a person's subjective degree of adherence with the respective claims of ideology and faith to absolute truth on the objective level.

Now of course a person's faith-inspired encounter with an objective font of absolute truth takes place in and through a process of ideological searching and has immediate ideological consequences. No one links up with absolute truth except in an effort to give truth and meaning to one's own life. There is an *ideological* intention at work. But it does seem that the fact of faith does relativize any and every particular ideology, even though it certainly does not relativize the general need for ideologies in orienting one's life.

Having faith makes no sense if it does not lead me to give direction to my life. At the same time, however, the direction that faith gives my life is relativized by that faith itself. My situation in the face of an ideological crisis will change, or at least it should change *objectively*. When some ideology linked up with my faith proves to be inoperative or grounded on uncertain suppositions, then the objectively absolute value of my faith should logically prompt me to a new and different encounter with the absolute revelation of my faith. If I am a Christian, for example, my ideological crisis should force me back to the gospel message.

If I am a Marxist, if I still have *subjective* trust in Marx, then of course an ideological crisis would force me back to the fonts of Marxism so that I could find my mistake without denying my basic principles. Here again we see that faith and ideologies can lead to the same results. But the balance between objective and subjective factors used in giving orientation to our search for truth and truth-based praxis is different.

Irrationality shows up as a threat, however, at both ends of the balance scale. For example, it would make no sense to cling doggedly to Marx when he himself never claimed that his views were worth more than the arguments on which they were based, and when we realize that his arguments were applicable to revolutionary conditions existing in an epoch very different from our own. What sense is there in saying that a particular analysis is or is not authentically *Marxist* when it presents new facts, new constants, and new conclusions?

It is equally irrational to have recourse to an objective font of truth that speaks to us only through ideologies. That, in fact, is what the Christian faith does. Christ, the supreme revelation of God, shows us a specific way of structuring our lives for the sake of love. If we know for certain that he did not thereby correct the whole process that led the Israelites out of bondage in Egypt, then we must conclude that Jesus Christ puts us in contact with absolute, objective truth through a relative ideology.

What, then, does the faith say to me in the concrete? What is its truth *content*? If I remain logically consistent in deducing conclusions from the above principles, then my only response can be: *nothing*. Let me repeat that in another way. If someone were to ask me what I have derived from my faith-inspired encounter as a clear-cut, absolute truth that can validly give orientation to my concrete life, then my honest response should be: nothing.

However, we are carrying the balance of faith to an irrational extreme in talking about *one* encounter with the objective font of absolute truth. If it is in fact a matter of only *one* encounter, then there is no solution to the problem. The absolute truth would remain totally obscured behind the ideology exhibited in that one historical encounter. It is quite clear that in history we can only have historical encounters, that is, encounters bound up with relative contexts.

This *reductio ad absurdum* prompts us to rediscover the decisive importance of the (historical) *density* of the Bible. Over a period of twenty centuries different faith-inspired encounters took place between human beings and the objective font of absolute truth. All of these encounters were historical; hence each one of them was relative, bound up with a specific and changing context. What came to be known or recognized in each of these encounters was an ideology, but that is not what was learned. Through the process people *learned how to learn* with the help of ideologies. This deutero-learning has its own proper content, and when I say that Jesus had two natures, one human and one divine, I am saying something about the *content* of this learning process. But these contentual items cannot be translated into one or another specific ideology because they belong to a secondary stage or level of learning. They are essentially methodological symbols. On the one hand they have no direct ideological translation; on the other hand they have no other function but to be translated into ideologies.

From these remarks it should at least be clear that one pretension of the ecclesiastical hierarchy makes no sense at all in theology. They often attempt, quite openly, to maintain a distinction if not an outright separation between faith and ideologies in order to safeguard the former. But while faith certainly is not an ideology, it has sense and meaning only insofar as it serves as the foundation stone for ideologies.

Regarding the attempt to separate faith from ideologies, I should like to cite the following remarks in an article by Thomas W. Ogletree:

> Man must answer for what he does. Being able to answer cannot be equated with success in "measuring up" to some pre-established standard. The openness of the historical process continually erodes the authority of such standards, unless they are given a highly abstract form, e.g., "loyalty to being," or "doing what love (agape) requires." Since the abstractness of such formulations makes their applicability to concrete situations problematic, it is clear that there is no precise measuring instrument by which human behavior can be tested . . .There is no way to remove the moral risk from human action, partly because no one can ever adequately grasp the nature of his situation or the possible consequences of his action, but also because the appropriate tack in a given context may be to innovate, to give rise to the new possibility which cannot be comprehended in terms of previous values and understandings."[6]

This passage is not alluding specifically to a Christian reading of the gospel message or to the difference between faith and ideologies. But it is perfectly applicable to those areas. Even though endowed with absolute value, the Christian faith totally lacks any precise instrument for measuring the historical life of Christians by pre-established standards. And since the human sciences also lack any such value standards, Christians cannot evade the necessity of inserting something to fill the void between their faith and their options in history. In short, they cannot avoid the risk of ideologies.

The problem is of course that we are used to picturing our faith as a plane of eternal certitudes which are destined to be professed on the one hand and translated into actions on the other. Rubem Alves comments on this fact in a reference to the thought of Ebeling: "There are elements in the consciousness of the community of faith, however, which suggest that it is not only possible but indeed necessary to understand faith in exactly the opposite sense, as a radically historical mode of being, as 'the acceptance of truly historical existence.' If this is the case, its language consequently must express the spirit of *freedom for history, of taste for the future, of openness for the provisional and relative.*"[7]

It is worth noting, by the way, that certain passages in the documents of Vatican II, particularly in *Gaudium et spes,* can only make sense if they are interpreted in this light. It is one more proof of the powerful ecumenism implicit in the methodology of liberation theology. The first passage deals with the orientation of faith, not towards other-worldly certitudes, but towards historical problems and their solutions: "Faith throws a new light on everything, manifests God's design for man's total vocation, and thus *directs the mind to solutions which are fully human"* (*Gaudium et spes,* no. 11). Are we to assume from this that the faith *possesses* such solutions? Vatican II unexpectedly rejects such an assumption, the standard assumption of classical theology: "In fidelity to conscience, Christians are joined with the rest of men *in the search for truth, and for the genuine solution* to the numerous problems which arise in the life of individuals and from social relationships" (*ibid.,* no. 16).

The latter passage by itself, and even more so when combined with the first passage cited, forces us to a different conception of revealed truth. It is not a *final* truth, however absolute it may be. Instead it is a fundamental element in the search for *the truth.* In other words, it helps to support and verify what was said about faith as a process of learning to learn, as a deutero-learning. However lofty it may be, it is ever in the service of historical solutions to human problems—even though the latter solutions will always be provisional and incomplete. Faith, then, is a liberative process. It is converted into freedom for history, which means freedom *for ideologies.*

IV. FAITH AND IDEOLOGIES IN BIBLICAL REVELATION

Our remarks so far suggest that we would do well to take a final look at certain biblical elements which must be considered if we wish to verify the path that has led us to those conclusions. We are particularly interested in one central point: the relationship between the revelation of Jesus and his own particular moment in history. We are interested in elucidating the relationship between faith and ideologies as it is to be found in this central event of Christianity. We want to consider the life and teaching of Jesus in his own moment of history within the overall historical process.

1. Insofar as content is concerned, liberation theology is known to have a preference and a partiality for the Old Testament in general, and for the Exodus event in particular. The reason for this is clear enough. The Old Testament, and the Exodus event in particular, show us two

central elements completely fused into one: i.e., God the liberator and
the political process of liberation which leads the Israelites from bondage in Egypt to the promised land. In no other portion of Scripture does
God the liberator reveal himself in such close connection with the political plane of human existence. Moreover, it is a well-known fact that from
the time of the Babylonian exile on, the *sapiential* literature became more
individualistic, inner-directed, and apolitical. And at first glance the
New Testament would seem to deprecate or even reject any connection
between liberation and politics, even though it might talk about the
former.

Jesus himself seems to focus his message on liberation at the level of
interpersonal relationships, forgetting almost completely, if not actually
ruling out, liberation vis-à-vis political oppression.[8] The same would
seem to apply to Paul[9] and almost all the other writings in the New
Testament.

Here liberation theology is faced with a pastoral problem of the first
magnitude. If concern and commitment constitute the elements fundamental to any encounter with the gospel message, then the results can be
and often are disastrous. Why? Because the Gospels seem to center
Jesus' main interests on another plane entirely, on an apolitical plane.
The young Christian is often advised in advance that he must "translate"
the language of Jesus into political dimensions. Aside from the fact that
such "translation" is not an easy process, the youth's first encounter with
the gospel message often proves to be disheartening anyway. That is not
one of the least reasons why liberation theology prefers the Old Testament and, in particular, the Exodus account.

In recent years, to be sure, various exegetes in Latin America and
Europe[10] have tried to read between the lines of the Gospels and find a
close connection between the activity of Jesus and the Zealots of Israel. I
personally think that their interpretations are a bit forced, quite aside
from the fact that they do not resolve the problem we have just posed in
pastoral terms.

Even though it does not solve the latter problem, I think it is more
sensible to realize that we are guilty of an anachronism when we assume
that the decisive and critical political plane—precisely in political
terms—was the opposition between Judea and the Roman Empire. It is
quite possible that some contemporary groups such as the Zealots
thought it was. But it seems to me that the political reality that really
structured the Israel of Jesus' time and determined people's role and
relationships in society was not the Roman Empire but the Jewish theoc-
racy grounded on, and controlled by, the religious authorities who had
charge of the Mosaic Law. We have already noted how Jesus destroyed

the foundation of that oppressive power structure by teaching the people to reject its theological foundations. His teaching was such a political threat that the authorities of Israel made use of Rome's authorities to eliminate this dangerous *political* adversary. That is precisely what Jesus was.

Whether my last hypothesis is correct or not, indeed even assuming that for a variety of sound reasons[11] Jesus had decided not to take an interest in any political sort of liberation, it is important to realize that we must still explain either attitude in terms of an *ideology*. We must explore the problem in terms of the necessity of combining means and ends vis-à-vis a concrete situation. And it cannot be approached in other terms that are not equally concrete.

More interesting in terms of our purpose here is the fact that two theological explanations are usually offered for liberation theology's preference for certain passages of divine revelation—or, if you prefer, for certain *ideologies* expressed in its content. The first, and more naive, explanation maintains that the Exodus event is the key to the interpretation of Scripture as a whole, including the Gospels and the rest of the New Testament.[12] I consider this position naive because it is very easy for a scientific biblical theology to tear apart any such pretension. To begin with, the Book of Exodus is an historical reconstruction. It is very important, of course, but it can hardly compete with the vivid reflections of living people who are facing the prospect and then the reality of the event—to take just one example.[13] Moreover, Exodus is certainly not the central axis of the sapiential literature. The latter relates to an era of foreign domination in which the historical vocation of Israel was either lost from view or projected into eschatological terms. Still less can it be the central axis of the New Testament unless we go in for a terrible process of mutilating the latter. We could maintain that liberation was the only theme of the New Testament, I suppose, but only if we were willing to go in for a great deal of abstraction.

That brings us to the second argument against this naive attempt to suppress the rich variety of biblical experiences and to replace them with an abstract summary. In any such attempt we lose the pedagogical intent of the whole scriptural process. We also cannot explain the why and wherefore of all that concrete content, if a few summary words could have done the job equally well.

The second theological explanation for the preferences of liberation theology is more complicated. At first glance it seems more immune to attack from critical scholarship. The argument in this case is that the pedagogical principle of the Bible as a whole not only justifies but demands partiality. God reveals himself to human beings who are preoccupied with their own concrete situation. We can only understand and appreciate the word of God if we take that fact into account. Only in connection with the problems that are embodied in the questions of the community can we comprehend who exactly this responding God is. If we fail to understand the situation and problems of the community, we cannot possibly come to know that God. At first glance there may seem to be contradictions in God's revelation and his responses, but they are clarified when we uncover the different historical situations and the different questions addressed to him from within those situations.

This more complex explanation does justice to the pedagogical principle of divine revelation. To cite a different example, let us consider the educational process of any child. If we want to understand that process but do not have direct access to the words or methodology of the educator—as is the case with the pedagogy of Scripture—then we must try to infer all that from what the child says about many different things, in different situations, over a long period of time. The first thing we must keep in mind is that the child does not tell us exactly what the educator is thinking. The educator is attentive to the child, and even the latter's mistakes can help in the pedagogical process. But that does presume that the educator is aware at every moment of the child's own situation, for that is and remains the starting point of education. The fact that at a given point in time the child may insist upon the real existence of Red Riding Hood does not indicate anything in the nature of a pedagogical error. Faced with a real-life situation at that point, the educator felt it made no sense to argue with the child over that point, but that it did make sense to try and draw certain lessons from the story, and so forth.

We can assume that in the Scriptures the people of Israel have accumulated and set forth for us an educative process directed by God. But God does not show up on the tape. All that we get are the *results* that flowed from the reflections and responses of the Israelites to that divine instruction.

2. That brings us to a second problem. What is the exact relationship between, for example, the revelation of Jesus in the New Testament and the revelation of God in the Old Testament? Though it may seem hard to believe, the fact is that this basic and important question has scarcely been given a clear answer over the past twenty centuries of Christian living. And that fact has conditioned the whole of theology.

The usual responses tend to move in two opposite directions. One response stresses the fact that Jesus represents one more link in a chain of revelation, the revelation itself being one basically and all of it being true. Jesus himself lends support to this view when he says: "Do not suppose that I have come to abolish the Law and the prophets; I did not come to abolish but to complete. I tell you this: so long as heaven and earth endure, not a letter, not a stroke, will disappear from the Law until all that must happen has happened" (Matt. 5:17–18). As we all know, "the Law and the prophets" was a common shorthand way of referring to all of Sacred Scripture in Jesus' day; it did not refer solely to the legal or prophetical books. Jesus, therefore, is referring to the whole of what we call the Old Testament; and he seems to be saying that he himself and his message represent an additional element that is directly and positively a continuation of past revelation.

The implication seems to be that the Scriptures are not a body of law in the modern sense of the term. Instead they embody a divine plan of long-term duration. Jesus did not come to alter this plan, but to bring it to its fulfillment and completion. And if we consider that plan as an educational one, then we are forced to conclude that Jesus is making himself a part of that plan rather than upsetting it. Thus when he goes on to say, on several occasions, "But I tell you . . . ," he is simply trying to purify the moral law of the Old Testament of its grosser material features.

But other features of the Gospel accounts point us in the opposite direction. They show us a break in continuity, a qualitative leap in Jesus' revelation beyond the older divine teaching—even though the exact nature of this leap may be hard to spell out. At the very least it looks more like outright correction than mere continuation.

At the end of the Sermon on the Mount, for example, Matthew informs us: "When Jesus had finished this discourse the people were astounded at his teaching; unlike their own teachers he taught *with a note of authority*" (Matt. 7:28–29). Now this special air of authority by contrast with the teaching of the Scribes could be viewed as a revival of prophetic authority in Israel after a long period of prophetic silence. There is no doubt that Jesus presented himself as a prophet and was taken as such from the very beginning. But in this connection we must note that it would never have occurred to the prophets to challenge the very content of the Mosaic Law. That is precisely what Jesus did, Matthew's previous remark notwithstanding. Mark certainly saw Jesus in that new light, for he notes that Jesus declared all foods clean when in fact there was a huge corpus of Mosaic Law and related commentaries on the matter of pure foods (Mark 7:19).

Then there are Jesus' authoritative statements on gratuitous love (Luke 6:27–36), which Paul sums up in his letter to the Romans: "Let your aims be such as all men count honourable. If possible, so far as it lies with you, live at peace with all men. My dear friends, do not seek revenge, but leave a place for divine retribution; for there is a text which reads, 'Justice is mine, says the Lord, I will repay.' But there is another text: 'If your enemy is hungry, feed him; if he is thirsty, give him a drink; by doing this you will heap live coals on his head.' Do not let evil conquer you, but use good to defeat evil" (Rom. 12:17–21). Now if we take Jesus' authoritative statements in this vein as authentic moral precepts, then he certainly did *correct* passages which the Old Testament attribute to God himself and which command such things as the slaying of neighboring peoples who might constitute a threat to the freedom and religion of Israel (e.g., Deut. 7:14 ff.).

Some time ago another view was popular, particularly in Catholic circles, which stood somewhere between the *continuation* view and the *correction* view. It was the notion of the *sensus plenior,* the "fuller sense," of Scripture. Jesus' revelation allegedly pointed up the true sense of older revelation, a sense that had not been appreciated even by those who wrote down God's revelation. With his revelation, in other words, Jesus provided people with new light for understanding the real import of persons, doctrines, and events in the Old Testament; e.g., Moses and the law, Adam and sin.

Now in some way or other we will always be compelled to recognize a fuller sense in God's later revelation. But the notion of the *sensus plenior* presents two very serious difficulties to any attempts to explain and resolve the contradictions cited above. The first difficulty is that unless one chooses to appeal to miracles as part of the scientific hermeneutic process, then one must assume that the whole notion of *sensus plenior* extends to all the different stages of the Old Testament as well. But, to take one example, can one really maintain that the authentic import of the Exodus event is more clearly spelled out in the more spiritualistic and subjective interpretation of the sapiential books? Are we to assume that in analogous circumstances the Israelites should henceforth act in a very different manner than they did the first time around? Clearly that is a basic and important question for any liberation theology.

Let us consider another example from the New Testament. Paul can certainly be considered a proponent of the *sensus plenior.* Looking at Moses and his law in the light of Christ, Paul believes he can pinpoint the true significance of that early legislation. The Mosaic Law was not a restrictive condition imposed by God on the unconditional promise made to Abraham. Rather, it was a preparation for Christ insofar as it revealed the reality and enslaving power of sin. This logically leads Paul to assert that with Christ human beings cease to be subject to the Law. It no longer makes any sense to ask whether some course of action is *licit* or not, when one is faced with some moral doubt. The new meaning brought by Christ serves to correct old, outmoded attitudes and approaches. But that brings us back to the critical question: if we do find thoroughgoing correction in divine revelation, can we really say that there is a oneness of faith from past to present? Can we Christians really say that we have faith in the Old Testament, in the Exodus revelation for example? Is it worth going back to the Mosaic Law when its real meaning is spelled out in the New Testament, to the point where the Law itself is abolished? And in such a case what is the point of preferring the Exodus account to the New Testament in our liberation theology?

3. The first response of liberation theology to the problem posed above involves going back to the notion that there is real continuity in the whole of divine revelation and distinguishing two elements in it. One element is permanent and unique: *faith*. The other is changing and bound up with different historical circumstances: *ideologies*.

If God's revelation never comes to us in pure form, if it is always fleshed out in historical ideologies, then we cannot appeal to the historical Jesus in order to throw out the solutions of the Old Testament. If circumstantial conditions and exigencies are decisive, then Jesus' remarks about turning the other cheek in no way correct the command of Deuteronomy to physically exterminate certain foreign peoples.

Our theory, in other words, assumes that there is an empty space between the conception of God that we receive from our faith and the problems that come to us from an ever-changing history. So we must build a bridge between our conception of God and the real-life problems of history. This bridge, this provisional but necessary system of means and ends is what we are calling *ideology* here. Obviously each and every ideology presented in Scripture is a human element even though in the intensely unified psychological processes of human beings it may seem to be a direct and straightforward translation of the proper conception of the God who has been revealed.

Consider the Israelites who arrived in the promised land. For them the extermination of their enemies was concretely the most clear-cut way of conceiving who God was and what he was commanding in the face of specific historical circumstances. Thus the extermination of enemies was the ideology that faith adopted, with or without critical thought, at that moment in history. And to be logical here, we must say the same thing with regard to the gospel message. When Jesus talked about freely proffered love and nonresistance to evil, he was facing the same problem of filling the void between his conception of God (or perhaps that of the first Christian community) and the problems existing in his age. In short, we are dealing here with another ideology, not with the content of faith itself.

This view of the matter gives liberation theology greater freedom to move, in principle, through the Scriptures and to work with the faith. Moreover, it is actually the scientific approach used by exegesis in dealing with the content of both the Old and the New Testament. For exegesis regards that content as a succession of religious ideologies, each one being bound up with its historical context and being comprehensible only in terms of that context. As a scholarly science, biblical exegesis is much less concerned about the oneness or unity of the whole complex. It does not decide, for example, whether a specific orientation or line of thinking is incompatible with the rest or not, is heretical or not. Of course it assumes some sort of unity between the Exodus and Jesus, since it is dealing with a process going on in the same cultural world, a world that differs from other cultural worlds of the same era. But it refuses to make a theological value judgment as to whether one of those ideologies is superior to another or not. Each ideology has its historical function to carry out.

Needless to say, liberation theology cannot accept or adopt that impartiality. Its concern is not to describe what happened in the past but to make a decision vis-à-vis new problems that either were not dealt with in Scripture or were dealt with in a very different context.

In this situation theology has two ways open to it in trying to relate the faith to new historical situations—e.g., to the situation of sociopolitical oppression that prevails in Latin America. One way is to seek out the biblical situations most akin to those of the present day and to accept the ideology that Scripture presents in those situations as the correct response of faith. If, for example, the relationship between the Exodus situation and our own today seems closer than the situation of the Hebrews in the time of Christ and ours today, then the Exodus rather than the Gospels should serve as our source of inspiration in trying to find a present-day ideology that will dovetail with the faith.

The other possible approach is to invent an ideology that we might regard as the one which would be constructed by a gospel message contemporary with us. What would the Christ of the Gospels say if he were confronting our problems today? If the faith is one amid the diversity of history, then there must be some ideology that can build a bridge between that faith and our present-day situation even as there were such ideologies in the past.

These would seem to be the only two approaches open to us. The problem is that the first approach becomes more unrealistic and antiscientific as time goes on. There seems to be less and less sense in trying to look for similar situations in cultural milieus dating back thirty-five centuries, particularly since the pace of history seems to be accelerating every day. The second approach does call for creativity here and now. But if we must try to imagine what the gospel message would be if it were formulated today, it is becoming more and more obvious to Christians that *secular* inventiveness and creativity is more appropriate and fruitful.

4. These difficulties prompt us to take a further step and to ask a further question: Can the content of faith offer us the precision we so far lack? Here we run into a serious problem. For while ideologies are defined by their content, we run into problems when we try to do the same thing with our faith. What is the faith in *objective* terms, in terms of information rather than merely subjective attitudes? Is there anything left in Scripture once we have discarded the ideological element?

It is too easy to say that what remains is precisely the conception of God that runs through the centuries and that the various ideologies attempt to relate to specific historical circumstances. It is too easy because that conception of God is never found separated from the ideologies that attempt to interpret God by applying his demands to a specific historical situation. Both processes are inextricably linked. You cannot get rid of one without emptying the other of content.

In other words the idea of a liberating God cannot be separated from historical situations and actions, such as the slaying of the firstborn, because no liberating God is revealed outside of such historical situations. As James Cone noted, there are no universal truths in the process of liberation; the only truth is liberation itself.[14] Though some people may feel disappointed, there is no "universal God" in the ordinary sense of the word "universal."[15]

Now this view frees us from the necessity of *reducing* the whole Bible to one singular conception of reality for the sake of maintaining the oneness of our faith. But it does not offer us much help in trying to use our faith as the orientation we need to solve our problems in history. But is it possible that we are confusing the issue for ourselves? When we talk about some objective content of faith and try to dissociate it from the content of various ideologies as if the two were disputing the same ground, may we not be confusing *two simultaneous but different levels of learning?* To borrow the terminology that communication theory uses with reference to such fields as cybernetics, biology, and psychology, may we not be confusing a *proto-learning* with a *deutero-learning*, a first-level learning with a second-level learning?[16] The former is *simple learning,* the latter is *learning to learn.*

Consider Pavlov's experiments, for example. His dogs learned that the sound of a bell signified food, and their salivary glands began to secrete as soon as the bell sounded. Here we clearly have a process of *simple learning*. The dogs learned to react to a specific stimulus, and that is all. They could be taught in the same way to react to a second stimulus. Now the characteristic feature of learning at that stage is that information is *added* or *subtracted*. Information about two stimuli tells the dogs nothing about a possible third stimulus, and a mistake represents a subtraction. Thus if a dog were given food one hundred times after a bell was rung and not given food one hundred times after a bell was rung, the sum of information at the end of the experiment would be exactly zero.

On the human level, however, we repeatedly experience a second-level learning, a process of *learning to learn*. The main characteristic of this process is that new information *multiplies* or *divides* the balance of previous information. Let us take mathematics as a case in point. After a certain period of learning, a child is able to solve a certain set of problems. But suddenly we notice that he or she is solving a problem that is not a mere copy of, or addition to, the previous problems. We have reason to assume that in the process of learning mathematics the child did more than merely learn isolated answers to isolated problems. The child acquired a bibliography, as it were, which it could then consult in order to solve a new problem. The information possessed by the student is not a simple sum of the problems already learned and the bibliography previously acquired. It is the product of a multiplication of those two factors. The student, in other words, possesses objective information that enables him to solve new problems which he has not studied before. An inadequate or jumbled bibliography, on the other hand, does not represent a mere subtraction of information already learned; it represents a division of that information because it wipes out much of what had been previously learned. But when they are part of the overall process and do not disorient the child, even errors are helpful. They do not represent subtraction or addition of information; they represent a multiplication of information.

The important point here is that simple learning and learning to learn do not dispute control of the informational content. The bibliography, for example, is not a mathematical formula. The mathematical formulas that the child may retain or construct are dependent on the bibliography, but they are not in competition with it.

Perhaps this allusion to a bibliography may not be the most satisfactory way to explain or comprehend the relationship between faith and ideologies, since a bibliography always remains external to mathematical knowledge and understanding itself. A student who is truly creative in mathematics might afford us a more suitable example. Once introduced to the learning process, such a student not only acquires specific formulas but also the possibility of creating them when faced with new problems. The relationship between simple learning and learning to learn becomes more intimate, and it becomes more difficult to distinguish beween the content of the two levels. But even in this case what we said of the bibliography above remains true: on one level information is added or subtracted, on the other it is multiplied and divided.

We can say without fear of error that the ideologies present in Scripture belong to the first level. They are responses learned vis-à-vis specific historical situations. Faith, by contrast, is the total process to which man submits, a process of learning in and through ideologies how to create the ideologies needed to handle new and unforeseen situations in history. The Scriptures can and should be examined and studied from both points of view since both processes are in the sacred writings and do not compete with each other over content. This means that fighting one's way out of bondage in Egypt is one experience and turning the other cheek is another experience. Someone who has gone through both experiences and has reflected on them has learned how to learn; he has multiplied his faith-based information, not subtracted it to zero.

V. FAITH OPERATING IN TERMS OF IDEOLOGIES

These remarks will help us to better understand two basic problems of liberation theology, even if they will not enable us to fully resolve them. The *first* problem has to do with the continuation of revelation. It seems clear in the thinking of John the Evangelist that divine revelation is destined to continue after the physical disappearance of Jesus. Classical theology, however, talks about revelation as a "deposit" closed at the death of the last apostle, the last eyewitness to the teaching of Jesus.

In the fourth Gospel Jesus has this to say as he is about to bid farewell to his disciples: "There is still much that I could say to you, but the burden would be too great for you *now*. However, when he comes who is the Spirit of truth, he will guide you into all the truth; for he will not speak on his own authority . . . He will glorify me, for everything that he makes known to you he will draw from what is mine" (John 16:12–14).

Jesus clearly affirms that many things remain to be said and that they will be said, although in a different manner. The *Spirit* of truth will take many things which Jesus himself had not spoken and will make them comprehensible as obviously belonging to the same divine revelation. Jesus' language is very clear. It points not towards a better understanding of what has already been spoken but towards the learning of new things.

Can we, in that case, substitute the word "ideologies" for "things"? We have already seen that the concrete responses of the Israelite community or the Christian community at any given moment necessarily constitute ideologies. Well, we have exactly the same situation here. There are things that Jesus *cannot say* because they do not dovetail with the historical situation in which his disciples are living. They could not bear them *now*. When they are spoken by the Spirit, however, they will automatically be converted into ideologies associated with a specific historical situation that renders them comprehensible and useful.

What will be the relationship between these new ideologies and *faith,* the latter being understood as a divine revelation that entails recognition of its revealer? The logical answer is that the former revealer, Christ, is replaced by the Holy Spirit. But the Spirit is not a visible, identifiable revealer, which would seem to indicate that one can really have faith only in past revelation. The only coherent hypothesis is to have recourse once again to the notion of a *deutero-learning* process, a process of learning to learn. This process is by its very definition the opposite of any sort of deposit, for it involves an unending process of acquiring new pieces of information that multiply the previous store of information. That being the case, the only visible guidepost is the presence or absence of the teacher outside of the pupil. At a certain point, however, the external teacher disappears from the scene; yet the internal process of learning goes on continually, based on external experience.

This seems to be the obvious import of Jesus' promise. The Spirit of truth is not an external teacher as Jesus himself was. Or we might say instead that no external teacher after Christ will add any information to the educational process. The process will go on internally, as the pupil confronts reality with new ideologies. Jesus is saying that one stage of the process is ended, but he is also promising that the process can continue through its own proper means. And those means are nothing else but a succession of ideologies vis-à-vis the concrete problems of history. In short, after Christ history itself is entrusted with the task of carrying on the process. The Spirit of Christ, that is, the dynamic, intrinsic result of the revelatory education process, ensures a process that will lead to the full and complete truth.

The *second* problem is intimately bound up with the first, and it is the same problem with which we have been dealing from the very start of this chapter. From what we have said so far it seems clear that it makes no Christian sense at all to try to separate ideologies from faith in order to safeguard and preserve the latter. Without ideologies faith is as dead as a doornail, and for the same reason that James offers in his epistle: it is totally impracticable (James 2:17).

From this standpoint it is very instructive to give a brief summary of Paul's interpretation of the Christian's moral obligations in the light of Christ's revelation. Remember that Paul's interpretation antedates the redaction of the four Gospels in their present form. His view can be summarized as follows:

a) Only concrete love gives meaning and value to any kind of law existing in the universe (Rom. 13:8–10).

b) Any and every type of law represents a decisive element for Christian conduct insofar as it points up more or less constant relationships between things and persons. But such laws are not decisive as moral laws (Rom. 14:14). They are decisive as constants in the service of the love-based plans and projects of human beings (1 Cor. 6:12 ff; 10:23 ff.), since they furnish these projects with criteria for judging what is or is not *expedient* in carrying them out (1 Cor. 10:23–29; Rom. 14:7–9).

c) Since this desacralizes the law as a static inventory of questions concerning the intrinsic morality of a given line of conduct, the conduct of the Christian must undergo a basic change. *Faith* rather than the law must serve as the springboard for launching into a new adventure. One's destiny will depend on this venture, but it possesses no *a priori* criteria established in advance. The Christian must accept the riskiness of projects that ever remain provisional and will often go astray (Gal. 5:6 and *passim;* Rom. 14:1 ff.).

d) Therefore this faith does not consist in intellectual adherence to a certain body of revealed content as the definitive solution to theoretical or practical problems. Nor does it consist in having confidence in one's own salvation, thanks to the merits of Christ. Instead it entails the freedom to accept an educational process that comes to maturity and abandons its teacher to launch out into the provisional and relative depths of history (Gal. 4:1 ff.; Rom. 8:19–23; 1 Cor. 3:11–15).

Faith, then, is not a universal, atemporal, pithy body of content summing up divine revelation once the latter has been divested of ideologies. On the contrary, it is maturity by way of ideologies, the possibility of fully and conscientiously carrying out the ideological task on which the real-life liberation of human beings depends.

NOTES

1. In his theology Bultmann is connected up with what is rightly or wrongly dubbed the philosophy of the "early Heidegger," that is the Heidegger who wrote *Sein und Zeit* (Being and Time). In this phase, or at least this particular work, Heidegger was apparently more interested in analyzing the *categories* within which man is forced of necessity to ponder his existence than in

approaching the being of beings. Thus *Sein und Zeit,* rather than spelling out a specific philosophy, provided a certain basic *language* concerned with existence. Quite logically Bultmann consistently refused to admit that he was basing his work on one specific philosophy. He maintained that just as any intellectual understanding of God's word depends on an intellectual understanding of language in general, so it depends even more on the possession of a profound and fruitful language dealing with the basics of human existence. In line with Heidegger's own distinction, we shall distinguish between *existential* analysis (categorical analysis) and *existenziell* analysis (purely factual analysis).

2. Karl Mannheim, *Ideology and Utopia,* Eng. trans. (New York: Harcourt, Brace, Jovanovich, Harvest Book, 1936), p. 192.

3. *Ibid.*

4. *Ibid.,* pp. 194–95.

5. We would go further here and say the following. Even though a person living a mature life differentiates the orientation of faith from the orientation of ideology, he cannot, without diminishing his humanity, forget the fact that they are complementary, if not identical. Take the two "failures" embodied in the figures of Christ and Che Guevara, for example. When faced with a failure, a lucid and mature mind ponders *two* kinds of questions. One kind of question considers whether the failure might have been avoidable with a sounder arrangement of means and intermediate ends, while preserving the basic values at stake. In short, it has to do with ideology. The other kind of question moves in a different direction. It tries to figure out whether the concrete failure was simply a result of ineffectiveness or has meaning and value in itself as a human happening. In short, it moves in the direction of faith.

From what has been said so far, it should be evident that the dimension of effectiveness and the dimension of meaningfulness are intimately bound up with each other but not to be confused as identical. Excessive concentration on one dimension to the exclusion of the other causes one to lose sight of an essential human dimension. This would apply to the childish Christian who forgets about effectiveness and concentrates exclusively on meaningfulness, and also to the technician or politician of whatever stripe who concentrates on effectiveness with no regard for meaningfulness. It is not easy to keep both dimensions together. For one reason, there are different rules of the game in each case, even in the very use of language. A mature human being must speak *two* languages, and must also connect the two without confusing them or distorting either one. Here we face one of the greatest challenges posed by our technological or, if you will, postindustrial culture.

6. Thomas W. Ogletree, "From Anxiety to Responsibility: The Shifting Focus of Theological Reflection," in *Chicago Theological Seminary Register,* March 1968. Reprinted in *New Theology* 6 (New York: Macmillan, 1969), p. 61.

7. Rubem A. Alves, *A Theology of Human Hope* (Washington, D.C.: Corpus Books, 1969), p. 71.

8. See above, note 5 of Chapter III.

9. See the passages where Paul exhorts slaves to obey their masters (e.g., Eph. 6:5; Col. 3:22; Titus 2:9, and Philemon), or the passages where he tends to

minimize but not reject the fact of slavery in the novel light of Christ (e.g., Col. 3:11; 1 Cor. 7:21–22; 12:13; Gal. 3:28).

10. See Gustavo Gutiérrez, *A Theology of Liberation,* Eng. trans. (Maryknoll, N.Y.: Orbis Books, 1973), Chapter 11.

11. One reason of utmost importance should be noted. Any liberation process—e.g., political liberation—would have concrete historical limitations of its very nature. That fact would have seriously diminished the universality of Christ's message about total liberation, applicable to all human beings and all phases of human existence. To be sure, it is impossible to *talk* about liberation without implementing some concrete forms of liberation if one wants to be credible to others. Jesus submitted to this basic law. But the obligation of summoning human beings to a universal liberation while bearing real witness to some concrete liberation is what explains the curious dialectic in Jesus' life. He first points up the concrete liberations he is effecting, only to try to draw people's attention away from them later in order to emphasize a broader and more profound message. That, in my opinion, is the proper explanation of the so-called "messianic secret" in Mark. The explanation of liberal exegesis is incorrect.

12. The most profound and scholarly effort in this direction is, in my opinion, that of Severino Croatto, *Liberación y libertad. Pautas hermenéuticas* (Buenos Aires: Nuevo Mundo, 1973).

13. See, for example, Gerhard von Rad, *Old Testament Theology,* Eng. trans. (New York: Harper & Row, 1965), II, Part II.

14. See Chapter I, p. 26.

15. See Chapter I, p. 32.

16. On this process of *deutero-learning* on different scientific levels, see Gregory Bateson, *Steps to an Ecology of Mind* (New York: Ballantine Books, 1974), especially Parts II, V, and VI.

CHAPTER FIVE

Ideologies—Church—Eschatology

As is often the case, the problems one thinks have been tamed at one point suddenly rear their heads and turn against one at a later point. Presumably the previous chapter has made clear a seemingly paradoxical situation: on the one hand it is impossible for human beings to get beyond the level of ideologies, all ideologies being partial and provisional; on the other hand faith, as a second-level learning process, clearly transcends particular and specific ideologies.

In my opinion it is most important that this basic tension be maintained in all that follows here. With faith or without it, we are all faced with new and unforeseen situations to which we must respond. Our potential responses are limited by our situation and our historical potentialities, and so they will always be partial in one way or another. In short, they will be ideologies. By the same token, however, human beings are capable of facing up to concrete historical situations without letting themselves be borne along by a chaotic flood of relativistic impressions. Learning to learn in and through historical experience is characteristic of man. A series of privileged historical experiences, such as those which go to make up our Scriptures,[1] only accentuate this deutero-learning process in man. Man does possess an objective capacity to formulate and confront ever new questions without being disoriented and dragged down by the novelty of the situation or being driven to retreat to the security of past beliefs and the status quo.

On the secular level it is obvious that this deutero-learning process requires some sort of community. This is even more true of the faith. The use of a specific tradition of faith, which is bound up with the interpretation of a privileged nucleus of historical experiences, requires a community. We call this community of faith "the Church." So the next question is: How capable is the Church of permanently living out the tension between the dynamic unity of faith on the one hand and the historical plurality of the ideologies to which faith gives rise on the other hand? Can the Church keep this revelatory process going without bursting into pieces, since it will take countless ideologies to make the faith a reality within history?

We can see readily enough that every ideology seems to go through a similar process in history. It begins as a protest against the limitations and ineffectiveness of a prior ideology and it ends up as a crusty refusal to give way to some newer ideology that is on the rise. It is difficult for ideologies to operate in history at all without giving rise to excessive hopes. And precisely because they are excessive, those hopes eventually harden into stubbornness and historical oppression.

Consider the Christian notion of *eschatology,* for example, which points to a transcendence of anything and everything in history. It would seem that this notion, linked up with the function of the Church, would be destined to keep de-ideologizing the human mind, to keep it open and flexible, to liberate it from its ahistorical pretensions. Yet there is reason to believe that this continuing function of de-ideologizing may in fact oppress our ideological creativity. Why? Because it wields the sword of criticism even before ideologies have time to be effective and to arouse real enthusiasm.

That this is a serious problem for liberation theology is evident from the fact that most of the attacks against it stem from a specific conception of the Church and its function as well as from a specific conception of eschatology, that is, of what God is fashioning above and beyond the reaches of history. These are the issues that we shall consider in detail in this chapter.

I. THE ANTI-IDEOLOGICAL STANCE IN THE CATHOLIC CHURCH

It can be said that the Catholic Church in Latin America was the first Catholic community to set out resolutely on the new pathway opened up by Vatican II. The new pathway was based on the assumption that faith has as its function the task of guiding the human mind towards more fully human solutions in history; that the Church does not possess those solutions in advance but does possess elements that have been revealed by God; that these revealed elements do not preserve the Church from ideologies; that instead the Church must take advantage of those elements to go out in search of (ideological) solutions to the problems posed by the historical process; and that such solutions will always remain provisional. The Medellín Conference was the first result of the new pathway opened up by Vatican II, embodying the enthusiasm of the early postconciliar days.

It might seem curious that a church community which had little to do with the preparations for Vatican II should be the first to draw radical consequences from the proceedings of the ecumenical council. Indeed one can detect more than a little ecclesiastical "imprudence" in the documents of the Medellín Conference. To phrase it in terms of Rahner's remark in an earlier chapter, at the Medellín Conference the Latin American Church took the risk of being proved wrong and refuted by experts. For it got down to sociological descriptions that specialists might well challenge as extreme, ill-founded, or even erroneous. How could any Church presume to lead all Christians on one pathway, a pathway not based entirely on faith, when some Christians are specialists in the very matters under discussion and other Christians can readily look to them for support or for refutation of the proposed position?

It would be difficult to explain the "imprudence" of Medellín if one did not keep an important and perhaps decisive sociological datum in mind. As opposed to the more or less competitive situation of the Church on other continents, the Latin American Church is supremely sure of its membership. Despite dire problems and predictions, and in a society that is urban for the most part, more than ninety percent of all Latin Americans still call themselves "Catholics." This fact can prompt imprudent calculations based on euphoria.

Needless to say, the "imprudence" to which I am alluding here does not consist in intermingling faith and ideologies. That the Church has always done. Indeed it cannot do anything else, if our analysis so far is correct. The difference lies in the position of the Medellín Conference vis-à-vis the status quo. In the past the Church adopted ideologies that were immersed in the status quo, and so they passed for just plain common sense instead of ideologies. At Medellín the bishops adopted ideologies that went counter to the status quo. This enabled a large number of Christians to perceive the intermingling of faith and ideology for the first time; and since they did not agree with the mix, they denounced it.

At the same time, however, it must be remembered that for some time back pastoral forecasts and evaluations had been growing more prudent and even pessimistic in certain Latin American circles. It had been growing clearer to many that the religious situation of the continent was changing at an accelerating pace, and sociologists brought forth convincing arguments to that effect. At least half of the Latin American population was now living in a modern urban civilization, and that clearly undermined the main tool that had been used for centuries to transmit the faith: i.e., the pressure of closed, wholly Christian communities. With the disappearance of such communities in an increasingly urban society, the Church could no longer entrust to society the task of transmitting Christianity from one generation to the next. One could hardly continue to talk about a "Christian milieu," since it certainly was not "Christian" any longer and probably was no longer a "milieu" in the strict sense.

If it is a matter of transmitting an authentic conception of life from one generation to the next, rather than just some vague sentiments, then a milieu must possess a certain homogeneity and a certain persuasive power. It can only do this if it remains closed to outside influences. That is no longer possible for any "milieu" in Latin America today. For they are all subject to the impact of mass migrations, the mass communications media, and a pluralistic hodgepodge of ideologies and values. In such a situation the Christianity handed down to people is totally different from the Christianity handed down in a closed milieu. In the latter, Christianity signifies a coherent picture of the world, of ultimate values and social roles, of personal conduct and the guiding rules. In open milieus, on the other hand, Christianity comes down to a vague sense of membership.

The census figures and other sociological data bear witness to the change that has taken place in Latin America. Mass attendance and reception of the sacraments no longer reflect a Christian orientation in people's lives. Various motives, tied up with the human search for security to a greater or lesser extent, continue to bring people to Mass and the sacraments. But their conception of life may have little or nothing to do with the Mass. Instead it may be fashioned to a large extent by such factors as television and social roles. Almost without anyone noticing it, a rapid change has taken place in the various milieus of Latin America. They have ceased to transmit Christianity from one generation to the next.

What is more, one cannot possibly envision reconstructing the pressure that was once exerted by a Christian milieu. For such pressure does not depend on a more or less strict morality but on socio-economic factors that are impervious to preaching. One cannot expect parents and educators to provide something which they obviously cannot provide. In such a situation we can detect a note of phoniness and desperation when we hear remarks such as those of the Filipino bishops: "The religious fervor of the Filipino people is a rich treasure. *Even though the underlying motivations are not always clear,* (religious) practice suggests that our people are open to God."

Once we manage to work our way out of a trap like that, we must recognize that the Church, even in Latin America, is faced with a tremendous challenge. It must stop relying on the surrounding milieu and start transmitting the gospel message to *each individual person.* As the Belgian sociologist, Kerkhof, puts it: we are faced with "voluntary consumers of religion." We can no longer convince persons through their milieu, we must reach the person themselves.

Now the main pastoral discovery in connection with these changing concerns and milieus is that the potential consumers of religion are much more interested in viable ideologies than in the faith. Indeed it could almost be said that it is only when ideologies systematically fail that people begin to show an interest in something that transcends ideologies and might offer better guidance: i.e., something like faith. So long as the ideologies function well, the allure of faith on the individual is extremely weak. So must we hope for an *ideological crisis,* so that the *faith* can take on meaningfulness and we can carry out the task of evangelization in the new terms posed by the new sociological situation?

This question brings us very close to the heart of the central problem pondered by Bonhoeffer in prison. Indeed the terms in which we have presented the problem here may be more accurate than those employed by Bonhoeffer himself, and more faithful to his underlying thought. If, as Bonhoeffer thought, we must refuse to take advantage of human frailty, crises, illnesses, and death in order to make people religious, then we must become capable of proclaiming the faith to people who are in the very midst of the process of creation. But that does not mean we delude people by disguising the language of faith under a secular idiom, as many current interpretations of Bonhoeffer's thought would have it.

The solution proposed here is that we let the faith be fleshed out in human, provisional ideologies. In this way it will not be a "cheap faith" that has been devalued by the existing crisis. When all is said and done, we encounter one fact in the Gospels to which current exegesis and biblical theology have not paid sufficient attention. The fact is that Jesus began to preach his message by uttering the magic word "kingdom." For us that word can only have a "metaphorical" and hence purely "religious" import; and so we forget that it was an ideologically explosive term in Jesus' day.

Jesus was well aware of that fact. He was conscious of the ambiguity that the ideology of the kingdom would confer on his message, and he may well have been aware of the danger such ambiguity held for himself. But he also realized that he could never demand faith from people if he addressed them in neutral, antiseptic terms: that he could not demand faith from people independently of the ideologies conveyed by faith—which is what we so often have tried to do.

If we want to gauge the difference between Jesus' attitude and that of the present-day Church, Chile will again serve as a fine example. When the coalition of socialist groups known as the Popular Unity Front came to power, that did not clear up the political scene in Chile. On the one hand there could be no legitimate doubt about their accession to executive power, even though they had received only a little more than one-third of the vote. Since the other two parties had not formed a united front against the Popular Unity Front, they were implicitly saying that they did not consider it of *primary importance* to block the implementation of the goals spelled out in Allende's platform. So it is definitely false to say that the minority nature of Allende's government, as opposed to the supposed majority of the other two parties, represented a political distortion. On the other hand, another fact must be kept in mind. While it is certainly true that the Popular Unity Front had committed itself to leading Chile towards socialism by legal means, the fact is that the structures of Chile continued to remain capitalist and that the executive branch could not effect the envisioned changes by itself. It would have to get absolute majorities in parliament. That could happen, at least in the initial stages, if the Christian Democratic Party (which was composed of Catholics for the most part) came to feel that it had more affinities with the construction of a socialist society than with the extreme right. Hence the political judgment made by Christians would prove to be decisive in spelling out Chile's future.

This critical judgment could be gradually influenced by another factor. On various occasions, and especially in the early sixties, the bishops of Chile had denounced the profound injustice of the established capitalist system. Using official statistics, they pointed out a host of unpleasant facts: e.g., that ninety percent of the national income was distributed among only ten percent of the population. Whereas the per capita income of the vast majority came to about forty-five dollars a year, the privileged ten percent of the population had an annual per capita income of $3,500.

Ten years later, then, the bishops of Chile were confronted with the new political situation we have just described. The political judgment of Christians would be a decisive and critical factor. What did the bishops do? During the first year of Allende's presidency, when many of the disturbing factors that would later show up had not yet appeared on the scene, the bishops issued a draft document entitled *Evangelio, política y socialismos* ("The Gospel Message, Politics, and Brands of Socialism"). Here I cannot give a full-length summary of that document, which is a history-making document in the relationship between faith and ideologies in the Latin American Church. But I do want to point up one important and curious fact which seems to have eluded the attention of the document's authors: on the one hand the document asserts that the Church cannot opt or choose sides, on the other hand it says that in

Chile socialism is not a real alternative to the existing capitalist system.[2] The explanation for this curious contradiction has a great deal to do with the relationship between faith and ideologies.

Why can't the Church choose sides? According to the Chilean bishops, it cannot do that because in practice it would mean excluding from the Church that portion of Christians who had opted for the other side. But in their view the Church belongs to all the people of Chile. In other words, to use our terminology, it means that the one faith must not be put in the service of ideologies, which are many and varied by very definition.

This is a very important point because it contains some critical underlying assumptions. Firstly, it is an admission that ideologies are in fact more appealing than the faith to the Christian people, even though they should not be. Indeed they are so appealing that they would separate a good portion of the faithful from the *practice* of the faith at least. Thus on the one hand the bishops are stating what ought to be: the faith that unites us is more important than the ideologies that divide us. On the other hand they are admitting that this is not the real-life feeling and disposition of Christians. Secondly, it presupposes a theological conception of the faith in which faith itself is the most important thing, quite aside from any and all ideological options one may make out of fidelity to that faith. But we are quite justified in asking: Why is it more important? I do not think any answer to that question can be found in the guidelines laid down by Vatican II, which suggest that the function of faith is to lead the human mind to fully human solutions. The implications of those guidelines are that the importance of the faith lies precisely in its connection with the different and even opposed solutions that are offered for our problems in history. So we have every right to assume that the Chilean bishops, despite the guidelines of Vatican II, continue to picture the faith as a direct means of eternal salvation whereas ideologies are seen as merely human options that can jeopardize that other superior value.

But as I suggested earlier, the most noteworthy and important point seems to be that the bishops, who claim they cannot choose sides, come out and say that socialism cannot be an alternative to the existing capitalist system, as things now stand in Chile. We are perfectly justified in asking: By what curious mental process did the bishops convince themselves that they were not choosing sides when they made that statement?

Remember that the Chilean bishops start out maintaining that it is not possible for the Church to choose between *ideologies*. It does not occur to them to deny that the *faith* is an option. What they say is that the option of faith should be divested of any and every element which is not the faith itself. In other words, no ideological option should condition the option of faith in any way. But right after they have said that the Church cannot opt for one (ideological) group against another, they go on to say: "The Church opts for the risen Christ." In the context it might sound a little odd, but actually it makes perfect sense in terms of their conception of faith. In their eyes, opting for the risen Christ comes down to making one possible option between the nooks and crannies of any and every ideology.

But how is it that the bishops end up opting for the capitalist ideology as opposed to the socialist ideology? The answer is obvious enough. In saying that socialism is not an acceptable alternative to the existing capitalist system, the bishops are not at all aware of the fact that they are choosing between ideologies. Strange as it may seem to us, they think that they are avoiding an ideological option in saying that.

The mental process at work here is clear enough. In the eyes of the bishops, the existing reality is not an ideology; it is simply reality. They have no doubt that it should be corrected but, as they see it, reality as such does not splinter the faith. So long as no ideologies about this *reality* arise, faith has nothing to fear from the *fact* that extremely wealthy human beings live alongside extremely poor human beings. The problem arises when an *ideology* challenges this *reality*. The great sin of "Christians for Socialism," in other words, is that there is no party of "Christians for Capitalism." Of course such people exist, but they do not have to join together under a banner to exercise their influence and carry out their program. But any attempt to put through a radical change in the existing structures must present itself as an *ideology*. It must knock on the door of the Christian heart and appeal to its relationship with the authentic values of the faith.

We must understand the language of the Chilean bishops in order to understand and appreciate their mentality and their theology. In saying that socialism is not a proper alternative to capitalism, they are not saying that socialist Christians are heretics. They are perfectly capable of remaining Christians in spite of their mistake, because it is a practical not a dogmatic mistake. But they should admit that the existing reality is sufficient for the faith. If they do not admit that, then they are relativizing the faith by imposing a condition on it: i.e., that the existing structures be changed, that people accept an ideology proposing such change. The episcopal document summons Christians to maintain a certain brand of prudent reserve. They must recognize the fact that the really important and decisive thing, faith, is possible in any and every set of circumstances. And since it is the decisive thing, it cannot be subordinated to those circumstances and their attendant ideologies.

That this is the great sin of an ideology is evident from the way in which the Chilean bishops analyze the *socialist* ideology. The various steps in their analysis are quite clear. Firstly, in any journey towards socialism Christians will be a minority and the socialist ideology must be given its proper label: i.e., *Marxist*. The second step is to take the feature of Marxism which seems to be most directly connected with the Christian faith—that is, *atheism*—and link it up with all the historical defects and dehumanizing elements that are evident in those societies where Marxism has triumphed so far. It does not seem to strike the bishops that they have often denounced the same dehumanizing elements in capitalist society without making any reference to its atheism or its religiosity. And it is worth noting that the elements overlooked in their analysis are precisely those elements which link up faith with ideologies.

For example, they overlook the obligation of the Christian faith to put through a substantive change in the distribution of the national income—something which they had often stressed in their earlier documents. They also overlook the official doctrine of the Church which was expounded by John XXIII, to the effect that Christian faith should not view ideologies as dogmatic monoliths; that it should evaluate them in terms of their historical embodiments and the changes produced, by real-life implementation. Thus they also overlook the fact that Marxism is not an ideology that subordinates society to atheism but rather an ideology that subordinates atheism to the construction of a more just society. In that sense Marxism poses a real challenge to the Christian faith, which claims to have the same commitment: i.e., to subordinate the Sabbath to man, and the faith to the solution of historical problems.

II. THE ANTI-IDEOLOGICAL STANCE IN PROTESTANT CHURCHES

From what we have seen in the last section, it seems evident that a vicious circle threatens the whole pastoral function of the Catholic Church in Latin America. There is a growing recognition that opting for the faith must be a free, personal option. It cannot be brought about by the surrounding milieu. But this realization leads to panic when it becomes evident that people are really interested in the ideologies associated with faith. What are we to do? The most typical answer is to attempt to set aside the ideologies that divide people and to stress the importance of the faith that unites them. But that comes down to giving the faith an autonomous value of its own, wholly apart from the ideologies it is capable of generating. The value of such a faith becomes very hard to recognize. How can one transmit the faith of the gospel message and point up its value when it has lost the cutting edge that Jesus gave to it? When it no longer pierces through the most intimate interpersonal relationships, *dividing* people with the closest ties and making them enemies (Matt. 10:34–36)?

Our analysis of the document produced by the Chilean bishops seems to indicate that it is not easy to pinpoint the ideological mechanisms at work underneath the statements of the Latin American hierarchy. They seem to be embarrassed by the new guidelines spelled out by Vatican II and their own Medellín Conference. The case of Vatican II is complicated by the fact that its documents do not present one homogeneous line of thought. One can look to it for support as well in defending the older view of faith as an autonomous value. Consider this statement: "Christ, to be sure, gave His Church no proper mission in the political, economic, or social order. The purpose which He set before her is a religious one" (*Gaudium et spes,* n. 42). In setting a "religious" mission over against political, economic, and social functions, the statement would seem to be suggesting that we are dealing here not only with different *functions* but also with different *values.* Thus it has not been easy for the Catholic Church to move through the postconciliar world, for one can find at least two opposing views of faith within the very documents of Vatican II. The whole question is somewhat obscure even on the level of official documents.

For that reason, we might profit considerably from an examination of some Protestant viewpoints on this matter. The Protestant Churches are caught up in the same process which now confronts the Catholic Church. But they often feel less inhibited by authority in their attempt to explicate their basic underlying arguments on this whole matter when they take a stand against liberation theology. And their remarks may well give us a clue to the real bedrock outlook underlying opposition statements from the Catholic hierarchy, an outlook that often seems to be disguised somewhat.

A recent book by C. Peter Wagner will serve as a fine starting point.[3] It is simplistic and naive in certain respects, but it has the great value of presenting certain Protestant objections to liberation theology in a very straightforward and honest way. Wagner views liberation theology in Latin America as the "theology of the radical left." This is how he sees the crucial problem: "The important issue is not really whether a Christian can hold a Marxist-oriented political ideology or not. The issue is whether Christianity obliges a man set free in Christ to hold to *any predetermined* [author's italics too] ideology at all. The Christian world view transcends all social, economic, and political systems. As long as a

Christian's goals in his relationship to the world are noble and held with a clean conscience, he should be allowed to choose the political means to reach the goals that he feels are best without his very Christianity being called into question. This applies equally to the capitalist and the socialist, the pacifist and the violent revolutionary."[4]

The key problem for Wagner is clearly the transcendence of the faith vis-à-vis ideologies. He makes that point clear, not only in the abstract, but also as a criticism of liberation theology. With the latter, he notes, "we come dangerously close to depriving Christianity of its transcendence and making it just another social institution."[5] Wagner does not impute that intention to any of the theologians whose work he analyzes, but he suggests that they will inevitably end up doing that, whether they want to or not, because it is the logical conclusion of the methodological premises they hold.

In support of his own position, Wagner cites Gonzalo Castillo Cárdenas talking about "the temptation to identify the Gospel and the Church, implicitly or explicitly with a given revolutionary program which she sees as indispensable for the establishment of the Kingdom of God on the earth . . . I am under the impression that some of the brethren in Cuba fell into that error and now have repented of it." Wagner then goes on to say: "Castillo's conclusion is one to which evangelicals could confidently subscribe. He says, 'The Church has no right to deny her own nature, her divine message, *by identifying herself* with any human program of social transformation.' "[6]

It may well be that none of the authors studied by Wagner propound any such *identification,* but the very ambiguity of the word itself can add to the confusion here. The theological context of the authors examined by Wagner indicates that none of them are thinking of *identification* in the sense that they would establish a hard and fast tie-up between the Christian message and a given program or system—come what way. If, on the other hand, *identification* means "critical support" in this context, then the whole matter is open to debate and discussion. But whatever the outcome of that debate might be, it is clear that there is no sense to the argument that one is thereby losing the transcendence of Christianity; for the critical nature of the support derives precisely from that transcendence.

However, that is not the most interesting and noteworthy feature of Wagner's critique of liberation theology, and in particular, of his conception of the relationship beween faith and ideology. The most noteworthy point shows up in six *ecclesiological* points which Wagner detects in the Bible. They bring us directly to the matter we are considering here: i.e., the relationship between ideology and the function of the Church.

1. The function of the Church is the *individual reconciliation* of all human beings with God. Criticizing an issue of the *International Review of Mission,* Wagner says: "Expressions such as 'relate to the Latin American context,' 'stimulate interest in the study of Christian social responsibility,' 'undergird involvement in mission by means of studies related to the social, political, economic, and cultural dimensions of the context,' 'express the growing sense of ecumenical commitment which is inseparably related to the task of mission,' 'awaken the masses,' 'point out the roots of the evils in the Latin American socio-economic-political situation,' 'struggle to remove the principal causes of massive injustice,' all are good statements, but the mission of the church—*which is to persuade men and women to be reconciled individually to God* and to become responsible members of the church of Christ—is not further mentioned."[7]

2. Among the different functions of the Church, priority goes to *the salvation of souls.* Promoting social justice is important but secondary. The "theology of the radical left" has turned this proper order upside down: "They judge evangelical theology not in terms of how true it is to the Bible or how it will result in *the salvation of souls,* but what it will do to promote social justice."[8] For Wagner, moreover, the secondary function is not achieved apart from the primary function. Indeed it is a direct result of the latter: conversion of the individual not only procures his salvation but also brings about more justice without attacking any structures. Criticizing the theology of Emilio Castro, Wagner says: "In some of his writings, he seems to have an aversion to a soul-saving ministry. He criticizes his opponents' hypothesis that 'if we change the heart of man, the society will also change,' by asserting that 'No such thing as the heart of man exists.' "[9]

3. The work of Christ is reduced to his activity through the gospel message *within the Church.* In criticizing the thinking of José Míguez Bonino, he first offers this summary of it: "The task of participating in the work of redemption involves not only preaching the Gospel, but 'participating in the work of Jesus Christ who works in the world creating peace and order, justice and liberty, dignity and community.' " Wagner comments: "This reference to the work of Christ in the world is perhaps one of Míguez's most serious departures from Biblical teaching. One searches the Scriptures in vain to find a commandment that would have Christians move into the world with this kind of mission."[10]

4. The *unity of the Church* and membership in it is more important than any socio-economic-political option. In commenting on the conclusions of the First Evangelical Consultation in Church and Society (held in Huampaní, Peru in 1961), Wagner presents a counter-argument that

seems to mirror that of Rahner and the Chilean bishops: "Even under the generous assumption that the church as an institution would possess the technical competence to judge the world's socio-economic situation accurately, not even the most convinced optimist would suppose that the church could bring its members to agree to one single political point of view as a possible remedy."[11] He then goes on to say: "But as Per Lonning asks, 'Can a Christian who chooses a particular historical option claim that this is the option Christ makes?' Nothing could stand as a clearer warning of the possibility that the passion for social action can become such a strong drive that it inverts Biblical priorities. 'Fear and trembling' should characterize Christians not in relationship to the risk of jumping into ambiguous worldly situations, but in relationship to the possibility of *failing to make the offer of salvation available to mankind.*"[12]

5. The "theology of the radical left" does not take into account the *dualism* of the Bible and, in particular, the *negative supernatural forces* that rule this world. Criticizing Rubem Alves, he says: "Alves does not seem much disturbed by the haunting contradiction in a philosophy of history that indicates that for at least twenty centuries God has been hard at work trying to 'humanize mankind,' but apparently with little success. Two world wars, Korea, Hungary, Viet Nam, Biafra, Czechoslovakia—all are dirty smudges on the twentieth-century world's canvas . . . Alves' exposition of the 'forces that oppose the action of God' does not come to grips with the Biblical concept of a temporal dualism in which the supernatural forces of evil play a sinister and important part. He rather searches for *natural* causes of evil."[13]

6. Finally, according to Wagner, there is no *universal promise or plan of salvation.* The only salvation around operates through evangelism and individual conversion. In this connection Wagner criticizes the views of Emilio Castro and Richard Shaull. Castro, he says, "approaches the heart of the issue by asking: 'What is the final destiny of those who die without having known the name of Christ?' but he never satisfactorily answers the question he raises. He does hint, however, that we need not be too concerned, for 'in the New Testament and in the Old Testament there are clear indications for us to affirm that the plan of God in Jesus Christ incorporates all humanity.' "[14] Of course Wagner does not agree with Castro, but his position will be clearer if we first see his criticism of Shaull. Shaull himself writes: "We can no longer think exclusively in terms of rescuing lost pagans from the imminent flames of hell. The missionary today may not have too great an opportunity for direct evangelism though his work is no less important for the proclamation of the Gospel. And most of us do not feel that we do justice to the Biblical

faith if we limit it to providing people with an entrance ticket to heaven."[15] Here is Wagner's comment: "With this rejection of the eschatological urgency of the mission of the church in the world, Shaull makes a decisive break from evangelical theology. It is quite remarkable that he feels that by rejecting the *urgency of saving people from hell* he is being faithful to the Bible. One wonders if Bonhoeffer's exaggerated emphasis on the Old Testament has not caused New Testament theology to become so diluted among secular theologians that the terrifying thought of a human being cast into the lake of fire no longer has as much power to move the heart as does a ragged peasant who has become disinherited by moving into a favela."[16]

The simplistic nature of this criticism and its line of argument as well as its forthright honesty may disconcert the reader. Wagner is uncommonly frank in spelling out the theological foundations underlying the Church's function, and the reader might entertain the suspicion that I am using him to paint a caricature. That is not so at all. Indeed my purpose is precisely the opposite of caricature.

The real merit of the points spelled out by Wagner is that they explicate the real underpinnings of the criticism that Catholic ecclesiastical authorities have made against liberation theology. The bishops of Chile, for example, would have performed a real service to the Church if they had explicated the same six points instead of trying to arrive at the same conclusions while hiding their underlying theology. Many sincere Christians in Latin America rack their brains trying to figure out how the hierarchy can cite extensive passages from the documents of Vatican II and Medellín and then arrive at exactly opposite conclusions. They would benefit from knowing that the latter conclusions derive from a different theology, a theology that is kept hidden because it does not dovetail with the main thrust of those two recent events.

Hence, as we noted above, one of the most difficult problems for liberation theology after Vatican II and Medellín was the inhibition surrounding the opposed theology. The real bases of decision-making remain hidden from view and hence impervious to discussion. The same principles are invoked, but one side draws just the opposite conclusions. Protestant thinking does not have to go by way of Vatican II and the Medellín Conference, and that has some advantages. At least one can see against what sort of ecclesiology one is fighting.

III. JUSTIFICATION BY FAITH VERSUS IDEOLOGIES

As we just saw, liberation theology is confronted with a serious methodological problem: its anticipated conclusions are in conflict with a particular theology of the Church which continues to remain decisive for

its authorities and its structures. It would be naive to imagine that liberation theology can be accepted in any consistent or serious way by the
ecclesiastical structures now in existence.

Insofar as criticism of the existing ecclesiastical function is concerned, it would seem that liberation theology has a greater affinity with
the current European "political theology," also known as the "theology
of revolution." Indeed one of the authors criticized by Wagner, Rubem
Alves, might be regarded as closer to that current of thought than to
Latin American liberation theology. Moltmann has probably exerted a
greater influence on him than any Latin American theologian has.
Moltmann himself is quick to criticize the triumphalist pretentiousness
of a Church which assumes it will be able to preserve its universalist
potential by maintaining impartiality: "Only in and through the dialectic
of taking sides does the universalism of the Crucified become a reality in
this world. The phony universalism of the Church is something very
different. It is a premature and untimely anticipation of the *Kingdom of
God.*"[17]

Yet, despite surface appearances, we shall see that this "political
theology" puts liberation theology in a difficult position vis-à-vis a factor
even more profound and definitive than the Church itself. The factor in
question is mentioned in Moltmann's statement quoted above. It is the
kingdom of God, the ultimate reality. In short, it is *eschatology.*

All Christian churches contain an eschatological element, since our
faith "gives substance" to the things for which we hope (Heb. 11:1). And
what we look forward to is the kingdom, or reign, of God. Wherein lie
the differences in the eschatology of the various Christian churches? I
think we can say that basically it lies in their differing conceptions of the
relationship between events in history on the one hand and the kingdom
of God on the other hand.

Since the time of the Reformation at least, the characterizing feature
of the Catholic Church in this area is its emphasis on the *merit* of human
endeavors for *gaining entrance* to the eternal kingdom of God. And this
notion of merit is of the utmost importance for liberation theology.

The fact is that in the Catholic view the merit of a human action had
no direct relationship to its historical effectiveness. Neither successful
endeavors nor unsuccessful endeavors are meritorious *as such.* The historical end result of human actions, in other words, does not have anything directly to do with totalling up a person's merit. What really counts
is the effort expended and a God-directed intention. To use a doctor as
our example here, the current conception of merit is not concerned at all
with whether the patient is cured or not. What gains merit for the doctor
is the effort he makes to cure the patient and the intention to do that for

the glory of God rather than for the sake of fame or the life of the patient. The latter merely serves as the occasion for merit.

It is quite apparent that this conception of merit assumes that there are two very different, if not opposed, planes of value and efficacy. For society, for the human and historical plane, the value of a doctor is in direct proportion to the historical results he obtains. For God, for the plane of eternal values, those historical results not only do not count but are actually dangerous. They are dangerous insofar as they are historical *values*, real satisfactions that can compete with the effort and intention that count for eternity.

In Catholic theology and spirituality these two planes have been given characteristic names. The *supernatural* plane is the plane of eternal values; the *natural* plane is the plane of temporal values. In *A Theology of Liberation,* Gustavo Gutiérrez rightly notes that such a theology could only arise insofar as the "theology of the two planes" lost its hold on people's minds.

How did the theology of the two planes come to exert such a strong hold over the Catholic Church? It did so because for a long time it seemed to be the only logical and feasible way of expressing a dogmatic datum that had been gradually minted during the earlier struggle against Stoicism. The dogmatic datum was that only *grace,* only God's free gift, enabled man to do anything worthwhile in terms of such a divine destiny as eternal life.

Underlying the translation of this dogmatic datum into the theology of the two planes were two assumptions: (1) that a free gift can be recognized by the fact that some people possess it whereas others do not, without any fault on their part; (2) that the absolutely gratuitous nature of the gift, its supernatural nature, presupposes the existence of purely natural states, persons, and values in real-life history.

Some years before Vatican II, these two presuppositions began to be challenged. It began to appear that we did not need these presuppositions to maintain the theological principle of the gratuitous nature of the supernatural—if you will pardon the redundancy. The fact is that a gift need not be recognized simply by the fact that some possess it and others do not. Everyone can possess something, yet that something may still be a gift. You don't have to go looking for some human being in history who lacks grace, at least for the moment, in order to be able to affirm the supernatural or gratuitous nature of God's grace. In short, the two prevailing suppositions only applied to the petty gifts that we human beings give to each other.

Let me clarify this point with an example. Even before he is born, a certain child might be endowed with a fortune. That would mean, of course, that his birth and subsequent development would be surrounded with lavish preparations and extraordinary care. I say "extraordinary" because other children presumably would not enjoy the same fortune. To the child in question, however, his way of life would seem to be the most "natural" thing in the world so long as he did not compare it to that of other children and come to realize how he had benefited from a gift. But now let us further assume that the gift-giver is so generous that he gives the same gift to every child of a given generation. That would change the life-styles of all of them, and the gift could not be recognized by making comparisons. Yet the gift does not cease to be a gift, for the children could have been born without it. To realize and appreciate this decisive factor in life, the one child or all the children would have to ponder that alternative possibility. But we cannot ask the child or all the children (in the second hypothesis) to imagine what a purely "natural" existence would have been for them, because they do not have around them the elements they would need to fashion such a picture: *everything* has been changed by the gift.

Something very similar, if not exactly the same, holds true for the theology of grace. If it has been given to all human beings to live in essentially *gratuitous* conditions, then they insofar as they are believers must recognize that God was free to create them without that gift, to create them in a state of *pure nature*. But one cannot ask human beings to *imagine* what that state would have been like because they have no such example in their present-day existence or in that of their contemporaries. Thus the concept of pure nature is what is called a "limit concept." It is necessary to understand and appreciate another concept (i.e., grace), but it cannot point out any concrete thing in history.

This point of view, worked out in particular by Karl Rahner, served as the background for Vatican II's statement that all human beings are called to one and the same supernatural vocation and, thanks to the grace of God, possess the means needed to fulfill this vocation (*Gaudium et spes*, n. 22). This holds true both within and outside the Church. The effects of grace within the Christian are the same as those produced by grace in all human beings of good will (*Gaudium et spes*, n. 22).

Thus it was that the Catholic Church officially abandoned the theology of the two planes and opened the way for a theology that was quite different: i.e., liberation theology. Of course that does not mean that all resistance to liberation theology based on the older notion of the two planes was thereby terminated. As we have already noted, ecclesiastical authorities have continued to describe the function of the Church as a purely "religious" one, finding support in other conciliar statements which clearly seem to set a "supernatural" realm over against the realm of "natural" human history. My point here is that the statements of Vatican II are clear enough to ensure that the basic theological foundations of liberation theology may not be declared heterodox.

One could say that the eschatological element opposed to liberation theology is stronger and more resistant in Protestant circles than in Catholic circles. This is not to suggest that the eternal, metahistorical factor is not of equal importance in both. It is, but the *historical* factor is not of equal importance in both. The disappearance of the notion of *merit* from Protestant theology, dating from the time of the Reformation, seems to have undermined the possibility of any theology of history.[18] In Catholic theology the only thing that united the plane of human activity in history with the plane of God's eternal kingdom was the notion of *merit,* that is, the "eternal" worth of human effort and right intention. But even this tie was cut in the Protestant theology of salvation by faith alone: i.e., salvation by virtue of Christ's merits alone.

By the time of the Reformation, the struggle with Stoicism which had laid the foundation for the theology of the two planes was a thing of the past. So was the struggle between pope and emperor, which had helped to give new life to the theology of the two planes as a possible solution to a real-life problem. By the time the Catholic Church was confronted with Martin Luther, in other words, the theory of the two planes was no longer a critical issue; it had become a point of orthodoxy in the Catholic Church.

Luther's doctrine of the *two kingdoms,* by contrast, became the politico-theological foundation for the whole edifice of the Reformation, as James S. Preus has pointed up again recently. The Reformation could not survive without the armed political support of princes. To make themselves independent of theological criteria, it became necessary to defend the difference between the plane of religious authority and the plane of secular authority. According to Preus, that was the price that had to be paid for other more liberating aspects of the Reformation. But as time went on, as it became evident that the Reformation no longer needed any political support, the price came to seem too high. That at least is the view of Preus, to mention one name. He writes: "The political character of Luther's theology has to be judged against that of the Bible, which in its repeated calls for justice and righteousness and in its concern for the poor and oppressed makes no distinctions between bodies and souls, but proclaims a Gospel for the whole man. The Lutheran doctrine of the two realms evades that calling by narrowing that Gospel. *The fastidious depoliticization of the doctrine of justification, via the two-kingdoms doctrine, has served the church's interests well–politically.* But has it served the world?"[19]

Reinhold Niebuhr offers us an example of this theological influence on the political realm. He is talking about religious opposition to Hitler in Nazi Germany:

> Lutheranism, which in my opinion has the most profound religious insights on ultimate questions of human existence, has remained defective on problems of political and social morality, until the encounter with Hitler cured it of some of the most grievous errors: its doctrine of the "two realms"—the "realm of heaven" and the "realm of earth"; the one the realm of grace "where nothing is known except forgiveness and brotherly love" and the other the realm of "law" where "nothing is known except the law, the sword, the courts and chains." This might be a good description of the two dimensions of life and morals, but the fatal flaw in the doctrine of the two realms was that the one realm was that of private and the other of official morality. Politics, in short, was designed to maintain order in the sinful world. The purely negative function of the state was aggravated by an absolute religious sanction of its authority and the prohibition of all resistance.[20]

It would be unfair, however, to pretend that the Lutheran doctrine of the *two kingdoms* was the outcome of a specific political situation or a political tool for confronting said situation. The doctrine of the *two kingdoms* is intimately bound up with other central themes in Lutheran theology: e.g., with the doctrine of justification by faith alone and the key notion that glory belongs to God alone (*soli Deo gloria*). In short, it has much to do with something that Karl Barth stressed once again shortly before his death: i.e., the rejection of the Catholic attempt to connect God "and" man, faith "and" good works. Thus the Lutheran rejection of this "and" in the problem of justification turns faith into the confident but essentially passive acceptance of God's fixed plan for human destiny and the construction of his eschatological kingdom. Indeed some Europeans in the field of "political theology" use that precise argument to counter any attempt to attribute to mankind an historical *causality* in the construction of God's kingdom.

For example, Rudolf Weth writes: "*God himself* brings about the revolutionary action that is decisive for the *coming* of his kingdom. His action cannot be effected or replaced by *any human action*." Weth bases his view on a central text of Luther in which he comments on the passage in Matthew's Gospel (Matt. 25:34) where the universal judge summons the elect to take the places that have been set aside for them from the beginning of the world. Luther's commentary is all the more important insofar as the Letter to the Romans, not the Gospels, was the initial basis for his doctrine of justification by faith alone. Here Weth applies the doctrine to other parts of the New Testament, and specifically to one that talks about the definitive establishment of the kingdom of God.

Luther's own text is this: "How could they [Segundo: the children of the kingdom] merit what already belongs to them and what was prepared for them long before they were even created? It would be more correct to say that it is the kingdom of God which merits us as its inheritors . . . The kingdom of God has already been prepared. But the children of God must be prepared for the kingdom. So it is the kingdom that merits the children of God, not the children of God who merit the kingdom."[21]

Leaving aside the whole question of the correctness of Luther's exegesis here, we can readily see that it thoroughly rules out any attempt to find or establish a causal relationship between activity in history and the construction of God's kingdom. It situates that kingdom in the remote past and the remote future (the *eschaton*), thus detaching it wholly from historical activity in the present.

Now German "political theology" is markedly dependent on the Lutheran theology of justification.[22] So it should not surprise us that it systematically tries to eliminate from theologico-political language any term that might suggest a causal relationship between historical activity and the construction of the eschatological kingdom. And this is true even when it is talking about revolution. Except in rare exceptions, the historical reality produced by human effort is described as "anticipation" (Moltmann), "analogy" (Weth), "rough draft" (Metz), and so forth.

This stress on the eschatological element, to the detriment of the historical element, has important consequences for liberation theology. Two critical ones must be considered here.

1. This eschatological relativization of any and every existing historical reality, this desacralization of any and every political regime, initially has a liberating impact. It disestablishes the world we know; it de-absolutizes the hallowedness that any and every political regime claims in order to perpetuate itself and deny its historical relativity. The key word in this political theology, *hope*, is intimately bound up with that kind of liberation. The future is liberated from the weight of the past. *Faith* enables people to imagine new possibilities and to escape the mesmerizing allure of the established order.

But when we go in for a more concrete examination of the specific circumstances in which this liberative function is to be carried out, its liberating character does not show up so clearly. We live in an interconnected world where different socio-economic systems and regimes hold sway. In such a world it is unrealistic to think that relativization of the established systems will produce some sort of cyclic efficacy.

Let us consider this point more closely. Relativization of any and every political system, in the name of God, can serve initially to stimulate creativity and imaginative thinking. And it can also do the same thing after a newly created project has begun to harden into another fixed and unimaginative system. But we live in a world where new and old systems coexist and communicate with one another. In such a situation there is a tendency for eschatological relativization to be generalized. Even before some new regime is worked out, it is criticized in the name of some new hope. At the same time, the opposed regime is being criticized under the same head but for opposite reasons. And even the search itself is relativized because there is no element in history that can be related causally to the construction of God's eschatological kingdom.

My suspicion is that this sort of generalized disestablishment and relativization ends up being a politically neutral theology. The "revolution" it talks about seems to be more like a Kantian revolution than an historical revolution. It merely revolutionizes the way we formulate our problems. Real-life revolution must have enthusiasm behind it, but the concrete circumstances in which this eschatology operates at present seem to throw a dash of cold water on any such enthusiasm—not only on the phony ideological enthusiasm created by the status quo but also on the imaginative enthusiasm for new projects spawned by criticism and hope.

In this connection I think we would do well to examine certain passages written by Rubem Alves, who is a disciple of Moltmann. One immediate consequence of the aforementioned principles is particularly worthy of note: the most radical means of bringing about change are rejected. The reason for this rejection is simple but basic: no one can adopt such means without losing his "cool," without losing his modicum of relativization which enables him to maintain control over events. Here is what Alves has to say about violence: "From the viewpoint of the man who is free for the future, violence is a totally different reality. It is whatever denies him a future, whatever aborts his project to create a new tomorrow; it is the power that keeps him prisoner of the futureless structures of a futureless world. Violence is the power of defuturization, which strives to close man's consciousness to the future and the future to man's consciousness."[23]

Hope is paradoxically translated into a radically pessimistic view of the whole process of change, even when the latter is not violent, precisely because any and every change prompted by man cannot help but lose out to world-dominating sin. The kingdom of God can only be fashioned by someone who is free from sin, and that comes down to God alone. Opting for "messianic humanism," Alves writes: "That is why messianic humanism refuses to draw its hope from the slave's faithfulness to the protest that is intrinsic to his condition of slave. Its historical experience shows that those who once were the negative slaves, and therefore the bearers of freedom, become, once they achieve their freedom, dominated by concern for the preservation of their present and are then infected with the sin of their masters: they are now those who want to forestall the future . . . The structure of oppression, accordingly, is able to create a man in its image and likeness, a man whose consciousness is as unfree as that of his master. He is the slave who does not want to be free. His will to freedom becomes will to domestication. The history of freedom, therefore, cannot be based on the powers of *man alone*."[24] Is Alves suggesting that there is a better chance for success when man works *with* God? The question is offbase, for the reason we cited earlier: a theology derived from Luther finds it very difficult to conceive of any such collaboration.

If Alves' remarks presume to describe objective historical reality, as they clearly do, then one must conclude that man always works alone. And Alves goes on to forget man completely in the remarks that immediately follow: "The slave may forget about his suffering, but God does not. God is the suffering God, the God who does not ever allow the pains of history to be overlooked and healed by the hypnotic power of the politics of preservation. Because God . . . is the God in history, and since his presence in history is always resisted by the powers of the old, God is a suffering God."[25]

This standpoint also leads Alves to reject *de facto* cooperation of any sort with revolutionaries in history:

> But messianic humanism also rejects the opposite sin of the revolutionaries. Since the repression and the restoration of the erotic sense of life depends on the powers of *man alone*, he finds it necessary totally to discipline his present in order to gather his energies for the task of liberation. In order to destroy the repression imposed upon society he finds it necessary to impose upon his present a similar structure of repression. The present loses itself. It exists only for the sake of a future. . . Man is absolved from inhumanity and brutality in the present, as the time of transition, the time that does not count. And the future, once it is brought about by the revolutionaries, tends to become closed, because it is believed that it is the presence of the *eschaton*. This is why revolutions that were once the bearers of new hopes soon became crystallized, rigid, and dogmatic, a veritable resurrection of the sins of the conservative.[26]

That is why God must operate *alone*. In the strictest theological sense of the word, he must "create" the liberation that man denies himself and will never manage to procure: "The normal unfolding of the politics of the old cannot give birth to the new. The new is here nothing more than the old under a different form, a different mask. It regenerates itself, thereby perpetuating the old world of unfreedom under a different guise. But because God's politics negates the natural unfolding of the old, room is made for the new. And one can truly say that it is created *ex nihilo,* since the new cannot be explained in terms of *the logic of natural causality.*"[27]

Here the distinction between the supernatural and the natural as two separate planes which never touch each other unexpectedly crops up in this radically eschatological vision of the kingdom to rule out any and all commitment of Protestant theology to liberation in history. When this theology remains consistent with itself and its fonts, the revolution it speaks about is transformed into faith and hope in something metahistorical and a disgusted turning-away from real-life history.

2. The second critical factor in the relationship between political theology and liberation theology is a language difficulty. The fact is that Alves, with his ahistorical conclusions, does not represent the majority of Protestant theologians of liberation.[28] Many of them, such as Richard Shaull, are far more pointed in proposing historical solutions for the problem of liberation. Indeed Shaull's paper at the Geneva Conference on Church and Society (in the summer of 1966) scandalized many of the participants with its concrete revolutionary content. But even so, the Lutheran tradition considered above continues to have an impact on the language used, if not on the content and the options proposed. Thus, if my observation is correct, we get two different languages. When Shaull is talking about the historical realm, the language is intensely committed and revolutionary. But when he tries to translate all that into theological terms, a certain reserve takes over and his language seems to be inhibited. Here I should like the reader to examine a few remarks of Shaull from the standpoint of a Latin American Christian who wants concrete guidance amid the thorny issues of the existing political situation and who looks to his Christian faith for this guidance.

Here is Shaull's remark: "The kingdom of God always stands over against every social and political order, thus exposing its dehumanizing elements and *judging* it. At the same time, the Kingdom is a *dynamic* reality; it is 'coming' through the work of him who is restoring the nations."[29] The very first phrase could only prove disconcerting to the Latin American. Total relativization of historical realities, far from being dynamic, ends up as merely static contemplation. Shaull is too intelligent and honest to overlook that fact, which is why he brings in the qualifying word "dynamic" in the next sentence. He tells us that the kingdom is coming. Through whom or what? The Latin American waits anxiously to see what Shaull will say. What group or thrust or ideology is ushering the kingdom of God into historical reality? Alas, the turn of Shaull's remarks can only produce despair in the Latin American. No human being, no human group, no human ideology, no human process of change is responsible—only *God alone*. Just as the bishops of Chile end up opting for the risen Christ alone, so Shaull ends up opting for God alone. Both choose not to opt for anyone or anything in concrete history.

Must a theology give that sort of response to be Christian? Such a response clearly would deal a fatal blow to the credibility of Christian theology and to liberation theology as such. Of course it is a fake death in a sense, because one and the same person, who is both a human being and a Christian theologian, can be drastic and intensely committed in his or her historical judgments when not talking in theological terms. But when a shift is made to the latter, the answers seem to lose all contact with history and the decisions that must be made within it.

Let us consider another remark by Shaull, of particular interest because it specifically alludes to the theology of Moltmann: "As Professor Moltmann (*Theology of Hope*) has worked this out, the Christian symbols point to a God who goes ahead of us and who is bringing a new future into being. His word is essentially a word of promise, that awakens in us the hope for a new future. It is a word that upsets old stabilities, arouses dissatisfaction with the old order, and frees us to expect and serve the things that are to come."[30]

Once again we find the same two elements noted above. Firstly, the fact that God "goes ahead of us" does not mean that we are co-workers with him. Only God is the subject of "bringing a new future into being." Nothing is said about mankind, though it is man and woman who are anxiously trying to figure out what decision they should make. Moreover, the phrase "bringing into being" is an evident allusion to creation *ex nihilo*. No human collaboration is involved. Secondly, here again it is evident that a critical attitude is the element in man and the Christian which corresponds to God's creation in history. The word of God "upsets old stabilities, arouses dissatisfaction with the old order." Here we seem to see a partiality and a partisanship that should be translated into some sort of decision in history. But Shaull cannot be unaware of the fact that it is very difficult to make a concrete choice in terms of *old* and *new*. Quite aside from the fact that the new is not always preferable to the old, there is the more important fact that the same things can be new or old depending on historical circumstances.

Consider capitalism and socialism, for example. One cannot choose between them in terms of old and new. Both systems have their own history in different countries. Socialism can be "old," as is evident from the remarks of a theological journal in Prague about Latin American liberation theology. After acknowledging the merits of our theology, it goes on to complain that liberation theology has not pointed out clearly that liberation is already a fact in the socialist countries.[31]

The point, then, is that the use of "new" and "old" in Shaull's theology does not really presume to provide us with a criterion for making judgments and finding direction in history. It merely represents man's trusting and reverent response to the creative activity of God alone. But there is a third feature in the above remark of Shaull that was not evident in the earlier citation. Here Shaull depicts a broader range of human attitudes. Besides alluding to the critical attitude, Shaull presents three positive attitudes. The word of God *awakens hope* for a new future, and *frees* us to expect and *serve* the things that are to come. Hope, freedom, service: are we to regard these things as characteristic features of a revolutionary option? The obvious answer would seem to be "no," unless we are dealing with a very queer sort of revolution.

Hoping and the freedom to hope can indeed be the first or initial steps towards revolution, its starting point. But a real revolution will subsequently call for attitudes of a very different sort. Shaull himself is perfectly aware of that fact, and he can scandalize an audience with his descriptions of a revolution that is real in every sense of the word. His third element, service, could very well be synonymous with real-life revolution if it were given its full scope and import. But that assumption is ruled out by the final turn of his thought. We are to serve "the things that are to come." Once again a potentially explosive option loses all its historical force when the verb is complemented with an object. The bishops of Chile *opt* . . . for the "risen Christ." Shaull says that we *serve* . . . "the things that are to come." Somewhere the historical thrust and content of decision-making gets lost.

IV. GRACE IN A THEOLOGY OF LIBERATION

It should be clear at the end of this chapter that the intimate and unavoidable relationship between faith and ideologies poses serious problems: (1) to the theology and structures of the Church; and (2) to a specific conception of eschatology which has been very operative within the Catholic Church and still remains powerfully active and central in the Protestant Churches. I shall have more to say about the function of the Church and its relationship with ideologies in subsequent chapters. So here I should like to say a few more words about eschatology to finish up with that topic.

Liberation theology is a profoundly ecumenical theology. It seems that the Christian's concern to collaborate in the process of liberating mankind unites him more effectively and surely with other Christians than does any attempt to resolve age-old theoretical problems. Libera-

tion poses problems of such magnitude that Christians of whatever denomination feel closer to those who have made the same option in history than they do to other members of their own denomination. This
ecumenism extends beyond the boundaries of Christianity, in fact, unit-
ing all men of good will in decisive options and separating them from
those of "ill will" wherever they are found.

But when liberation theology examines its own methodology, it runs
into a second level of ecumenism where a new light begins to dawn over
all the old and critical controversies. Let us adopt Paul Lehmann's assumption that God's policy is to make human existence human and
maintain it as such.[32] This assumption may help us to appreciate better
what happened in the past, particularly at the time of the Reformation.
Our previous remarks in this chapter will serve as the backdrop for the
point we are trying to stress here.

In contrast to the Lutheran view of justification by faith alone,
Catholic theology stresses justification by good works in accordance with
the moral law. At first glance it would seem to be hardly Christian at all,
or very Old Testament in cast at best. There is only one thing that would
seem to justify it, but that one thing is very important. However shakily,
it does try to preserve the principle that human liberty is liberty *for*
something definitive and indeed eschatological: the building up of the
kingdom of God. It differs from Luther's notion of the servant will (*servo
arbitrio*) in that important respect.

On the other hand, the Lutheran principle of salvation by faith
rather than by good works does seem to be central to the New Testament
message of people like Paul, for example. But following Fromm's distinction between freedom *from* and freedom *to* (or *for*), one would be
inclined to say that Luther was faithful only to the former aspect of
Paul's thinking, that Paul also discussed freedom *to*. In short, Luther
clearly and correctly pointed out that faith should free the Christian
from the law and preoccupations with it. That was his creative intuition,
welling up from his own consuming inner problem.

On the one hand, then, we find Catholic legalism; on the other we
find Lutheran passivity. The element that might have helped to reconcile the two—freedom *to* construct the kingdom—was lost in the shuffle.
The two sides hardened poles apart instead of melding into a fruitful
and liberative synthesis.

Faith liberates man from a preoccupation with the law so that he can
launch out into creative love rather than remain paralyzed by the problem of personal security and individual salvation. The only criterion for
the latter things can be the static criterion of the law. But in entrusting

our destiny to God, we should not imagine that God simply wants us to leave him alone because any cooperative effort on our part would somehow diminish his glory. On the contrary, the Christian God is a God who loves and who, as such, needs to be loved. He needs our creativity for his work, and so he asks us to entrust our destiny to him in faith. So the Catholic doctrine was clearly inadequate insofar as it made the law the object of our liberty, and the Lutheran doctrine was inadequate insofar as it turned faith into a deprecation of human liberty.

Are we being too presumptuous when we say that liberation theology must be grounded on a profound reconciliation of these two Christian viewpoints and their work of mutual correction? I do not think so. And the concrete experience of dialoguing about liberation, seeking proper decisions, and making appropriate commitments would seem to justify my opinion.

NOTES

1. As I noted in note 22 of Chapter I, it is far from evident to many North Americans that our hermeneutic must go back specifically to the "Christian" sources, to our biblical writings. I think this calls into question the very possibility of faith, starting from Bultmann's assumption that any and every divine intervention in the realm of phenomena must be regarded as mythical. On that assumption any "revelation" in the strict sense would be mythical by that very fact. Thus, even though Bultmann feels that his assumption is compatible with the Christian faith, strict logic should compel him to offer a new definition of faith or of Christianity. For in his view the divine revealer is absent from the "Christian" message, and one is at least forced to say that any other message in history, even one opposed to the "Christian" message, has as much right to be believed. The problem does not face Latin American theology in this form, and so its solution is not critical here. But I think that the dualism suggested by Bultmann between transcendence and a phenomenal world is one of those false dualisms typical of the nineteenth century and all subsequent evolutionary thought: either spirit or matter, immanence or transcendence, instinct or reason, and so forth. Teilhard de Chardin tried to show how such dualisms could be overcome while preserving their truth. I think his approach holds equally true for a revelation in history. See, in particular, the text cited in note 20 of Chapter II.

2. The first affirmation is expressed in such passages as these:

"The Church opts for the risen Jesus Christ" (p. 67).

"Today in Chile we are faced with the opposing alternatives of capitalism and socialism. It is important to remember that they are not the only possible ones—since there is nothing to prevent us from trying a third approach—and that there are many forms and degrees of both capitalism and socialism" (p. 68).

"Thus we can arrive at different political options while remaining united in our basic, absolute option for the risen Jesus Christ" (p. 69).

"If we take the word 'opt' in the strict sense, that is, in the sense of choosing one group and excluding the other, then it is clear that the problem is being posed on the basis of a simplistic and dualistic view of the world that attempts to draw a neat dividing line between groups of 'good guys' and groups of 'bad guys' and to force us to speak out *in favor of* one side and *against* the other side... The Church *does not choose between* different human groups. In and with Jesus Christ, the Church makes a decision for all those whom Jesus himself opted for: *for all the people of Chile*" (p. 65).

Their second affirmation is supported by all sorts of reasons grounded on historical experiences. I cannot sum them up here. But here is how the affirmation itself is stated:

"Hence ... the concrete embodiments of Marxist socialism so far cannot be accepted as an *authentic alternative* to capitalism" (p. 82).

As I indicated in note 2 of Chapter II, this document is reproduced in an anthology of episcopal documents designed to bear witness to the active witness of the Chilean episcopate during the years of Allende's presidency (1970–1973). But it is sad and almost embarrassing to find that the last document in that anthology was finally approved by the Chilean episcopate on September 13, 1973, *two days after* the military coup and Allende's own death. When their partisans were being persecuted and sometimes killed in the streets, the Chilean bishops were meeting to make some final observations on the "Christians for Socialism" movement and to condemn them. For this document and further background material on the Chilean situation, see the anthology *Christians and Socialism*, Eng. trans. (Maryknoll, N.Y. Orbis Books, 1975).

3. C. Peter Wagner, *Latin American Theology: Radical or Evangelical?* (Grand Rapids, Mich.: Eerdmans, 1970). The author served as a minister in Bolivia.

4. *Ibid.*, pp. 61–62.

5. *Ibid.*, p. 51.

6. *Ibid.*, p. 26.

7. *Ibid.*, p. 23.

8. *Ibid.*, p. 26.

9. *Ibid.*, p. 50.

10. *Ibid.*, pp. 29–30.

11. *Ibid.*, pp. 31–32.

12. *Ibid.*, p. 32.

13. *Ibid.*, p. 42.

14. *Ibid.*, p. 53.

15. *Ibid.*, p. 55.

16. *Ibid.*

17. Jurgen Moltmann, "Dieu dans la révolution," in *Discussion sur 'la théologie de la révolution,'* French trans. (Paris: Cerf-Mame, 1972), p. 72.

18. See, for example, Harvey Cox, *The Secular City,* rev. ed. (New York: Macmillan, 1966), pp. 91–95. At the time of the Reformation Bucer may have been the only person who attempted to clarify the relationship between justification by faith alone and historical effort to build up the kingdom of God. The point deserves further study.

19. James S. Preus, "The Political Function of Luther's *Doctrina,*" *Concordia Theological Monthly* 43 (October 1972) 598.

20. Reinhold Niebuhr, "Germany," in *Worldview* 16 (June 1973) 14–15.

21. Rudolph Weth, "La 'Théologie de la révolution' dans la perspective de la justification et du royaume," in *Discussion, op. cit.* (note 17), p. 120. The citation from Luther is from *De servo arbitrio.*

22. Catholic theologians in this circle, and even more those outside it, betray a clear Lutheran influence on this point. They do not make the distinctions I propose here between individual justification on the one hand and an extrapolation of the problem insofar as the construction of the kingdom is concerned. This convergence is due in part to the ecumenical climate prevailing since Vatican II. But it is also due to the fact that Catholic theology has honestly admitted the fact that it had simply overlooked Paul's teaching on justification by faith. See, for example, the joint study of the Letter to the Romans which was written up by Hans Küng. Even though this admission is not made uncritically by Catholic theologians, in my opinion they are not critical enough when it comes to extrapolating Paul's thought to the work of constructing the kingdom. In short, they tend to overlook the authentic feature of his thought which the Catholic Church did defend at the time of the Reformation.

23. Rubem Alves, *A Theology of Human Hope* (Washington, D.C: Corpus Books, 1969), pp. 111–12.

24. *Ibid.,* p. 116.

25. *Ibid.*

26. *Ibid.,* p. 155.

27. *Ibid.,* p. 127.

28. As the title of Wagner's book would indicate, liberation theology is so "radical" that it would cease to be "evangelical" in his eyes.

29. In *Christian Social Ethics in a Changing World,* edited by J.C. Bennet (New York: Association Press, 1966); cited by J.M. Lochman, "Ecumenical Theology of Revolution," in *New Theology* 6 (New York: Macmillan 1969), footnote 22, pp. 121–22.

30. Richard Shaull, "Christian Faith as Scandal in a Technocratic World," in *New Theology* 6, p. 130.

31. See Adolfo Ham, "Introduction to the Theology of Liberation," in *Communio viatorum* (Prague), Summer 1973.

32. Paul Lehmann, *Ethics in a Christian Context* (New York: Harper and Row, 1963), p. 101 and *passim.*

CHAPTER SIX

Ideologies and Relativity

If our observations in the preceding chapter are correct, then we can say a few basic things about faith and its relationship to ideologies. Faith is an absolute insofar as it is a truth revealed by God, an absolute truth. But insofar as it is destined to perform a function that is not faith itself, even revealed truth and our adherence to it constitutes something *relative*. In other words, the absolute feature in the plan of God who reveals some truth is not that this truth be accepted but rather that it be placed in the service of historical problems and their solution. The solution of such problems, as we have seen, is brought about by an ideology; that is, by an historical system of means and ends related to the problem in question.

From the viewpoint of value, then, *ideologies* constitute the absolute feature of a functional faith; in that respect the latter is relative *to* the former. At the same time, however, ideologies ever remain *relative* to the historical circumstances that produce and condition them. No solution to an historical problem can lay claim to absolute value, if absolute implies complete independence from the conditioning influence of historical circumstances.

But paradoxically enough, it would seem that we now have once and for all subjected the absolute aspect to historical relativity. This may well be the *major difficulty* facing any theology that tries to maintain that faith and ideologies are both different and complementary. Hence it is a critical methodological problem for liberation theology. If we cannot solve this problem, then liberation theology will be accused of relativism and condemned on that ground.

I hope our previous remarks have made it clear that the claims of academic theology to absoluteness are quite illusory. Yet that does not alter the fact that academic theology continues to parade in the garb of absoluteness whereas liberation theology is accused more pointedly every day of lacking any such character.

In my opinion the clearest example of this whole problem, and the most concrete and propitious area in which to treat of it, is the whole subject of violence. What ought to be the relationship between Christians and violence? Tackling that question will, I think, provide us with a methodological approach for dealing with many similar issues. And the advantage in this case is that we have a wealth of material at our disposal for examining and evaluating the process of discernment that goes on in connection with the issue.

Let us begin with the well-established fact that Christians do not seem to have any problem in agreeing that the commandment of Jesus was mutual love. The difficulty begins when we try to spell out more concretely what goes to make up mutual love for Christians. There seem to be two major Christian opinions on the subject. *According to the first opinion,* the deeds and teaching of Jesus *spell out clearly* what sort of love is required. Perhaps the best summary of this spelling out is to be found in this counsel of Paul: "Do not seek revenge. . . Do not let evil conquer you, but use good to defeat evil" (Rom. 12:17, 21). The summons is to take the risk of wholly gratuitous love. Even though Jesus' remarks about turning the other cheek and surrendering one's coat as well as one's shirt are not material precepts, they do clearly specify the kind of love that Jesus demands from his followers.

According to the second opinion on this matter, Jesus *did not spell out* the exact kind of mutual love that his followers had to display. And he did not, precisely so that Christians would be left free to operate imaginatively and creatively, to figure out what would be the most effective and comprehensive sort of mutual love at a given moment in history. This second opinion certainly does not ignore the Gospel passages adduced by the first line of opinion, but it does stress their functional and relative nature. In such passages, it says, Jesus is calling attention to a gratuitous sort of love that almost seems to be a useless luxury—and that is all. He is not imposing specific commands on people. The only perduring rule is that one should try to display the most effective and wide-ranging love possible in a given situation.

It is important to realize that these two different outlooks presuppose different conceptions of the relationship between faith and ideologies. In the first outlook, the specific type of love demanded by Jesus is part and parcel of *faith,* not of a specific ideology in history. It is part of the content of divine revelation and, as the last and latest part of that content, it becomes an absolute and irrevocable criterion of faith. In the second outlook, on the other hand, the concrete kind of love proclaimed by Jesus constitutes an *ideology*—that is, a concrete system conditioned by history. It represents a way to attain the most love possible in a given concrete situation which, as such, will never be repeated in exactly the same terms. The element of surprise in the future can range from the reappearance of situations analogous to those of the remote past to the appearance of totally new situations that cannot be tied in with the suppositions of Jesus' concrete message. Moreover, the form in which his message is presented in the New Testament might very well be the product of the ideology which the primitive Church felt obliged to use in confronting the problems of its day. In short, the second outlook is clearly more relativistic than the first outlook.

In the preceding chapter I outlined the reasons for adopting the second outlook, so I shall not repeat them here. What we must do now is go back and provide a fresh phenomenological analysis of what exactly is entailed in the New Testament's unique commandment of love. That will get us into the problem of violence on a more profound level, enabling us to consider the relationship between normative theology and historical relativism in terms of that issue.

I. WHEN AND WHERE DOES VIOLENCE BEGIN?

Any phenomenological study of violence and its relationship to love must begin by discarding the terrible superficiality that surrounds many analyses of this issue.

Summing up the proceedings at the World Conference on Church and Society (Geneva, 1966), J.M. Lochman cites the first paper presented. That paper, presented by H.D. Wendland, describes the Christian contribution to revolution in these terms: "the 'quiet,' unarmed, loving action and service of Christian groups."[1] The three characteristics are noteworthy and highly significant.

First of all, this definition does not even tackle the essential point: Who is the subject of the violence? Is it the armed person as such *completely aside from* the question whether he is trying to kill someone, or defend himself, or defend others from death? Nor does this definition consider the question as to whether violence is a moral or immoral action only for the person who is armed, or also for individuals, societies, and institutions that support and pay those who are armed or else force them to take arms. In the same article Lochman wonders whether Christians can take part in revolutionary activities that presuppose *the use of force*. Are we, therefore, to assume that the use of force and violence are synonyms? Is it violence to compel another person to obey the law by the use of armed force? Or will laws always require the use of armed coercion, so that Christians will be obliged to abandon any and every society established by law?

The terrible superficiality of this kind of definition shows up even more clearly when one tries to decide what sort of instruments are to be regarded as arms. Would the term apply to a firearm, a stick, a punch, an insult, a prejudice, a pervasive social structure? Without suggesting that there is any hypocrisy at work here, I do think that it is sociologically significant that all the talk about violence comes in connection with the subject of revolution, but not in connection with such subjects as the police or the army, for example. And even if we were to find Christian groups inclined to fight equally against armed revolution and an armed government, we would still face the task of correcting a dreadfully superficial definition of what constitutes "arms."

It is quite clear that conscious and unconscious mental tendencies can constitute a weapon more effective in killing millions of people than any weapon that is traditionally viewed as armament. So why focus the whole problem of violence around the picture of a person bearing arms? Let us grant that the nuclear weapons possessed by the superpowers might *eventually* destroy our whole planet. But the fact is that human egotism is *already* destroying our planet, for it is systematically and perhaps irrevocably eating up the resources of this planet during a nuclear "peace."

The purpose of these comments is simply to indicate that the problem of violence must be studied in depth, not superficially, and that we must undertake a serious phenomenological analysis of its relationship to love.

Let us begin that analysis by considering the most radical polar opposites in human conduct: love versus egotism. Where does violence stand in this basic opposition? In my opinion, any phenomenological analysis will readily show that violence is *part and parcel of both of these opposed tendencies,* a sort of no man's land between them. Egotism is no more violent than love; love is no less violent than egotism.

Psychology, biology, and physics clearly show us that love, like any other human or natural activity, must be understood within the framework of an existing *economy of energy.* To put it in more simple terms: if we truly love a specific number of persons, we cannot incorporate other people into our love by distributing our available energy differently without taking energy away from certain areas of our love for the first group. If our love for humanity in general remains vague and ineffective, that is not due simply to our egotism; it is due to the human condition, wherein each individual person has only a certain quantity of available energy. We can fashion infinite combinations with it, to be sure; but we cannot increase the supply in any absolute way.

Thus our love must place in its service *the very same instruments* that can and usually do serve egotism: e.g., sex in its direct and sublimated forms, aggressivity, and the fundamental tendencies which Freud called Eros and Thanatos. There is no other energy available for effective love.

At this point it is interesting to note that the gospel message commands us to love our neighbors, those *near* us. It is curious that it should advise us to do something that has always been one of the major pretexts for all sorts of human egotism. And it is even more curious when we realize that another Gospel passage bids us to love our enemies.

The only logical and possible answer to the problem is that love can only be effective and therefore real when it possesses motives and instruments for being feasible. Such is the case with our neighbor. Love for our enemies is possible, in terms of energy, only as an *extension* of our love for our neighbor—not as an alternative to the latter.

For this reason I find it very difficult to comprehend a position such as that which John Swomley defends in *Liberation Ethics:* "An antiwar movement that is willing to share power with or be the 'loyal opposition' to the military-industrial complex ceases to be a real force for peace. It must seek the elimination of that complex or become its captive."[2] This text, and the whole context of his book, would seem to suggest that there is a whole set of means which are related exclusively to love and peace whereas another set of means are related exclusively to egotism and violence. The obvious question is: How can one eliminate the military-industrial complex without fighting it for power? The members of that complex in the United States must be amused to find such unexpected and unwitting allies among their severest critics. By falsely assuming that love possesses its own exclusive means, real-life love ties its own hands and stops up the very source of its energy.

It is quite understandable, of course, that the corruptive force of power should be called to our attention. The same could be done with respect to money, sex, and everything else of an instrumental sort. While these things are essentially neutral, they do possess an inner thrust and mechanism of their own. It is always easy for human beings to lose sight of their original intentions and end up enslaved to the inner mechanism of their supposed tools. Choosing not to use them, however, offers no guarantee against enslavement. Indeed it may permit the existing enslavement to go on indefinitely. Love for one's mother, for example, clearly has the same psychic roots as patriotism, prejudice, racism, and war. Does this mean we must uproot the facility for maternal love in order to free ourselves for peace?

When Jesus was asked by someone who was to be regarded as our neighbor, he gave the parable of the Good Samaritan. It indicated that anyone can make use of countless occasions that crop up to turn another human being, even a stranger, into one's "neighbor." Jesus seemed to criticize the attitude of the priest and the Levite, who did not take advantage of the opportunity presented to them. But can a human being truly love at all without bypassing many possible occasions to answer the cry of human need? Jesus' parable is just that, a parable; it is not a moral precept. If we try to force it and turn it into a concrete precept governing every similar occasion, we will not end up with love but rather with an incredible dispersion of energy and an irreparable loss of time for real, effective love. This point is brought out magnificently in François Mauriac's novel *The Lamb* (*L'agneau*, 1954). It deals with an odd character of extreme sensitivity who feels compelled to imitate the attitude of the Good Samaritan to the utmost extreme. The ultimate tragedy of this character is that he becomes totally incapable of systematically and effectively loving any concrete human being.

Jesus does not end up his parable saying that every human being *is* our neighbor. His point is that we can make any given human being our neighbor if we take advantage of the countless opportunities offered us in life. That is a very different point. Consider the Good Samaritan himself, for example. If he found himself there on the road by the wounded man with money to pay for his lodging and a burro to carry him, he did so because previously he had bypassed many other human misfortunes. Otherwise he would not have had money, a burro, and a trip.

Thus the economy of energy in the process of love implies that there is some mechanism whereby we can keep a whole host of people at arm's length so that we can effectively love a certain group of people. Some such mechanism is necessary until we hit upon another combination of energy that will enable us to broaden the circle of our love and bring new "neighbors" into it. The mechanism is very simple in psychological terms. It entails not letting some other person get close to us *as a person* so that we might be tempted to take a *personal* interest in him. Obviously this mechanism can serve the interests of egotism as well as those of real love. That is why it ever remains a danger and must be watched carefully. What is more, this process of discriminating between real people must be attended with anxiety, crises, and sins. But that is the condition for being a human being. Man ever remains *simul justus et peccator,* just man and sinner at the same time. The *wholly* good samaritan does not exist. Indeed that would be a contradiction in terms.

But the main point I want to bring out here concerns the mechanism we use to keep other individuals or groups at arm's length. This mechanism is not precisely hatred, it is *violence*—at least some initial degree of violence.

We are able to love our neighbors to the extent that we keep other human beings from showing up as neighbors on our horizon. To strip the latter of the feature of being neighbors, we resort to the familiar mechanism of treating them as *functions* rather than as persons; we reify them. We have time and energy to love our family, for example, thanks to the mechanism whereby we take no interest in the countless people who cross our path each day. We would consider it an improper intrusion if the baker, the butcher, or the telephone operator tried to get us interested in their *personal* history. Our inclination is to treat them in terms of the role or function they represent and perform.

Now no one can doubt the fact that this mechanism *does violence* to the one and indivisible reality of those persons. That reality is suppressed by the force of our mind if not by the force of external, material arms. Furthermore, even though this violence begins as an internal thing, the need to make this segregation and economy effective means that the underlying violence soon surfaces directly. For example, certain people have free access to our time, our attention, and our home; other people are kept at a distance both mentally and physically. Our relatives, friends, and compatriots are treated differently, mentally and physically, than are other people who do not fall into those categories.

Why do I stress the material quality of the segregation that the economy of love demands? Because the fact that some people are recognized as our neighbors quite logically places them above and beyond all laws. On the other hand, our relations with people who do not fall under the category of neighbor, whom we do not wish to treat as persons in the deeper sense of the word, are regulated by law. Law constitutes the most generic expression of these functional, impersonal relationships with other human individuals. And an intrinsic characteristic of law is the fact that it is always backed up by coercive power, that is, by some sort of physical violence that compels compliance. We do not pass laws if we do not possess the violent means required to force people to obey those laws whether they wish to or not.

There is, then, no break in continuity between a necessary mental process of segregation and physical violence, however legal and widely accepted the latter may be. This means we must abandon the simplistic notions that prompt us to discover violence only when a revolutionary shoots a gun on the one hand, and to talk about nonviolence as if it were compatible with impersonal laws and their attendant coercive force on the other hand.

This little phenomenological conclusion can be corroborated and clarified with a homely example. Suppose we surprise a burglar robbing our house some night. Two lines of conduct are open to us. On the one hand we can treat the burglar as a person in the deepest and strictest sense of the word. We can show an interest in his side of the story and try to place ourselves in his shoes. Or, on the other hand, we can treat him as an impersonal human being, that is as someone with certain rights and obligations fixed by law. And since the law permits us to repel unjust aggression, whoever the attacker may be, we can use physical force and even arms against our nocturnal assailant. If we are reluctant or afraid to use violence personally, we can do so indirectly by making use of the violence paid for by our taxes; we can call in the police.

At first glance the first alternative might seem to be more compatible with love, at least with a love that purports to be as broad and efficacious as possible. But it is precisely at this point that we realize that the example itself is oversimplistic and highly unrealistic. We have been considering our relationship with the burglar as if we were alone in the world, or as if we were alone in the house. But the fact is that we already have prior commitments of love, of effective love, to many people. The latter may depend on us, and they may be living in the same house. So we are inexorably forced to calculate our store of energy vis-à-vis two possible directions of love.

Now if that in fact is the case, we must conclude that *violence is an intrinsic dimension of any and all concrete love* in history just as it clearly is an intrinsic dimension of any and all concrete egotism. The efficacy of our love must be worked out within the context of the laws that govern the economy of energy. Of course we must do all we can to narrow down the proportions of the violence required to maintain that efficacy. But speaking in general, we can say that any attempt to choose between love and violence makes no sense at all.

On the basis of the above analysis, I think we can postulate five basic points:

1. There is no such thing as instruments proper and exclusive to love on the one hand, and instruments proper and exclusive to egotism on the other hand. One and the same set of instruments are available for use in either direction.

2. Since there is only a limited store of energy available, love calls for a prudent distribution of this energy if it is to be effective. This will entail painful options very much akin in appearance to those of egotism.

3. These options will always entail some danger insofar as they are ambiguous and can be used unwittingly for egotistical ends. They will always cause some pain to the people who are affected by them. Nevertheless they basically have nothing to do with hatred or egotism as such. The mechanism at work in them entails subjecting real people to the law that regulates our relations with impersonal things and impersonal functions.

4. From the very first, and down to its deepest level, this reductive process which is necessary in our thinking and acting is real violence. For

it puts an internal and external impersonal force in the way of the free personal expression of other human beings.

5. This basic, structural violence is not opposed to love. It is an essential and intrinsic dimension of any and all effective love within the context of the human condition. The dynamic of love, however, tends in the direction of reducing the quantum of violence required for efficacy to the lowest possible level.

II. AN EXEGESIS OF THE GOSPEL ON VIOLENCE

Keeping those five points in mind, we can now attempt to delineate the main features of a Christology insofar as it bears on violence. A liberation Christology is forced to combat an insidious heresy that has been silently and inadvertently creeping into it. Its underlying presupposition, never stated explicitly, is that Jesus, being God, somehow could not have been completely human. He is often given such labels as "the man for others," "the man without sin," "the man of gratuitous love," and "the man of nonviolent love." While these labels can be and sometimes are interpreted in a correct sense, they generally tend to place Jesus above and beyond the basic law that regulates any truly human life: i.e., the law of the economy of energy with all its painful consequences.

But suppose we start from the opposite hypothesis. Suppose we assume that Jesus, being truly man, had to conceive and orient his existence in history by taking due account of this inexorable law. We will be surprised to find that the Gospels, which are often accused of idealizing Jesus in the glow of their postpaschal faith, actually seem to be perfectly aware of the "imperfect" features in Jesus' life and bear eloquent testimony to them.

Mark seems to make a simple statement: "After John had been arrested, Jesus came into Galilee proclaiming the gospel of God" (Mark 1:14). But the very juxtaposition of the two phrases points up a painful alternative. John the Baptist was Jesus' precursor (Mark 1:2), and he was arrested for proclaiming the same message that Jesus is proclaiming (Mark 10:10). Jesus did not hide his admiration for John, calling him the greatest prophet of Israel (Matt. 11:9; Luke 1:76). May we not assume that abandoning John to his fate, not siding with him publicly and perhaps sharing his fate, was a painful choice for Jesus to make? We do not have to exert our imagination to arrive at that conclusion, however, for John the Baptist himself lets us know how he feels. He had baptized Jesus in the Jordan reluctantly, protesting his own unworthiness (Matt. 3:14). But Jesus' reaction to his imprisonment, his apparent lack of concern, hurts John deeply. He sends his own disciples to find out if

Jesus really is the one to come or not (Matt. 11:3). The evangelists are certainly aware of the fact that "the man for others" chose not to be "the man for John the Baptist" in this concrete case. Or, to put it another way, he was for John the Baptist in such an indirect way that he deeply wounded his friend and confronted him with a painful crisis.

A sin? If we define sin as any evil inflicted on a person which was not absolutely necessary, then it certainly was. But this materialistic or literalistic conception of sin must be framed within the real-life coordinates of the economy of energy. And in that context we can appreciate the fact that Jesus, without sinning, could make a choice between two unavoidable material "sins." We can see, in other words, that the impeccability of Jesus Christ is not synonymous with an inhuman innocence. Strange as the formulation may seem, we can say that sin had a positive place in the life of Jesus.

Consider universality, for example. It certainly is a quality of love. Reading the Gospel message, however, we readily forget that the universality of Jesus was only appreciated after his resurrection. Following the instructions of Jesus himself, his disciples were supposed to restrict their ministry to Israel. They were not to go into pagan territory or Samaritan cities (Matt. 10:5–6). We are so used to thinking about Jesus in universal terms that we automatically interpret those prohibitions as a superficial and temporary strategy grounded on a vision that saw a Church without boundaries or frontiers from the very start. And so we do not give heed to the violent segregation that those prohibitions would entail for pagans and Samaritans. We just cannot imagine that this segregation and violence directed against human beings was rooted in the mind and emotional life of Jesus himself.

In this connection it might be well for us to consider the Gospel incident where Jesus speaks with the Phoenician woman from Syria. She is a pagan who comes to ask Jesus to cure her daughter. Jesus' answer alludes directly to the economy of energy involved in the process of loving: "Let the children be satisfied *first*; it is not fair to take the children's bread and throw it to the *dogs*" (Mark 7:27). Going against all the laws of exegesis, one can assume that Jesus is merely testing the faith of the woman rather than expressing his own thinking about the relationship between Jews and pagans. But even in that case is it permissible and nonsinful to use a brand of violence that attacks the very roots of a person's national identity in order to test that person?

In short, the efforts to exculpate Jesus actually condemn him even more severely. It would be much more logical to assume that Jesus' concrete and effective love for his neighbors, for those of his own country, had to operate with the same mechanisms used by all human beings.

He had to put some people at arm's length in order to let other people get close to him as real human beings. And putting them at arm's length meant accepting the common prejudices against aliens in order to maintain them in that status. How could Jesus have wept over Jerusalem if there had been no trace of nationalistic prejudice in him? And all prejudice is latent or expressed violence in relation to something or someone on the outside. Without such violence, however, love dies; human beings are left at the mercy of an even worse violence.

At this point one might justifiably be inclined to ask: What distinguishes this brand of "love" in Jesus from the worst forms of racial segregation in South Africa? Once again we are compelled to say that the difference certainly does not lie in the means. We cannot decide whether love or egotism is at work by examining the means employed. Both use the same means because at bottom both make use of the same energy, the same canalizations of instinct and reason. Jesus was no exception to this rule. What is more, when theology and ethics forget this, they wittingly or unwittingly help to perpetuate exploitation, segregation, and egotism.

In the preceding section we saw the mechanism used to keep some people at arm's length so that we can love other people effectively. Basically it involves submerging some real people in the anonymity of a group, a category, a prejudice, or a law. Categories and laws obliterate the personal and historical features of the people who fall under them. Once again Jesus was no exception with regard to the use of this essentially violent mechanism. There is no doubt, for example, that each and every Pharisee was a unique person. In the abstract, no reason can justify cutting short our dialogue with a person, because the very notion of person includes freedom, the possibility of reflection and change, and the absolute value of personal existence. From this same abstract viewpoint, cutting off dialogue is doing violence to those qualities and reducing the person in question to the category of an instrument.

All that is true in the abstract, but in the concrete we must choose between one person and another in order to dialogue. Neither our life nor our energy is infinite. Jesus, for example, openly breaks off dialogue with the Pharisees, using the mechanism already described. He takes these unique and concrete persons and submerges them in a mental category where they lose their individual features: "You hypocrites" (Mark 7:6 and *passim*). Once you have placed people in such a category, you can begin to lose interest in them, cut off dialogue with them, and turn your attention to others whom you choose to regard as neighbors. And Jesus did precisely that, focusing his attention on those "around him" (Mark 4:10 and *passim*).

Only idealistic oversimplification of Jesus' real attitudes can paint a picture of him as a human being dedicated to limitless love without a trace of resistence or violence. That he came to the point of taking a whip in hand to drive the merchants from the temple is of minor importance (Mark 11:15 ff.; John 2:13 ff.).

III. RELATIVE FACTORS CONDITIONING AN ABSOLUTE FAITH

So far our phenomenological and exegetical analyses have led to results that are basically negative. Insofar as they are correct, they can help us to demolish the oversimplistic notions that have accumulated around this whole topic. However, they also force us to confront the central problem we mentioned at the very beginning. It is the problem of the *criteria* governing any evaluation of this subject.

Our analyses here have ruled out any possibility of a gospel-inspired ethics or morality deciding in advance whether some line of action is consistent with divine revelation or not. It seems quite unbelievable that theologians versed in biblical exegesis can maintain that the commandment, "You shall not kill" (Exod. 20:13), provides a divine criterion that enables us to rule out the use of fatal weapons, revolution, and war under any and all circumstances.

First of all, any serious investigator of the Bible knows very well that the so-called Ten Commandments—be they ten or not—show up in different biblical passages and different editorial settings not as intrinsic exigencies of a moral code but rather as a complex of behavior patterns required to maintain and preserve a particular group of people in a particular historical setting. Rather than being a moral law, they are more like a civil "Constitution" of a religious nature. And they embody profound changes as the people of Israel are obliged to confront new situations in history. Only a spiritualistic interpretation of them, coming much later on and being far removed from their original import, could view them as intrinsic dictates of an absolute moral law dictated by Yahweh.

Secondly, anyone who is at all familiar with the Bible knows that such a commandment as "You shall not kill" cannot purport to constitute an absolute moral rule. For the very words of the Bible itself obligate the Hebrews to kill people in different circumstances, which presupposes that killing is legitimate. The Israelites are obliged by God himself to fight against his enemies and to slay those who oppose his plans. And they are obliged to kill not only the enemy soldiers but also the whole population of some enemies (see Deut. 7:16; 1 Sam. 15:3, etc.).

The Israelites are also obliged by God to kill members of their own nation who are guilty of certain crimes, of social crimes in particular (see

Deut. 22:13 ff.; 24:7; Num. 35:9). There is a further point that is worth noting and it was very important in a society where it was impossible to obtain legal justice. Certain private individuals, who took it upon themselves to avenge bloody crimes and to punish criminals who would otherwise go unpunished, were accorded the right to see that justice was carried out (see Num. 35:22 ff.).

In short, the Bible itself indicates that the commandment not to kill was not universal in any absolute sense, that it was equivalent to saying that one could not kill *without a justifiable reason.* So once again we are forced to confront the question: What criteria enable us to know when violence that takes away another's life is justified? The biblical commandment not to kill never was seen as divine repugnance towards the human instrument of physical violence.

At first glance it would definitely seem that Jesus did interpret this commandment in an absolute sense, enforcing it with a rigidity that is hardly tolerable in normal human relationships: "You have learned that our forefathers were told, 'Do not commit murder; anyone who commits murder must be brought to judgment.' But what I tell you is this: Anyone who *nurses anger* against his brother must be brought to judgment. If he *abuses* his brother he must answer for it to the court; if he *sneers* at him he will have to answer for it in the fires of hell" (Matt. 5:21–22).

Well, it seems that Jesus took special pains to disregard his own counsels and precepts in this regard, undoubtedly so that we would not regard them as material additions to the material contents of the already existing decalogue: "Then he turned to them. . . looking round at them *with anger*" (Mark 3:5); "If anyone is ashamed of me. . . in this *wicked and godless age*. . . " (Mark 8:38); "Isaiah was right when he prophesied about *you hypocrites*" (Mark 7:6). We are forced to choose. On the one hand we can interpret "brother" in Matthew's text above as referring only to those who do good. We cannot get angry with them or insult them, but we can sneer at those who really deserve to be sneered at. Or, on the other hand, we must accept the fact that the violence of these attitudes is a relative means and that Jesus is urging us to use the least amount of violence compatible with truly effective love. The proper proportion, then, must be figured out in the context of each different historical situation.

To put it another way, all the remarks we find in the Bible about violence or nonviolence are *ideologies*—necessary, of course, since we will always be confronted with the task of filling the void between faith and concrete historical realities.

Thus, as Paul reminds us forcefully, the gospel message teaches us that the law, viewed as a type of ideology arising from a given point in divine revelation, is not *above* man but rather *beneath* him. Christian revelation desacralizes the ideologies that had served as our pedagogy in the past (Gal. 4), but it then places us before an even greater problem. If we are to choose the ideology that is simply "good for us" (1 Cor. 6:12; 10:23), what criterion is to guide our selection?

The language of Paul, even more than that of the Gospels, points us towards a kind of love that depends on the concrete situation of the loving person and the one loved. This preoccupation with the concrete is perhaps brought out quite clearly in Paul's version of the commandment to love: "He who loves his neighbour has satisfied every claim of the law" (Rom. 13:8). He seems to be saying: *if your love really affects another person,* you have fulfilled the law. And that forces us to consider the countless historical factors that necessarily condition our love and determine whether it is effective or not. More than once Paul himself reminds Christians that their moral conduct may have to change in line with significant changes in the circumstances of their neighbors. Something permissible and useful in one situation may be improper and useless, and therefore prohibited, in a different set of circumstances (Rom. 14:1–21; 1 Cor. 8:7–13; 10:23–33).

So once again we are forced to ask ourselves: Can a more effective and wide-ranging love serve as the adequate and principal criterion in our moral options? Or would that come down to relativism and "situation ethics"?

The supposition is that faith is the only recipe against relativism in history. Without faith we would be at the mercy of different values, and we could only establish scales of value as relative as the values themselves. Another supposition, one which Sartre took the trouble to demonstrate and spell out quite fully, is that an absolute moral code in an atheist can only represent a lack of logic and a nostalgic clinging to some religious past. Dostoyevsky has one of his characters in *The Brothers Karamazov* say that everything is permitted if God does not exist. Dostoyevsky himself, or his character, may not have alluded to the fact that Saint Paul suggested that everything is permitted to the Christian precisely because God does exist.

The point, in other words, is not that without faith we live in the midst of relativism. It is that even with the Christian faith we live in the very same situation. As will soon be evident, that does not mean that man lives in chaos, oscillating between contradictory values. In everyday language we tend to equate relativism with caprice, with crude pragmatism, and with the egotistical exploitation of other human beings as mere tools. But none of these traits have any essential tie-up with atheism or with lack of faith in a God who provides absolute truths. Many human beings without theological faith can live a highly moral and coherent life. What is more, a curious mixture of absolute and relative factors, characteristic of many believers, allows them to rationalize lines of conduct that are intrinsically capricious and contradictory.

For this reason I think it would be useful to reflect briefly on the essentially relative factors which condition an absolute faith and upon which the latter depends.

Right off we can say that no such faith can exist unless it has a foundation or guarantee that is equally absolute. Obviously such a foundation or guarantee exists insofar as God himself exists. What then are we to say about the present status of the whole problem of the existence of God? I think we can say that the proofs for the existence of God depend upon two equally unverifiable suppositions: (1) that the mechanisms of our knowledge-process work as well outside of the realm of sense life as they do within it where we can check them out; (2) that when our mechanisms of knowledge and desiring cannot be explained —even when operating within the boundaries of normal experience—except on the supposition that there does exist some real infinite goal for this knowledge and desire, then we must accept that as proof that such an entity really does exist.

Obviously the second presupposition takes the first for granted. Quite aside from that fact, it is evident that if our faith claims to break through the relative condition of all human knowledge, then its logical presuppositions would have to be endowed with a character of absolute certainty which they obviously do not possess. Rational argumentation can show that faith is not irrational, and that is all.

Faith also presupposes an historical encounter with this God, who reveals what we have to believe. Once again it is quite easy to demonstrate that we possess no absolute criteria with regard to any such encounter. To bypass the broader realm of "religions," we can simply say that in the concrete we find traditions about such an encounter with God and divine revelation in the bosom of various churches. But each and every church, like every human group in history, presents itself to us as something ambiguous and relative; it certainly is not without its values, but it also is laden with mistakes and sins. The only way to point an infallible finger at one specific church would be to derive that certainty from divine revelation itself. Yet it is precisely to find such a revelation that we must try to distinguish between the different churches.

The obviousness of the vicious circle involved in all this, insofar as we are talking about the absolute nature of our certitude, becomes even clearer when we realize that God's revelation depends on the Church. For it is the Church, the Church alone, which distinguishes between the countless number of human books and establishes the "canon" or catalogue of books that are to be accepted as vehicles of divine revelation. The process by which we attain certitude would have to be able to follow and verify the historical process of fixing that "canon" of books which would determine whether we did or did not encounter a divine revelation in history. But the whole process of establishing that canon remains uncertain and obscure—and even more importantly, ambiguous and human. In most instances we do not advert to the relativistic implications of all this: we choose the tradition of one Church because that same Church scanned human scriptures and selected certain divine scriptures which accredited it, and the whole process whereby the Church did this is no longer exactly clear even to the Church itself.

But let us suppose that the Church was faithful and upright in recognizing and singling out divine revelation among the infinite store of specific books in history. Even then we still have to determine whether the books of revelation do or do not claim to possess some divine truth that is valid for all times and circumstances in history. If we examine the history of the Bible's redaction, for example, we will see that it does not show us a continuing process of growth in the body of doctrines that are supposedly revealed. On the contrary, we must say that opinions about God and morality contradict and oppose each other in the process.

Suppose we concentrate the absolute aspect of our faith in the divine revelation of Jesus. Quite aside from the fact that the historical Jesus lies hidden behind the different interpretations of him which the various authors and communities of the New Testament offer, what criterion can we have that in him resides the truth, the whole truth, and nothing but the truth? Do we have signs that permit us to affirm, for example, that God spoke in history through Jesus but not through Socrates or through the religious authorities established by God in what is now called the *Old* Testament but once was the *one and only* Testament?

Jesus did not think he had offered any heavenly sign to his own generation. Presumably that would be even more true with respect to us. The judgment that his contemporaries might form about him depended upon their ability to appreciate and evaluate his liberative actions. Such ability would obviously be vague and relative. And there hardly seems to be any need to point out that the criteria we use today to recognize an absolute truth in his message must necessarily be based on the fact that somehow his actions seem to belong to a plane very different from that of all the previous and subsequent heroes of human liberation whom we do not regard as bearers of an absolute truth. Paradoxical as it may seem, the criterion for singling out this absolute cannot possibly get beyond the plane of the relative.

If Jesus wanted his resurrection from the dead to represent an exception in the way of signs or proofs, we must admit that he failed. The witnesses are all partisan ones, and the accounts are particularly incoherent and inconsistent as compared with the accounts dealing with the rest of his public life. Then there is the acknowledged difficulty of recognizing this resurrected Jesus, and the latter's almost total lack of interest in making his resurrection an argument to convince people of the absolute validity of his teaching. All this reinforces the case for the relativity of anything and everything historical.

And there is more. We say that we have faith in Jesus, when in fact we do not possess any direct trace of his life or his words. What we are really saying is that we have faith in those who were acquainted with him personally, interpreted him, and gave us their version of him. And this applies to the evangelists, to the other New Testament writers, and to the main line of thought in the Church which, over the course of centuries, defended one interpretation of Jesus against other interpretations that we *today* regard as heterodox. But when these other interpretations were under discussion, they posed as the one and only authentic interpretation of Jesus' life and doctrine. When we declare that the life and teaching of Jesus have absolute value, in other words, we are presuming that we can recognize them with absolute certainty. But this assumption runs directly counter to the relativity of the countless historical judgments which serve as the logical basis that is required in order to affirm that there actually has been an encounter with God in the midst of human history.

IV. THE MORALITY OF THE MEANS

The reader might well wonder why anyone would go into such a lengthy, though far from complete, exposition of the relative factors that serve as the basis for what claims to be an absolute faith. And the reader might also wonder how we managed to get from the problem of violence to the relative factors that serve as presuppositions for the faith.

Let us tackle the latter question first. The problem of violence was introduced into our methodological discussion as an example of the relativity that surrounds any attempt to decide what concrete moral attitude corresponds to our faith. It is precisely that difficulty, however, which has led theology wittingly or unwittingly to entrench itself in dogma in order to preserve its assumed absolute character in the midst of the pervasive relativity of history. Academic theology has gone in for all sorts of escape mechanisms such as that. For example, it has tried to avoid making any moral applications to the realm of the changing and the relative, or it has tried to claim that no such change exists with respect to most of the morality that derives from faith, or it has dealt with dogma quite independently of the plane of moral conduct and its concrete problems.

It is precisely for that reason that we had to tackle the problem at its roots. We had to show that not only does the application of the faith to concrete moral problems in history entail an acceptance of the relative but also that theological dogma itself is sustained and supported in and through the very same relativity.

In enumerating the list of factors cited above, it was not at all my intention to undermine the foundations of faith or strip it of its absolute value. As Nikolai Berdyaev points out, the absolute character of my faith does not depend on the success of historians in proving with absolute certainty that Jesus actually existed in history and in pinpointing the "objective" content of his life and teaching—contradictory as that may seem at first glance. What is or at least should be ruled out is any and every attempt to evade the relative aspect by appealing to the absolute character of faith. As we have already noted and tried to show, faith can be absolute and still have no value whatsoever unless it is used to give us orientation in the realm of the relative. And to do this it must be willing to accept the relative as something that naturally and inevitably conditions it.

Let us turn right now to the problem of Christian morality, so that we can move from there to faith itself and its relationship to the relative in history. Our phenomenological and exegetical analysis of the problem of violence leads us to the logical and obvious—but scandalous—conclusion that *the end justifies the means.* We did not even need to be told this explicitly by the gospel message, though we are so told: To faithfully paraphrase several passages, we can say that "it is not what comes to a man from outside but what results from his own plans that makes him moral or immoral" (see Mark 7:16, 18–23). We need only analyze the term itself to realize that a "means," because it is precisely that and nothing more, cannot have any justification in itself. Its value derives from the end for which it is employed, if we are talking about its moral value rather than merely its value as a neutral instrument. By very definition, the end justifies the means.

At this point it might be in order to point out that the scandalous reaction to such a clear and logical conclusion operates on two levels. The first is a more superficial and commonplace one. When one says that the end justifies the means, people assume that is equivalent to saying that anything is justified, since any nut or egotist or sadist can say it is a means to his or her end. But such an assumption forgets that Christian morality is precisely a *morality of ends,* that the specific task of the Christian message is to lead mankind to ends that are the most communitarian and generous-hearted ends imaginable.

The great challenge that Christian morality hurls down to traditional and legalistic morality is its affirmation that *there are certain ends which are bad,* which cannot justify any means, *however sacred or legal they may be,* that are used to achieve them. Yet today we find a curious situation with regard to Christians and birth control, for example. In the minds of most Christians the decisive issue has come to be deciding what methods can or cannot be used to control procreation. Yet they seem to be hardly concerned at all about the need to integrate some sort of birth control with the most critical and decisive ends to be pursued by the human species. They do not ask which means would be the most suitable to achieve those decisive ends, nor do they try to find out what obscure motivations are at work in a reckless and thoughtless process of birth control by whatever means.

On a deeper level, where the real underlying motives are kept hidden better, the shocked reaction to the possibility that the end justifies the means in Christian morality stems from the difficulty that will ensue in trying to determine valid criteria for justifying or rejecting means in relationship to a given end. If a certain end can be subsumed under the general category of love, in other words, how and when can it justify certain means and reject others?

Right off we must admit that to use the word "love" as the definition of a moral end is to use a false singular. Rarely if ever do we choose between love and egotism as the goal or end of our actions. Instead we opt for one specific love over against another love. Each human situation furnishes multiple if not infinite possibilities for different types of love.

We cannot eliminate the difficulty in question simply by saying that it is the *quality* of our love that is to serve as the criterion for Christian morality. Though that might be true, quality cannot be measured in the abstract; due account must be taken of the real-life possibilities open to us in each case. There is no use opting for some sublime love when we do not have at our disposal the means to carry it through. Opting for a quality that is incapable of realization helps no one actually, whereas we might have been of help if we had chosen a form of love that was less sublime but feasible with respect to real living people.

All that compels us to go back and study the *means.* The difficulty here is that we cannot consider the means in the abstract, wholly apart from their relationship to a concrete situation. Their morality stems from their relationship to an end, not from their intrinsic nature. They must be studied in the context of a given historical situation in order to determine which means represent the richest and most promising possibilities for love. Here "means" takes on all the relativity that the term implies, injecting a note of doubt and anxiety into Christian morality.

Does that mean that we are here proposing and espousing a "situation ethics"? For many people, the latter would mean a life lived in complete relativism; it would be a chaotic and dismal way of solving moral problems, or if you will, of not solving them at all.

Obviously the first thing to do is to find out what we mean by "situation ethics" here. If we accept John Swomley's definition of situation ethics, then our position here would fall under that label. As he puts it: "Situation ethics differs from rules ethics in beginning with the assumption that each situation is unique and therefore requires a different application of love or respect for persons."[3] If that is enough to justify labelling an ethical system as "situation ethics," then it is hard to see how any other brand of ethics could be compatible with human reason, and hence with the Christian message.

It seems that Swomley is out to frighten us by pointing to the logical consequences of such an ethical criterion: "Love is to be used as a norm for conduct at each point of moral choice so that the validity of any action *including stealing or murder* is determined by the situation plus love." I must admit that such a consequence does not frighten me, nor am I disturbed by the possibility that certain situations can turn stealing or killing into licit actions. As we have already seen, such has been the case from the earliest days of the Old Testament; and the most conservative manuals of Christian morality still furnish examples of situations where both courses of action are licit.

There is no doubt that Swomley himself sees more or less clearly that on the basis of such definitions "rules ethics" is bound to appear pharisaical and devoid of any sound basis. In any case he feels obliged to throw in a new and decisive element as he proceeds to discuss "situation ethics": "The illustrations or case studies used in books on situation ethics often reveal a very parochial concept of love, such as love of party or love of country. . . There is *no analysis of the consequences or probable consequences.*"[4] And a little further on he adds this comment: "The situationists' problem of history, however, is not with the rules of the past but with the failure *to take history seriously.* They do not seem to be clear about the meaning of the term *situation* [Swomley's italics too]. Sometimes it seems related to a larger context but more often situation ethics is distinguished from contextual ethics by appearing to be confined to *a relatively short period of time* in which a decision has to be made. It thus appears to concentrate on immediate facts to the exclusion of a larger context."[5]

Swomley's concern is perfectly understandable. What is not clear is whether we have to include that *defect* in the very definition of "situation ethics." And since there is no question of solving any sort of problem on the basis of definitions, since the latter are arbitrary, we can conclude that if one chooses to limit the term "situation ethics" to an ethics that confines its attention to the moment of decision alone, then such an ethics must be rejected because no single *moment* in itself possesses any ethical principle for defining human conduct. But Swomley in turn must admit that a "rules ethics" suffers from the very same defect. Wherever the rules come from, in themselves they possess no morality apart from the broader context of human historical reality. So we are left with what Swomley himself calls "contextual ethics."

The problem is that no matter how much amplitude we give to the context, the latter will always be subject to a certain amount of relativism. However broad they may be, contexts change with history.

Let me cite an example. One of the most penetrating Christian specialists in the area of development ethics is Denis Goulet. Here is what he has to say in one of his books: "Painful options must also be made regarding which values must be changed in a transitional society. . . Should a merit system in the distribution of economic rewards be adopted *in a given society*? Should men be forced to enter 'necessary' professions against their will? What are the moral limits of manipulating incentive structures in order to induce behavior compatible with 'modernity'? There are no clear answers to such questions. They can be answered only if development, like all historical enterprises, is seen as a *relative*, not an absolute, value."[6]

Shortly thereafter Goulet spells out clearly the exact nature of this relativeness and its tie-up with morality: "Ethics must become a 'means of the means': a transfiguration of means into something more than purely technical, social, or political instruments. Circumstances alone can reveal whether any given strategy is progressive, regressive, or ambivalent. What, for instance, is the ethical merit of such measures as nationalization, the imposition of stringent monetary controls, the freezing of wages under inflationary conditions? We can never answer the question: is this moral or immoral? *Each of these measures can be moral or immoral, depending on total circumstances.*"[7]

Goulet's line of argument is so clear, so grounded on common sense, and so measured in its formulation, that no one would be inclined to protest the fact that a Christian thinker has abandoned "rules ethics" for "contextual ethics" and has invoked the relativity of any and every value in history. Why is it, then, that something that is obvious in the realm of social and international ethics is not obvious in the realm of personal ethics? And the fact is that it is not. One need only replace the social terms in which Goulet speaks with other terms that relate more directly to "personal" morality to see that fact. Simply replace such terms as "inflationary conditions" and "stringent monetary controls" with terms like "abortion," "premarital sex," and the use of violence against the police. Most Christians would shrink back in horror from the obvious consequences of the principles they had readily accepted just a moment ago.

But why? Apart from the possibility of pharisaism and the scandal that it might take, there is a sincere reason involved here. The exigencies of social and international morality are exigencies that are viewed as somehow new. The exigencies of personal morality, on the other hand, have been stated over and over since the days when the gospel message was first proclaimed. They are "external" exigencies whereas the others, however important they may be, cannot lay claim to the same status since they have been introduced by history.

Of course someone might interpose a legitimate objection at this point. It could be argued that social, political, and international exigencies existed long before the gospel message and clearly were part and parcel of the law of God. The Old Testament itself laid down rules for the treatment of war prisoners, for the proper ownership of slaves and land, and for the rights of the destitute. But since all that talk seemed to disappear from the language of Jesus, the supposition is that it was displaced by absolute moral obligations. The exigencies of the past and of the future are attributed to the relativity of the times. Thus the gospel message becomes a safe haven of the absolute amid the swirling vicissitudes of the relative and the historical. We have faith in Jesus, not in Moses. We certainly do not have faith in some theoretician of development.

And so the problem of relativism in moral attitudes takes us by the hand and leads us right to the problem of relativism in relation to the faith itself.

V. DOGMA IS NOT AN ENCAPSULATED VERSION OF THE ABSOLUTE

In the preceding section I tried to show that Christian conduct, like non-Christian conduct, is subject to a "human" dose of relativism; and also that this dose of relativism does not turn it into something chaotic, indulgent, capricious, or contradictory. We need only look to everyday experience to confirm that fact, but there is also a weighty theological reason in its favor. It would be impossible to imagine any divine plan of universal salvation if the absence of faith entailed such consequences.

For faith was not around for thousands of years, and absence of faith continues to be a necessary state of affairs for many people, quite aside from their good or bad will.

And we can look at the matter from the other side of the coin too. Insofar as we can judge human conduct from the outside, the moral attitude of many Christians seems to be much more inconsistent than that of many non-Christians who are obliged to undertake an ongoing process of moral discernment. For these Christians accept absolute criteria on the one hand, and then disregard critical fields of action for love as morally indifferent realms on the other hand.

One thing may well have remained obscure to the reader, however. What exactly does an authentically Christian morality owe to faith itself? When I spoke of a "dose of relativism" at the start of this section, was I implying that some portion of Christian conduct does depend on absolute criteria? If the answer to that question is "yes," then how do we combine the absolute element of faith with the relativity of historical circumstances to form a unified and meaningful whole? If the answer is "no," then am I simply trying to say in a nice way that all our conduct is based on relative criteria and that our faith itself is subject to the same condition?

We can put the question another way, using the basic terms that we have established in this book. So far we have equated the relative element with ideologies and the absolute element with faith. But after our considerations in this chapter one might well ask: Isn't it true that everything is relative? What is left after we strip away the ideologies? What is faith? What content does it have?

To answer these questions, we must consider several critical and decisive facts. The *first* fact is that our freedom is precisely the capacity to absolutize what nature and history always present to us as something relative. We must rid ourselves of the prejudice that we are most free when we have absolute values inscribed in things and events and need only choose between good and evil. Our liberty, which is the capacity to make absolutes, is triggered and starts to operate precisely insofar as the absolute is not inscribed in the things and events that we come across in reality.

Thus we need not fear this type of *relativism*, nor need we change the word to *relationism* as Mannheim does in order to evade the pejorative connotations of the former word. As H. Richard Niebuhr puts it: "Relativism does not imply *subjectivism and scepticism*. It is not evident that the man who is forced to confess that his view of things is conditioned by the standpoint he occupies must doubt the reality of what he sees. It is not apparent that one who knows that his concepts are not universal must also doubt that they are concepts of the universal, or that one who understands how all his experience is historically mediated must believe that nothing is mediated through history."[8]

Niebuhr then goes on to establish an essential element for theology in its relationship to the ever-relative reality of history: "The acceptance of the reality of what we see in psychological and historically conditioned experience is always *something of an act of faith;* but such faith is inevitable and justifies itself or is justified by its fruits."[9]

Insofar as the mediation of the Church is concerned, Niebuhr says something very similar:

> Furthermore historic faith, directed toward a reality which appears in our history and which is apprehended by historic beings, *is not private and subjective, without possibility of verification.* To be in history is to be in society, though in a particular society. Every view of the universal from the finite standpoint of the individual in such a society is subject to the test of experience on the part of companions who look from the same standpoint in the same direction as well as to the test of consistency with the principles and concepts that have grown out of past experience in the same community. A theology which undertakes the limited work of understanding and criticizing within Christian history the thought and action of the church is also a theology which is dependent on the church for the constant test of its critical work.[10]

There is a *second* decisive fact here. If the whole concrete content of faith and all the attitudes and beliefs in which it is embodied are dependent on the relative context in which they occur, how can we possibly call faith *absolute?* Or, to put it another way, *what exactly is this absolute faith* whose content always is relative, however certain it may be? As I noted above, and as we saw at length in Chapter IV, our freedom focuses our whole being on some value which it declares unconditional, that is, absolute. It puts its trust in that, or if you will, it entrusts everything else to the carrying out of that particular value (the image of the kingdom in Matthew 6:33). We cannot check the matter out in advance and determine whether the value chosen by us is worth the effort involved in realizing it. So we are confronted with a *subjective* absolutization, with an act of trust and surrender that logically deserves to be called "faith" even though it may not entail belief in God or in a specific religious tradition. Thanks to such figures as Tillich, H. Richard Niebuhr, and Richard R. Niebuhr, Protestant theology in the United States has made a fine analysis of this common *faith* shared by Christians and non-Christians.[11]

Before engaging in any criticism of that line of analysis we must admit that whatever its limitations may be when it deals specifically with Christianity, it does present a consistent picture of an absolute faith whose historical content materials are always relative, however much they may provide a certainty that allows one to make a total life-commitment. It also makes clear that we cannot look for the absolute element of faith in some interruption in the relative happenings of history; that we must look for it in perfectly reasonable human decision-making, which centers a person's whole life around some value that thereby becomes an absolute and an object of faith for mankind's freedom.

To get to the *third* important fact involved in our quest for the absolute in Christian faith, we might pose a question to the conception of faith just outlined. Indeed I think the question is very much in order. To what extent can we say that such a faith is explicitly Christian? The works of the theologians just mentioned at least imply that it is explicitly Christian. And this conclusion stems from a very simple fact. Their conception of faith stems from a *reduction* of Christian faith to rational, modern terms.

Sometimes these theologians explicitly refer to *human* faith. Tillich does, for example. But the whole approach of these theologians as well as the frequent allusions to Christianity indicate quite clearly that this is in fact the faith professed by a Christian who has stripped away the veil of illusion and has come to realize that this is the process whereby a Christian value such as love becomes something absolute in the midst of relative realities.

Now it seems to me that in such circumstances the relationship between Christians and faith is logically one of mere coincidence. *In fact* my absolute subjective choice and the Christian tradition coincide—using Christian tradition here in its most generic sense. What is really chosen is a value, not one specific line of tradition among many others.[12]

The *third* important fact in this whole area—or so it appears to me—is that there is a real and valid way of explicating a faith that is *intrinsically* Christian and biblical without denying the relativity of the historical realm or subjectivity as the source of absolute value in history. This explication is closely bound up with the existential experiences analyzed in Chapter IV. It starts off from the fact that a *Christian* option does not absolutize a value or a doctrine but rather an educational *process* dealing with values.

We have already had occasion to see that the process of faith begins by absolutizing persons rather than disembodied or abstract values. However, it does not absolutize a static person. Instead it attributes absolute value to the person as a companion in existence, as a guide through the wilderness of the unknown and the unexperienced. In short, it attributes absolute value to a person as educator. Faith in one's parents, for example, does not absolutize some monument erected in their memory. Instead it absolutizes them as persons who are part and parcel of an educational process. We confidently entrust our life and its meaning to this educational process.

We learn to be human beings under the guidance of other human beings. It is a process of *deutero-learning*, of learning to learn. In the case of Christianity or, if you prefer, the Bible, we learn to learn by entrusting our life and its meaning to the historical process that is reflected in the experiences embodied in that particular tradition.

Thus, in and through faith, we absolutize one concrete pedagogical process in history, placing it above and before any other such process. We entrust ourselves to it in a free act that cannot help but be an absolutization, since we give our all to it. And to absolutize this process is to say that God, the Absolute, is guiding it in some special way.

In principle this absolutization is subjective and free; it is not imposed on us by necessity, logic, or reality itself. Indeed that has always been the most traditional view of the act of faith in the Catholic Church. It has always held that faith is not demonstrable, that it therefore demands a free decision on the part of our will. But this free decision does not consist in choosing some value; it consists in entrusting the meaning of our life to a process of illumination and knowledge directed by God himself, to an *objective* process that has taken place in history—in a specific history.

The problem for Catholic theology begins when one tries to define the precise content of this revelatory process. I think we can find—and debate—three interpretations of what this content is.

The first interpretation makes *God,* and God alone, the content of the revelatory process. Only what the Bible says about God is taken seriously, everything else is discarded as mere "context." This interpretation sees no particular value in the historical or mythological statements about man, the human situation, human nature, and human history.

Obviously this interpretation is not faithful to the Bible itself, for the latter has much more to say about man and his experiences than about God. Even more importantly, however, it ignores the educational process that is embodied in the Judeo-Christian tradition. Quite aside from the fact that the extant Bible is a complete waste of paper if it was God's intention to *provide us with information about himself,* there is also the fact that this interpretation forgets that a process of *education* is concerned with the one being educated and differs radically from a process of information. And learners cannot be separated from their circumstances because it is in and through those circumstances that the educator will really educate.

The second interpretation assumes that the final purpose of the process can be found at its end. It is embodied, in other words, in the level of knowledge that we attain about our relationship with God at the end of the process. If God did spend centuries educating his people, it was so that they would be prepared to receive the final and definitive message of the gospel. And the latter must be culled from the accounts and circumstances of the New Testament. In other words, the Bible is a long and poetic process of education that is to be translated into some definitive *dogma*. The poetic presentation is the early and primitive approach to a truth that reason must comprehend and translate into unvarying propositions.

Now while this second interpretation does more justice to the biblical process, it also reduces that process to a preparation for some definitive content acquired at the end of the process. Once that content has been translated into dogma by the Church, there is no longer any need to keep going back to the Scriptures. This interpretation also eliminates the sense and import of the process as a process of learning to learn. Dogma becomes the definitive thing, and later history must accommodate itself to that dogma and dovetail with its terms in order to be interpreted in Christian terms. Thus we remain on the level of a *proto-learning* process, where we are taught ready-made answers for familiar circumstances.

The third interpretation, which is the one espoused here, attempts to do full justice to divine revelation as a *deutero-learning* process. If we learn how to learn in and through the Bible, then we must keep going back to this learning process and entrusting ourselves to it. We must keep in contact with this process which reconstructs the historical experiences of a people and a community. We must keep living those experiences over, thereby giving them an absolute value. In this case the absolute value is not just subjective, since we absolutize one objective tradition among many possible traditions.

In addition, we reject the idea that dogma is a translation of the *outcome* or result of the educational process. As we noted in an earlier chapter, there is no end to the process of learning to learn. We began it in an historical process guided by an absolute educator. At a certain point in time we continue the process in and through the unfolding of history itself. Dogma merely defines the boundaries within which we can say that we are still operating inside that same educational tradition. Ancient Israel had norms, established by the Mosaic Law and the prophets, which indicated who really was a member of the community that was being educated by God in history. In like manner the new Israel possesses in its dogmas such guidelines (not final facts) for its thinking.

An important consequence of all this is that faith, when properly understood, can never dissociate itself from the ideologies in which it is embodied—both in the Bible and in subsequent history. It certainly can, and should, dissociate itself as much as possible from the "ideological" tendencies that wrongfully subordinate it to a specific brand of historical oppression. But it makes no sense at all to ask what faith is when any and all ideology has been stripped from it. Faith without works is dead. Faith without ideologies is equally dead. Faith incarnated in successive ideologies constitutes an ongoing educational process in which man learns how to learn under God's guidance. We will never be able to reduce the faith to a specific book or page of the Bible, to a specific Creed, or to a specific dogma. All of these things point out *the road to be travelled* by faith, but they never provide us with the journey completed.

NOTES

1. H.D. Wendland, "The Church and Revolution." Cited by J.M. Lochman in "Ecumenical Theology of Revolution," *New Theology* 6 (New York: Macmillan, 1969), p. 106.
2. John Swomley, *Liberation Ethics* (New York: Macmillan, 1972), p. 47.
3. *Ibid.*, p. 21.
4. *Ibid.*, pp. 21–22.
5. *Ibid .*, p. 26.
6. Denis Goulet, *The Cruel Choice* (New York: Atheneum, 1973), pp. 114–15.
7. *Ibid.*, p. 116.
8. H. Richard Niebuhr, *The Meaning of Revelation* (New York: Macmillan paperback edition, 1961), p. 13.
9. *Ibid.*, p. 14.
10. *Ibid.*, p. 15.
11. See, for example, H. Richard Niebuhr, *Radical Monotheism in Western Culture* (New York: Harper and Row, 1970).
12. That is why Niebuhr's book cited in the previous note, in which he did not see a possible pluralism of value systems as compatible with the faith, prompted a book in response which bears a polemical but somewhat ambiguous title: David L. Miller, *The New Polytheism* (New York: Harper and Row, 1974). Indicative by way of illustration here is the way Tillich talks about the *objective* criteria of the truth of faith: "The truth of faith must be considered from both sides. From the subjective side one must say that faith is true if it adequately expresses an ultimate concern." We might expect, then, that the

objective side would provide us with a criterion for choosing between different traditions of faith. But Tillich goes on to say: "From the objective side one must say that faith is true if its content is *the really ultimate*. . . The other criterion of the truth of a symbol of faith is that it expresses the ultimate which is really ultimate. In other words, that it is not idolatrous. In the light of this criterion the history of faith as a whole stands under judgment. . . This is true of all types of faith" (Paul Tillich, *Dynamics of Faith* [New York: Harper and Row, 1958], pp. 96–97).

CHAPTER SEVEN

Theology and Popular Religions

Everyday experience tells us that conscientious Christians of our day do not possess ready-made certitudes in their faith which enable them to evade the relativism that operates together with their faith in new and changing situations. As the old adage goes, theory should cede to fact. Why, then, is such an intense effort made to formulate arguments and theories that fly in the face of facts? Why is so much trouble taken to deny facts that can be readily ascertained by psychological or sociological or phenomenological or theological analysis?

While the answer may seem to be obscure, it is actually very plain and simple. Faith does not need to absolutize things which in fact are not absolute and which, once absolutized, conspire against the absolute and transcendent character of faith itself. Neither does the Church need to do that for the sake of its mission in the world. Neither is it a necessity for "salvation," even if the latter could be dissociated from liberation in history. And the latter sort of liberation clearly depends on the active work of creative imagination, which is linked up with the relative value of any and all historical constructions.

What, then, is the factor that seems so intent upon absolutizing something that evidently is not absolute? The customary response to that question is not only superficial but also quite out of line with reality. It assumes that the quality of absoluteness, with its attendant notions of universality, certainty, and invulnerability to the ravages of time, is both important and essential for preserving and safeguarding the supreme values of humanity. In the realm of concrete facts and deeds, however, quite the opposite is true. The essential values of man, both as an individual and as a social group, call for an ongoing process of creation in the face of new situations and problems. Man absolutizes those things that are to be carried out in a mechanical and purely routine manner. Absolutization is in fact the psycho-sociological basis for structuring and handling the unvarying, and the unvarying is that which possesses no value in itself. It is our way of conserving energy within the framework of a specific and structured value system. Thus the things that are absolutized in this way are the nonhuman portion of human conduct.

At first glance, then, it seems odd that ecclesiastical authorities and academic theology are at one in their attempt to fix dogmatically things which are part and parcel of the realm of means, which are relative by their very definition. One need only look back over the pages of Denzinger to see that over the course of past history the Church and its dogmas have evinced great flexibility and relativity in those very areas.

The curiousness of it all disappears, however, when we realize another important fact. However inappropriate they may be for effectively implementing man's highest values, the absolutization, mechanization, and routinization of behavior patterns is the psycho-sociological precondition for individual security in social life and for the social consensus that permits a socio-political system to continue in operation.

Once again ideological analysis, which is an intrinsic element in the hermeneutic circle, leads us to the conclusion that the gospel message has been placed in the service of another set of interests—no doubt unconsciously. The point to be added and further studied here is that this distortion of the gospel message is intimately and intrinsically bound up with the rise of what are called "mass" phenomena in the West.

A liberation theology cannot ignore this whole problem: the relationship between creative relativism and *minority* lines of conduct on the one hand, and the relationship between mechanical absolutization and *mass* lines of conduct on the other hand.

One of the most important things we have learned from the political dimension of human existence is that an ideology of change is not communicated from one individual to the next by a process of contagion which eventually spreads to every member of a given society. Analysis of any revolutionary process clearly reveals that there are not only different levels of awareness about the complexity and facets of the ideological process but also different ideological mechanisms to be used, depending on whether one is trying to move masses or minority groups. The latter might also be called elites or vanguards, but the statement holds true in any case.

To talk about Christianity and about theology as a liberative factor without taking due account of these crucial differences would be to commit a sin of omission against liberation itself. Yet it is not easy to plunge into this topic.

I. THE SNARES OF LANGUAGE

First of all, there is the problem of *semantics.* I am referring here to the denotations and connotations of the words that are used to speak about both masses and minorities. Even the most enthusiastic defenders of "mass" Christianity cannot deny the fact that there are two very different types of Christianity in Latin America. On the one hand there is a majority Christianity of very low religious caliber, however much worth one may attribute to the people involved; on the other hand there is a minority Christianity which is characterized by a much more profound grasp of the Christian message and the commitment it demands, however much one may accuse it of being class-conscious and intellectualistic. In other words, the difference itself is inescapable, no matter which kind one may feel inclined to prefer on the basis of a personal set of values.

There is a semantic problem here because debate and discussion often end up as a dialogue between deaf-mutes. For the unfortunate fact is that the terms used are often fraught with valuational and emotional overtones. Such words as "masses" and "minorities," for example, are neutral in themselves; they are the product of statistics that anyone can verify. But they are wielded as arguments in themselves, often without any line of reasoning and in direct contradiction to the attitudes and ideological systems that are supposedly being defended. We are confronted with various terms that would seem to be synonymous but are not in terms of valuational judgments. So we cannot make our way through this semantic jungle without first trying to refine our concepts and to track down the underlying ideological and valuational connotations.

Three examples may help us to overcome the *verbal terrorism* that has come to surround certain words. The first example will help us to see how an unwitting equation has been developing in Latin America between three different terms: *Christianity, popular religiosity,* and *culture.* The terminology may vary slightly, so that the synonyms become *membership in the Church, popular Catholicism,* and *socio-cultural values.* But the basic process in the formation of these synonyms is the same.

To get some idea of what all this means, it will help to note the religious differences between the United States on the one hand and Latin America on the other. Important sociological studies[1] have shown that the secular American life-style (the "American way of life") has come to fashion a religion in its own image and likeness. The latter is a "civic religion" compounded of Protestantism, Catholicism, and Judaism. In other words, the culture has converted religion into just another cultural factor. In Latin America, on the other hand, a "religious culture" has resulted from a curious and powerful fusion of religious elements brought over by the Catholic conquistadors with indigenous and African religious elements.

This does not mean, of course, that the "civic religion" of the United States and the "religious culture" of Latin America do not share many features in common. At first glance there might seem to be a world of difference between the oversimplified and moralistic Catholicism of the middle class in the United States and the highly charged, superstitious Catholicism of the popular masses in most Latin American countries. But important parallels can be seen in the two. In both, Christianity has become an important factor in helping people to comprehend and endure the world, that is, the established social system. The latter is freighted with what Freud called social repression and what Marcuse, perhaps more accurately, has called "surplus repression": i.e., a society organized for the unnecessary exploitation of man by man.

One often hears interminable discussions concerning the motivations that bind the present-day type of *homo religiosus* with this particular brand of established and domesticating religion. Such discussions often lose sight of the fact that there is no real need to go into the infinite subjective variables that are compatible with the original, objective motivation. Once the visible factors are considered and the place of the religious process and its function within the overall system has been spelled out, it is clear that the varied subjective motivations can be subsumed under the objective motivation of the human quest for security. This function can be established, for example, once a person comes to see and admit that membership in the Church, the recitation of certain credal formulas, and the performance of certain rites are regarded as obligatory conditions for obtaining eternal salvation, getting in good with God, and influencing his providence in a positive sense. There is nothing to stop this basic motivation from leading to the acceptance of other authentic human values such as hospitality, self-sacrifice, and solidarity with others. But it would be senseless to attribute these conditioned values to autonomous motivations that could allegedly counterbalance the basic impact of the quest for security.

Over against Marx, we would affirm that religion can perform the function of "unsettling" people. At the same time, however, we must logically admit that such a function can only be comprehended and accepted by people who are secure enough to "disestablish" themselves from the prevailing system. They will always constitute a minority, however, as is evident from the difficulty involved in destroying such a system and replacing it with another.[2] In other words, a mass religion cannot be a "disestablishing" religion at the same time. It cannot appeal to the whole population and unsettle the existing order simultaneously. A religion with both characteristics would be a contradiction in terms.

That is not to say that a religion that begins on the individual level as a search for psychological security cannot evolve into a revolutionary force. Indeed we shall study the possibilities and the factors conditioning such a *process* further on. But it should be recognized here that a real *process* is involved in any such transformation. Existing reality must undergo a transformation before a religious structure, which was originally accepted by the masses for the objective motive of fitting themselves into the existing system, can be turned into a force for "unsettling" that system. Aside from such a process, one cannot attribute positive value to a religious structure simply and solely because it is part of the popular culture and may therefore evolve along with the people in the future.

But let us not jump to our conclusions here. For the moment we are considering the language problem, focusing on the "civic religion" of the United States as opposed to the "religious culture" of Latin America. We might describe the difference between the two in these simple terms: United States citizens feel "religious" sentiments when they consider their flag, their national anthem, or their national rites; the average Latin American feels "patriotic" or civic sentiments when he considers his religious symbols and ceremonies.

Thus there is an important difference in the level at which the domesticating function of religion works in the two cultures. In the United States the phenomenon is more clearly traced out because the utilization and import of the religious distortion is obvious, insofar as the tool in question can be separated from the machine to which it belongs. The social class that displays the religious traits mentioned above clearly benefits from them and could do without them on the cultural level. In Latin America the situation is quite different, for whatever reasons. There, religion is intricately bound up with the whole system of relationships that governs the mentality of the people. So true is this that one can say that the religious factors have ceased to be autonomous at the very least, and perhaps even religious at all. It is much more difficult to pinpoint motivations governing the specifically religious sphere, since the latter has more or less ceased to be a distinct sphere separable from other cultural ingredients. That explains why sociologists and anthropologists generally tend to advise the Catholic Church in Latin America against any *autonomous* effort at religious change, at least on the level of the popular masses.

Let me explain this a bit. Suppose it could be proved that the motivations underlying the religious practice of Sunday Mass attendance had little or nothing to do with the *authentically* theological significance and function of that rite. Suppose it turned out that the practice was much more akin to the mechanisms underlying the functions of a *sorcerer* or *witch doctor* in a primitive tribe. The professional deformation of a theologian, insofar as it was progressive, might lead him or her to the hasty conclusion that human liberation called for the suppression of the religious practice in question. But the real problem lies in the fact that one is using a fiction of language when one calls the practice in question "religious." Tribal witch doctor and tribal chief are *social* roles of equally fundamental importance in a primitive culture that does not distinguish—much less separate—the socio-political sphere and the religious sphere. You cannot introduce changes, on the pretext that they fall under the jurisdiction of religion, without upsetting the whole balance of the culture. And so we get a curious twist. Something may be regarded as a degraded form of Christianity in religious terms, even by those who defend it. But insofar as it is seen as part of the "people's religion," it takes on the positive value and the claim for respect that any and every culture merits—quite aside from the fact that in this case it constitutes part of the "national" culture. In other words, when something is labelled "mass religion," there is a clearly pejorative connotation. But when the very same thing is dubbed "popular religion," there is a subtle shift in the valuational overtones. This trend becomes most pronounced when it is seen as part of "the culture," for then it is seen as draped in the vesture of profound and sacrosanct values. The reader can readily see how difficult it is to operate in an area where language can prejudice one's conclusions in these subtle and not so subtle ways. One must pay close heed to these subtle shifts in connotation.

A second example of this process at work is the subtle shift in valuation that takes place in a discussion of Christianity when one shifts from the term *masses* to *majorities* and then on to *the people*. As we have already noted, the term "masses" has a pejorative connotation. At the beginning of this chapter we considered the fact that it is somehow associated with the more mechanical and routine aspects of human behavior. In addition, in Latin America it is associated with the whole notion of "alienation." Both liberation theology and the closely related liberation pedagogy of Paulo Freire have stemmed from the conviction that the Latin American masses are not only oppressed and exploited but also *alienated*. It is not just that they cannot express their own thoughts as liberated subjects of history. They cannot even think their own thoughts. One does not have to be a Marxist to see that the ideology of the oppressor has been introjected by the oppressed as modern civilization has progressed. Thus the term "masses" is associated with the notion of "alienation," as Lenin pointed out in *What Is To Be Done?* some time ago, and it shares the pejorative connotation of the latter. But the term *majority*, even when applied to the very same group of people, has very different connotations and suggests a very different value judgment. Our basic

context is one that tends to exalt democratic systems. In such a context
we are used to the notion of a governmental authority that represents
the majority, is responsible to the majority, and thus presumably serves
the majority.

As Raymond Aron has shown, it is quite obvious that every "democratic" society has worked out hidden rules and mechanisms that prevent the "majority" from exercising the power it possesses in theory. In
other words, the democratic majorities never exercise power directly.
Each and every one of the "democracies," be they capitalistic or socialis-
tic, is firmly grounded on the tacit principle that it would be disastrous to
allow that to happen. And the basic underlying assumption is that the
majority would not know how to use power for its own benefit, at least
over the long run.

In any case normal word usage, when it is dealing with majorities,
carries with it something of the historical backdrop connected with the
struggles for democratic ideals. So even though the terms "masses" and
"majorities" may refer to the same objective content, they are not
synonyms insofar as valuation is concerned. And one's choice of term
depends on what one is trying to prove.

This is even more apparent when we move to the other extreme, the
positive pole, and talk about "the people." And it is especially clear when
we add some adjective that identifies the country involved: e.g., the
American people, the Argentinian people, the people of Latin America.
Though the human content of the term may be exactly the same as that
of the term "masses," all the pejorative connotations disappear and we
are left with an emotional identification.

Thus you can hear one and the same person say that "the masses" are
alienated by consumer society on the one hand, and that "our people"
are creative revolutionaries and should be followed on the other hand.
And this person does not feel the slightest need to explain the evident
contradiction in what is said. The mere substitution of one noun for
another takes care of the whole matter, even though the very same
human reality is being discussed.

It is important to realize how commonplace this practice has become.
One appeals to "the people" to make revolutions or to justify oppressive
dictatorships. When one uses "the people" as a noun or describes some
reality with such adjective as "the people's" or "popular," it is very hard
indeed to evade positive connotations. Thus the religion "of the masses,"
without changing its clientele, takes on positive and nationalist color-
ation when it becomes the religion "of the majority," and even more so
when it becomes the religion "of the people."

One little sample of this process in the theological arena might be cited here. The bishops at the Medellín Conference were confronted with the thorny task of evaluating the mass religion of Latin America in positive terms. They had originally entitled the relevant document "Pastoral Care of the Masses." But at the very last moment they changed the title from *Pastoral de masas* to *Pastoral popular*.[3]

A third example of this sort of semantic shift can be seen in the use of the terms *sect, universal religion,* and *Church.*

As we have already seen, and as we shall see even more clearly further on, liberation theology represents a revolution in the classic conception of Christianity. It demands of the Christian a difficult political commitment which runs directly counter to the oppression that is sanctioned and imposed by the existing social systems. In addition, on the religious level, it calls for the disestablishment of customary certitudes and securities. Thus it is not surprising that liberation theology "takes" among groups of Christians who are prepared to shoulder the burden of such commitment and change. It is not just coincidence that the bishops at Medellín opted for basic or grass-roots communities at the same time that they opted for liberation.

Undoubtedly the bishops rather naively assumed or hoped that such grass-roots communities would *complement* the existing pastoral effort directed at the masses. Facts, however, soon gave the lie to any such hopes. The burgeoning grass-roots communities became very critical of a brand of "Christianity" that was closely allied with structural injustice, and they also challenged the claim of the "Church of the masses" to call itself Christian. Such were the criticisms that arose, not from theologians, but from average Christians as their faith became a more mature thing. The reaction to their criticisms was a cry of alarm, and they came to be designated by the pejorative term *sect.*

Now the fact is that the word "sect" is employed in the New Testament to designate the nascent Church. More directly it derives from the Latin translation of Acts 24:14, in which Paul acknowledges that he is a follower of the new way or "sect" of which people are speaking. The implication is that his way is a split-off (or "heresy") from the Jewish religion. Both the original Greek word and the Latin translation of it imply that Christianity is a minority group composed of dissidents who have separated from a larger religious tradition.

These latter connotations have become such an integral part of our own language today that we apply the term "sects" to elitist religious groups who form their own closed circles, who possess their own distinctive beliefs and charismatic features, and who are not structured in terms of the roles and official positions that are part and parcel of the great religious traditions.

In contrast to such *sectarian* groups Christianity, even though divided, displays all the features that would make it one of the half dozen *world religions* or *universal religions* existing today.

The notion of a "world religion" or a "univesal religion," as used by someone like Toynbee, for example, clearly suggests just the opposite of a sect—in sociological terms at any rate. A *universal religion* gains that appellation insofar as it has infiltrated the cultural life of broad areas of our planet. It clearly could not have done this without a great deal of routinization, without accepting minimum levels of participation and membership and stressing visible, cultic participation over interior obligations and demands. Belonging to a *sect* implies a certain amount of social inadaptation. Belonging to a *universal religion* ensures a certain amount of socio-cultural integration.

The concept of "world religion" is certainly not evident in the New Testament as a designation of the Christian message or the Christian community. But it does contain repeated allusions to a universal kingdom. The latter was soon associated with the spread of the Church, the religious community established by Jesus, and later with the wars against other "religions" that marked the period after the acceptance of Christianity by the Roman Empire. People were led to the conclusion that the gospel message was the foundation stone of a *universal religion* which was destined to compete with the other world religions on the scene. And since there were supporting statistics from around the world, they began to be viewed in terms of a world religion—though one can hardly imagine what it meant to be a "Christian" in terms of those figures.

This radical opposition between "sect" and "universal religion" eventually led people to apply the connotations of the latter to the term used most frequently by the New Testament to designate the Christian community: i.e., the *Church*. The unconscious power of language affected people's outlook. Since "the Church" was viewed as the direct opposite of a "sect," it would have to possess just the opposite traits. It should be open to the people at large, not too demanding, structured by administrative forms, suspicious of charismatic pretensions on the part of individuals and groups, and grounded on cultural values.

And so people have come to use these features as arguments against opposing points of view, without feeling any need to establish the validity of such features in and through the gospel message. The documents of the Medellín Conference are not wholly free of that tendency. Perhaps the most antiliberation stance it takes anywhere is to be found in the document on the *Pastoral Care of the Masses*. And its argument is based here solely on the connotative power of certain terms, nothing more. Consider this statement: "Given this type of religious sense among the masses, the Church is faced with the dilemma of either *continuing to be a universal Church* or, if it fails to attract and vitally incorporate such groups, of *becoming a sect.* Because she is *a Church rather than a sect,* she must offer her message of salvation to all men, running the risk that not all will accept it in the same manner or with the same degree of understanding and maturity. . . And while one may not presume on the existence of the faith behind all apparently Christian religious expressions, neither may one arbitrarily deny the character of *true belief* and of real ecclesial participation, no matter how weak, to every action *which manifests spurious motives or temporal motivations, even selfish ones.*"[4]

Here the bishops clearly take one of their most critical and decisive stands on the matter of pastoral activity, and it is closely bound up with the question whether the Church's function will be for or against liberation. Yet, incredible as it may seem, the only argument put forward is based on the connotative coloring of certain words. "Sect" is used in a pejorative sense, "Church" is not. The Christian community must be a "Church" and accept the consequences that choice entails, whether they have anything to do with the gospel message or not.

The three examples given above show how the verbal terrorism works. Different words, with different connotations and valuational overtones, are used to designate one and the same reality. The choice of vocabulary is determined by the position one holds and the point one is trying to make. The mere use of certain words is designed to settle an issue and provide ready-made solutions for profound problems. At the same time it often impedes serious study of the reality in question.

Many other similar examples of the process could be cited. One could show, for example, how the term "community" or "grass-roots community" takes on more pejorative connotations when it is labelled a "minority" group and eventually an "elitist" group. But we have said enough to alert the reader's attention to the positions and viewpoints we are going to study in this chapter regarding the relationship between the Christian religion and the Latin American masses. In the final chapter I shall try to give more careful definition to all these terms, and to explore the more basic question of the relationship between the Christian message and the liberation (not precisely the religion) of the Latin American masses.

II. THREE SAMPLE APPROACHES TO THE ISSUE

Keeping in mind the points about linguistic usage and terminological argumentation that were made in the previous section, we can now consider the three principal theories or approaches that have been formulated with regard to the relationship between popular religion and liberation.

A Typological Approach

Let us begin with the most simplistic and superficial approach. After what we said in the preceding section, it probably would not deserve detailed treatment here if it were simply a matter of its theoretical worth. But it is important for two other reasons. First of all, it offers an easy way out, a solution that can offer peace of mind and assuage the consciences of the Church's pastors. They can take satisfaction from the fact that "the people" are still responding as usual to the religious stimuli being offered them in both an active and passive sense. The bishops can go on providing them with sacred ministers and sacred ceremonies, and they can simply overlook the complex motivations involved as well as the rites that are added to the official stock of orthodox practices.

Secondly and more importantly, this approach was the one presented at the Medellín Conference and endorsed in some of its documents, particularly in its document on the "Pastoral Care of the Masses." As we have noted before, the documents of the Medellín Conference are not a homogeneous corpus. Sometimes in a given document one can almost sense the tension between a particular description of the real-life situation on the one hand and the theological reflections or pastoral recommendations on the other hand. But the most clear-cut tension of all lies between two blocks of documents: those which talk about the commitment of the Church to justice and peace and those which refer to the internal structure and activity of the Church. This obvious contrast led one observer to remark sardonically that the Church was prescribing severer measures for society at large than for itself. But the contrast becomes more understandable when one realizes that the first set of documents bears the imprint of Gustavo Gutiérrez whereas the latter bears the imprint of Renato Poblete. And Poblete had a special hand in the document on the "Pastoral Care of the Masses."

The essential lines and features of Poblete's religious sociology are summed up in an article entitled "Religión de masa, religión de élite," which appeared in a 1965 issue of *Mensaje*. This article was cited extensively by Bishop Luis E. Henríquez, who presented a paper on this topic to the Medellín Conference.[5]

Accepting as his basic framework a Weberian typology, Poblete starts off with the assumption that an organized Church is not a *sect;* that as such it naturally tends towards universality and the conversion of all human beings—the two being synonymous for all practical purposes;

and that this obligation to expand over the whole world will necessarily "dilute" the original message to some extent, so that it loses something of its spontaneous and charismatic character. That is the price that has to be paid when an early charismatic approach gives way to institutionalization and routinization.

As Poblete sees it, religious movements possess the same features to be found in any social group. In particular, religious movements, like other social organizations, are composed of concentric circles of members who live out their religious values at different levels of intensity and profundity. We thus get four levels: (1) the dedicated disciples who are wholly devoted to religious activities; (2) the militant workers who are not quite as devoted as the full-time disciples; (3) the broad circle of average believers; and (4) the masses at large who are still open to receiving and accepting the religious message.

Poblete feels that the great temptation facing the first circle of dedicated disciples is the tendency to interpret the demands of their religion in radical terms and separate themselves from the world. Hence a religion destined to be worldwide and to influence if not convert all men cannot ignore popular beliefs and simply adopt the forms that are peculiar to the first circle of disciples. It must remain open to the masses and try to keep them within its organization and its sphere of influence.

It seems almost unbelievable that this superficial notion of sociological membership, unsupported by any theological criteria, should come to define the decisive thrust of the Church's pastoral activity. Yet it is not so unbelievable when we realize that there is a general tendency to use "science" to justify hazardous options that have *already been made* for other reasons and that one does not wish to weigh in the balance scale of critical judgment.

Let me indicate how superficial Poblete's analysis is. Any serious sociological analysis could readily show that the first circle of believers, the circle of totally dedicated disciples, is just as exposed to "mass" tendencies; that the most obvious temptation is not the tendency to absolutize the gospel's demands and to move apart from the world but rather to minimize and amputate the gospel message in order to accommodate oneself to the ideological and pragmatic mechanisms of an alienated world. If we correct Poblete's typology on this basic point, what remains of his whole argument?

Moreover, any competent sociologist knows that typologies can be useful only insofar as the terms are not taken as entelechies but simply as attempts to lay hold of regularly recurring phenomena. Thus they must be corrected in the light of facts, not *decide* the facts themselves. The fact is that what is today called the Church of Christ began as a sect, and that its radical understanding and interpretation of the gospel message did not separate it from the world or its worldwide vocation (see, for example, 1 Cor 5:9 ff.). It is also difficult to see how a theology that places the Church in the service of liberation could lead that Church, however minority it might be, away from the world. For the liberation of the world is its very reason for being.

Needless to say, Weber was not familiar with liberation theology. But the fact that something is new does not disturb Poblete in his use of typology. Something that might have happened in the past, though in fact it did *not* happen in the case of Christianity, is absolutely bound to happen in the future. And if it resists this tendency, then one must force it to happen. So it seems to Poblete in any case.

In addition, the most cursory sociological analysis will reveal the superficiality of Poblete's notion that the Church, precisely because it is a "social group," must have four concentric circles of adherents. The formation and makeup of a "social group" depends on its commitment—whether the latter is fixed by society at large or the vocation of the group itself. If one does not accept that principle, then one would have to say that an anti-bomb squad, insofar as it too is a "social group," would be composed of four circles: (1) the members totally dedicated to the defusing of bombs; (2) the militant but less dedicated defusers; (3) the broad circle of those who are familiar with technology and explosives and believe in them; and (4) the masses who are open to the idea that explosives are dangerous. In short, Poblete makes use of a particular notion of "social group" that dovetails with his own theology of the Church. And the latter is that of a social group rooted in the fact that its members *share in a privilege.* If the gospel message or theology should prove that the Church really has a very different function, his whole argument falls apart.

That is true even if in the past the Church did structure itself precisely as a group enjoying a special privilege and having to manipulate social conditions so that this privilege would reach as many people as possible. At some stage of its existence, but certainly not at the very beginning, the Church married itself to the notion of "universal religion," that is, to the notion that it was a group of believers who had special ways and means for relating to God and obtaining special prerogatives from him.

But what if Christianity, when it is at its most authentic, cannot possibly be a "religion" in that precise sense? Such an idea, according to Bishop Henríquez, seems to make a distinction between faith and religion that is "of Protestant origin" and that "we cannot accept in its entirety."[6] Quite characteristically, Henríquez adopts and accepts the terminology pointing towards a "world religion" without presenting any "Catholic" argument based on the Bible or theology to prove that this indeed is the vocation of the Church. In all likelihood he is unaware of the fact that it was only during the Middle Ages that Christians began to use the term "religion" to describe Christianity in relationship to other "religions."[7]

The "Protestant origin" of the distinction in question is no indication that it is false or wrong. Richard Shaull is not alluding to Lutheran tradition but to the tradition of Christ and his message when he writes: "The time has come when we must rediscover—in church and society—the meaning of our *sectarian* heritage. Those who are *in* but not *of* the established order will be the agents of revolution in our advanced technological society."[8] But since this possibility is not envisioned in the typology of Poblete (of Protestant origin, by the way), then it must be discarded as an hypothesis.

More significant and dangerous, however, is the attempt to turn sociology into the governing norm of the Church's function. All sociologists, right from Weber himself on, have realized that no typology can serve as a norm for deciding what reality is to be. Typology simply helps one to comprehend some regularly recurring reality. Poblete, however, thinks that any attempt to interpret the demands of the gospel in radical terms is a "temptation." Exactly where the temptation lies here is not too clear, of course. Against whom or what? Perhaps against his typology, but certainly not against the gospel message!

From what has been said so far it should be evident that any and every liberation theology must begin by rejecting the ideological supposition that Christianity exists in order to fill a certain pigeonhole in some typology. That is true, no matter what theological opinion one may hold about the problem of religion and the masses. The whole problem of the "Christian" masses simply cannot be solved that way.

A Populist Approach

A more complex and profound attempt to solve this problem is offered by Aldo Büntig, though I think it runs into contradictions in the last analysis. His views are presented in a paper that he read at the El Escorial theological meeting to which we alluded earlier.[9]

The Latin American standpoint is brought out clearly by Büntig when he points out that popular religion is not an autonomous religious phenomenon, that it is just as much a cultural phenomenon: "In few regions of the world can one still find such a close symbiosis between two sets of values [Segundo: religious and cultural values] as one can find in our homeland. In other words, Latin America still cannot be comprehended in socio-cultural terms without taking due account of Catholicism."[10]

Unlike Poblete, Büntig rightly assumes that it is theology, and specifically liberation theology, which should dictate our value judgments concerning the religious aspect of this phenomenon: "There is a pressing and immediate need to situate and integrate this popularized Catholicism, which is rooted in the very depths of our people, within the irrepressible process through which our continent is now living. Within this latter process Catholics are *summoned* to play a role as protagonists, with or without sacred gestures, as an historical precondition for survival and a theological exigency for fidelity."[11]

It is right at this point, however, that an element of ambivalence and confusion begins to creep in. Büntig talks about a *people* who, on the *religious level,* must be *introduced* into a liberation process *in which they are already living,* presumably on other levels. This antinomy is indicative of a very peculiar and specific situation in Latin America: the situation in Argentina. I don't think I am being unfair to his formulation when I point up this ambivalence, because the Argentinian movement of Priests for the Third World has run head-on into this problem, debated it for years, and, I think it is fair to say, divided over it; and yet the people involved have still maintained a consistent theology of liberation and a correct general approach to the whole question of the relationship between the gospel message and politics.

To get back to Büntig himself, it is clear that he does not sacralize the people, much less their religion. He openly criticizes the "naive attitude" found among the people, particularly with respect to religion. And he challenges the view that it must be left alone: "Since this undeveloped religion is the only thing the people really feel or live, and since everything that comes from the people must be good, then the processes of the people at large must be left untouched altogether or for the most part. Otherwise there is the danger that our people will lose the little faith they now have. So the argument goes. Those who criticize certain popular sacred rites as adulterated are Europeanizers who do not really understand the people. This acritical attitude used to be typical of old-line pastors, but recently it has been given rational backing by certain theologians and pastoral workers."[12]

But is it really true that religion—as opposed to politics, for example—is the only thing that the people feel deeply? Büntig is not very clear on this point. One cannot tell for sure whether he shares the "naive attitude" of the people or not on this question. He seems to accept it at the start, only to end up at the opposite pole: "We must *start from* the reality of the people, including their way of internalizing and expressing the religious element. By 'the people' here I especially mean those human groups who are neither oppressors nor accomplices in the oppression that marks our social system. . . We find in this people a growing and aggressive awareness of their dependent situation and a burgeoning struggle for their own liberation. We find in this people an extraordinary *reservoir* of Christian values, *both sacral and nonsacral,* which must be encouraged to grow and flourish in the light of the gospel message."[13]

In saying that the growing *awareness* of the people can find expression in both sacral and *nonsacral* forms, Büntig would seem to be forced logically to deny that "this undeveloped religion is the only thing the people really *feel* or live." For they also can apparently express their new awareness in nonsacral forms. Büntig must also logically deny that the religious forms are a decisive element in the whole cultural balance, and that runs directly counter to his earlier assertion.

Reading Büntig's paper, one suspects that he is not very confident that the Church can do very much in a religious way on the level of popular religion. But he does seem to have a lot of trust in the political forms through which the people attempt to express themselves, even though they may be bound up with religious excrescences that have little or no liberative content. This suspicion is confirmed when we read the following remark: "There is a twofold dimension in popular Catholicism that must be clearly underlined. On the one hand there are the *sacral gestures* . . . which go to make up the traditional dimension of popular Catholicism. On the other hand there is *the people* which expresses itself in these gestures. This distinction has basic pastoral implications and consequences. For us, in the long, hard, and complicated process of liberation through which our continent is living, the values of our poor and oppressed people which find spontaneous expression in and through these sacral gestures are *far more important* than *any salvageable values in the sacral gestures themselves.*"[14]

At first glance this distinction seems designed for a very clear-cut purpose: i.e., to discourage pastoral activity from undertaking an impossible task that might seem feasible and plausible in the abstract. One must not try to distinguish the wheat from the chaff in the religion of the Latin American masses in order to salvage the former and discard the latter. Büntig's distinction clearly seems to imply that a socio-political process of a secular nature will serve as an adequate vehicle for the transformation of the peoples of Latin America. The greatest contribution the Church could offer to this process would seem to be a prudent act of omission. It should keep its hands off the inflexible and relatively negligible factor of "popular Catholicism" and commit itself to

accepting and encouraging the forward movement of the overall popular process. Such has been the course of the most clear-eyed faction of
Priests for the Third World in any case.

To one's surprise, however, that is not the conclusion Büntig draws
from his premises. For some unexplained reason, he goes back and tries
to *salvage* the values to be found in "popular Catholicism." Right after
the remark cited above, he goes on to say: "Hence a pastoral effort
directed at the people cannot prescind from two dimensions which are
mutually complementary. It must (1) evaluate *what is salvageable in the
sacral gestures* of popular Catholicism; and (2) pinpoint the people's liberation values which find expression in these gestures, offering them
positive criticism and encouragement in their efforts at liberation."[15]

After saying that this was not very important, Büntig feels obliged
for some reason to undertake the task of separating the wheat from the
chaff, both with respect to the values of the people and with respect to
their religious embodiments.

It is at this point that Büntig's use of language takes some curious
twists and turns. How is this difficult function to be carried out, particularly in the ecclesial realm? Büntig rightly observes that "some sort of
theology is not enough. It is necessary to create *microstructures of membership,* ecclesial grass-roots communities. No one is a member of a *mass*
[Segundo: he resorts to this term here to avoid giving a pejorative connotation to the term "the people"]; we feel ourselves to be members only
of those human groups in which we can really participate in an active
way."[16]

But unless Büntig is thinking of some sort of Pentecostal group,
which is highly unlikely, this remark would seem to run directly counter
to his description of such communities and their evolution in an earlier
part of his paper. There he says: "The risk entailed in this approach is
clear, however attractive it may seem in theory. Such *elites* [Segundo: he
does not want to give pejorative connotations to the term "grass-roots
communities"] quickly tend to go ahead all alone, evolving exquisite and
precious experiences perhaps but staying on the margins of *the people.*
Yet it is the latter who are the fundamental agent of change in the last
analysis. Hence these *elites* frequently do not get beyond the level of
intraecclesial modernization or progressivism. They are advanced in
their liturgy, their catechetical methods, and their overhaul of certain
ecclesiastical structures, but they do not really perceive the contradictions entailed in the life of their respective national communities."[17]

It is obvious that in the last two passages cited, Büntig is talking about
the very same human groups. But depending on the evaluational impact
he wishes to convey, he calls one extreme "grass-roots communities" or

"elites," and the other extreme "mass" or "the people" or "national community."

Büntig clearly indicates that the "microstructures of membership" are not designed for the "mass," for he characterizes the former by "participation in an active way." The most elementary pastoral experience teaches us that mass conduct, at every level of society and in every social class, rejects such participation. It is looking for security, not responsibility, in its membership in the Church. This point is also implied in Büntig's earlier passage where he states that the pastoral effort for the people must be integrated *critically* in the popular process. Presumably mass conduct itself is not critical, otherwise there would be no need for the pastoral effort to add criticism to the popular mix.

It would seem, then, that Büntig is caught in a bind. On the one hand his own logic obliges him to admit that the only way to salvage the liberation values of popular Catholicism is to fashion participatory structures that are of a minority cast. On the other hand he seems to need an ecclesiastical and political stamp of approval, which leads him to maintain that he is anti-elitist and to point out the dangers of those very same microstructures.

Büntig is not alone in the stance he takes, and there are many worthwhile elements in his presentation. To fully appreciate his position, however, one must realize three operative factors: 1. The advanced stage of secularization and urbanization in Argentinian society gives Büntig greater leeway to make a theoretical and practical distinction between the popular element and its religious expression. 2. The populist thrust of Peronism exerts a strong influence here, forcing him almost to identify himself with the people and to show distrust for minority-based processes of conscientization and criticism. 3. In the ecclesiastical sphere, there is often a *sine qua non* condition attached to working in ecclesial organizations; either there is to be no criticism of "popular Catholicism" at all or one is to offer only discreet proposals for reform, the assumption being that popular Catholicism can salvage authentic values and the latent revolutionaries in its bosom without losing its mass character.

The first two factors are not exclusive to Argentina, of course. At the same time, however, it must be said that they do not apply in exactly the same way or to the same extent to all the other countries of Latin America. That is particularly true of the first factor, since many Latin American countries still have a large rural and aboriginal population. The third factor is applicable to all of Latin America.

An Approach Focusing on Societal Change

The relationship between liberation theology and popular religion is tackled in a somewhat different way by Segundo Galilea of Chile, a pastoral theologian who discussed the matter at the same meeting in El Escorial.[18]

Galilea perceives two decisive facts on the level of popular *culture*. The first fact is that primitive cultures are bound to disappear or to be transformed under the impact of modern life and that this transformation will be the result of real social change rather than of any modification of highly ideological factors. In other words, the transformation will be brought about by working conditions, migrations, urbanization, economic production, and living standards far more than it will be brought about by changes in religious gestures, religious notions, or the popular conception of life in general.

The second fact is that what is commonly called the pastoral effort for the people comes down to nothing more than taking religious advantage of those primitive traits of the people which persist, and for as long as they do persist. To think that the people are helped thereby is to entertain an illusion.

The conclusion is clear enough: "It is towards this popular Catholicism that pastoral activity is directed. Here I am not going to go into any detailed evaluation of it. I shall simply say that most of this pastoral activity maintains rather than transforms this brand of degraded Catholicism. Insofar as it simply continues, we must classify it as alienating and reactionary. At best it is naive. It thinks that it is preserving the "Catholic faith" when in reality it is paving the way for a grave crisis for this faith *at the moment that politicization and social transformations occur.*"[19]

In my opinion this formulation of the whole problem is not only more correct but also more useful in attempting to deal with the various critical data that are brought together in it. First of all, the most important factor in the transformation of the primitive cultures of Latin America is not the Church nor even a consciousness-raising form of education such as that of Paolo Freire. It is the *mass* demands imposed by such realities as migration, urbanization, the supply and demand of manual and industrial labor, and so forth. We may not agree with this process or we may have serious doubts that the transformation will take place in a properly balanced way; but the national and international forces underlying the process are far stronger than our humanist objections. Furthermore, it is not at all true that the Church is capable of instigating such changes or accompanying them with critical comment. The indubitable fact is that the Church will certainly be *the last element to change*. Remember that we are talking here about masses, not about minority grass-roots communities. Sociology shows us that masses who are almost fully integrated into modern culture-forms maintain relationships with their primitive past solely in and through religious practices that have no relationship whatsoever with their present roles and values in the everyday life of modern society.

Secondly, the hope of Latin American countries does not lie in an impossible attempt to preserve their more primitive cultures, however much respect we may show for their humane values and their proper pace of transformation. The only road open to them is to pass through the modernization that is a precondition for survival to a revolution that will thoroughly and radically humanize the social structures of the population as a whole. Now in this connection we can cite a pertinent remark of Richard Shaull: "Once again, revolution will depend upon a vanguard that is free to see what is happening, discern the shape of the future, and accept a new vocation over against the system."[20] It is with respect to this specific goal, and perhaps to no other goal of any sort, that the Church possesses a powerful instrument. It consists of those minority groups in possession of a mature faith which will not allow them to close in upon themselves in a "sectarian" way. In them the content of faith loses all meaning insofar as it is not related to acting as a revolutionary vanguard seeking to humanize the inevitable process of transition. Shaull's conclusion is corrective in every respect, both from the sociological and the theological point of view: "If a small minority of the Western middle class[21] is to become a vanguard in the transformation of technological society, is it too much to hope that some of its members might come from a [Segundo: Christian] community in which such symbols [Segundo: of liberation and transformation] are at work?"[22]

Thirdly, taking as our assumption this conception of cultural transformation and the role of the Church in it, we Christians can be free, within the context of our commitment to the masses, to inject into them *the crisis of an authentic evangelization process.* In Galilea's words, this crisis would entail:

> "Relativizing the religious expressions that 'popular Catholicism' tends to repeat cyclically and to absolutize into an enslaving thing. This is a first form of liberation.

> "Integrating into individualistic religious expressions the original dimension of the Christian religion which has to do with communitarian solidarity and fraternity as essential features of any religious act. . . This is a second form of liberation.

> "Revealing the element of protest against injustice and oppression that exists in religious attitudes. . . This is a third form of liberation."[23]

Fourthly, even though the second point cited above might seem akin to one that breaks down the consistency of Büntig's position, the whole context of Galilea's presentation shows that he is not aiming in the same direction. He is not asking us to salvage the values existing in sacral gestures. Liberation is his guiding criterion throughout. Both theory and practice indicate quite clearly that we cannot have two contradictory Churches existing simultaneously—one for mass lines of conduct (in whatever social stratum) and another for minority lines of conduct, one taking advantage of, or irrationally trying to preserve, the old outdated cultures and another committed to liberation. If the concrete experience of grass-roots communities proves anything at all, it proves that taking cognizance of the liberative function of the Church does not lead to liturgical preciosity and merely intraecclesial reformism. Instead such communities become the fiercest and most effective opponents of the compromises the Church is forced to make when it tries to expropriate the masses as such and thereby impedes the liberation of the latter.

III. PHONY UNIVERSALISM

The reader can make his or her own personal choice between the opinions just cited regarding the problem of popular religion. In any case I think it is evident that all three opinions, despite their differences, present similar data and formulations that point us towards a deeper underlying problem.

First of all, all three suggest that there is some peculiar difficulty in transforming popular religion from the standpoint of the Church's mechanisms. In Poblete's view the difficulty stems from the fact that Christianity, as a universal religion, is in practice forced to view itself as surrounded by masses who participate only slightly in its essential nucleus. In Büntig's view the difficulty stems from the fact that the motivating force for transformation is to be found in the people's profane awareness rather than in its religious expression. In his view the popular masses go through a political process that also serves to bring about a religious transformation, although the latter seems to evolve more slowly and in the wake of the former. In Galilea's thesis, the difficulty involved in religious transformation stems from the fact that the impulse behind change is rooted in the overall evolution of the people but it is not at all certain that the popular masses themselves are the impulse behind this process. Insofar as they are not politicized or conscienticized, they may simply be victims of it all.

Thus all three positions assume that we are faced with two types of religion which share very little in common. One is very monolithic. It is grounded on the coercion exerted by primitive mental attitudes, attitudes that are shaped by physical and psychic insecurity, environmental pressures, and so forth. Thus, even as religion, it is impervious to any large-scale purification of a liberative sort. The second type of religion is much more flexible. It is represented by "voluntary consumers of religion," by people who are interested in religion insofar as the latter bolsters, deepens, and corrects the human values to which they are committed. All three theses indicate that this latter group of people constitute a minority as opposed to the former group, but that they are more active and more inclined to commit themselves to the overall liberation process.

Having arrived at this conclusion and freed ourselves from the terrorism of mere words, we might expect and hope to be able to agree on some evaluation of popular religion in Latin America and on the possibilities and ways of exerting a liberative influence on it. That is not the case, unfortunately, for several convergent reasons.

The first reason is theological. The Christian community, the Church, has never fully resolved the question of the proper relationship between its *particularity* on the one hand and its *universal* destiny on the other. It has never satisfactorily worked out the relationship between its diminutive proportions in time and space within the overall human process and its supposed mission to the whole world.

The notion of a numerical universality *in the future* would not solve the problem, for even that would not satisfy the demands of a universal salvation plan designed for all of humanity throughout time and space. Even more important, however, is the fact that numerical universality itself merely aggravates the whole issue: for it presupposes the acceptance and manipulation of mass mechanisms. To what extent would such a Church really be in line with the Christian message? To what extent would such a Church be the satanic Anti-Christ represented by the Grand Inquisitor of *The Brothers Karamazov*? And the reader should note that the same questions can be directed at any revolutionary project, for the problem is not just a theological one.

This leads us into the second reason why we cannot readily evaluate popular religion in Latin America and suggest how to exercise a liberative influence on it. Here sociological, philosophical, and even biological data converge on us. The only way to reconcile qualitative change with numerical universality would be to assume that mass lines of conduct will turn into qualitatively minority lines of conduct in passing through a certain educational process. One must assume, in other words, that the masses, without ceasing to act with their customary mass characteristics insofar as numbers are concerned, can somehow acquire the qualities and expend the efforts that are typical of minorities. Thus if it used the right approach, a Church that is numerically universal could likewise become a leaven of light and critical judgment at the same time—though these latter qualities are restricted to minorities today, thanks to the effort they expend.

It is worth noting here that Marxism has never really solved this basic issue either, not in an explicit and convincing way at least. In the final stage of truly communist society, will the masses divest themselves of the structures of egotistical, immediatist, and oversimplifying conduct which at present prevent even socialist societies from introducing a division of labor that dovetails with the spontaneous vocation of each and all? We get no solid answer to that question.

So we are left with a major issue that must still be explored. On the one hand we find *majority* lines of conduct that are quantitatively supreme; on the other hand we find *minority* lines of conduct that are qualitatively critical and decisive. Does this division represent an inexorable law or the expected outcome of the historical processes and structures that are given? If the answer must be "yes," then we must consider a crucial theological question: How are we to picture the task of the Church to "expand"?

In my opinion, the suspicion that there is a radical ambiguity involved in this point constitutes an essential feature of any and every authentic hermeneutic circle in theology.

NOTES

1. Consider this passage by Will Herberg, for example: "Each on his own part—the Protestant, the Catholic, the Jew—may regard his own 'faith' as the best or even the truest, but unless he is a theologian or affected with a special theological interest, he will quite 'naturally' look upon the other two as sharing with his communion a common 'spiritual' foundation of basic 'ideals and values'—the chief of these being religion itself. America thus has its underlying culture-religion—best understood as the religious aspect of the American Way of Life—of which the three conventional religions are somehow felt to be appropriate manifestations and expressions" (Will Herberg, *Protestant— Catholic—Jew* [New York: Doubleday, 1960], p. 258).

2. As Gerth and Mills point out, the character of the dominant symbols alone does not determine the character of the social structure. If that were the case, then one who held a monopoly over the communication of those symbols could presumably create new institutions by broadcasting certain symbols as the main examples of what *ought to be.* But that does not happen. The propagation of symbols is effective *only insofar as they have meaningful relevance for existing roles. They cannot create such roles of themselves.* See Hans Gerth and C. Wright Mills, *Character and Social Structure* (New York: Harcourt, Brace, Jovanovich, 1964), p. 298.

3. The Medellín document was originally entitled *Pastoral de masas,* but changed to *Pastoral popular* at the last minute. Some editions and translations kept the original title, or were issued before the last-minute change. The edition published by one diocese in Uruguay starts off with this cautionary note: "This editon presents the *almost definitive* text of the documents. Only changes in literary style or corrections of a *stylistic nature* might be introduced." In this particular text, correction certainly went beyond the mere matter of literary style.

4. Documents of the Medellín Conference, *The Church in the Present-Day Transformation of Latin America in the Light of the Council,* 2 vols., Eng. trans. (Washington D.C., Latin American Division, United States Catholic Conference), Vol II, Conclusions, pp. 122, 124. Compare the passage cited above with the following passage from *Lumen gentium:* "He is not saved, however, who, though he is part of the body of the Church, does not persevere *in charity.* He remains indeed in the bosom of the Church, but, as it were, only in a 'bodily' manner and not 'in his heart'. . . . If they fail moreover to respond to that grace in thought, word, and deed, not only will they not be saved but they will be the more severely judged" (n. 14, *The Documents of Vatican II,* edited by Walter M. Abbot, S.J., New York: Guild-America-Association, 1966). It seems obvious that the committee charged with producing the Medellín document on pastoral care of the masses did not think thus.

5. The use that Bishop Henríquez makes of Poblete's approach can readily be seen in his position paper on "Pastoral Care of the Masses and the Elites," in the Documents of the Medellín Conference, *op. cit.,* Vol. I, Position Papers, pp. 186 ff.

6. *Ibid.,* p. 190.

7. See Wilfred C. Smith, *The Meaning and End of Religion* (New York: Mentor Books, 1964), Chapters 1–4, and in particular Chapter 2.

8. Richard Shaull, "Christian Faith as Scandal in a Technocratic World," in *New Theology* 6 (New York: Macmillan, 1969), p. 132.

9. Aldo Büntig, "Dimensiones del catolicismo popular latinoamericano y su inserción en el proceso de liberación. Diagnóstico y reflexiones pastorales," in *Fe cristiana y cambio social en América Latina* (Salamanca: Sígueme, 1973), pp. 129–50.

10. *Ibid.,* p. 131.

11. *Ibid.,* p. 132.

12. *Ibid.,* p. 134.

13. *Ibid.*

14. *Ibid.,* p. 135.

15. *Ibid.*

16. *Ibid.,* p. 145.

17. *Ibid.,* p. 133.

18. Segundo Galilea, "La fe como principio crítico de promoción de la religiosidad popular," in *Fe cristiana y cambrio social,* pp. 151–58.

19. *Ibid.,* pp. 152–53.

20. Richard Shaull, "Christian Faith as Scandal," p. 130.

21. The fact that it is a matter of the middle class here can be interpreted in two ways insofar as Latin America is concerned. On the one hand it could mean

that only the middle class on our continent is equipped to live the "civilized" European mode of life, which presupposes being adherents of Christianity. On the other hand it could mean something more provocative and promising. It could mean that in the light of the real situation of our continent, where the very rich and the very poor divide the arena between them, the middle class is the critical and decisive class for performing the activities noted by Erich Fromm in this key passage: "Finally, one other point of difference [Segundo: with Freud] should be mentioned. It concerns the differentiation between psychological phenomena of want and those of abundance. The primitive level of human existence is that of want. There are imperative needs which *have* to be satisfied before anything else. Only when man has time and energy left beyond the satisfaction of the primary needs, can culture develop and with it those strivings that attend the phenomena of abundance. Free (or spontaneous) acts are always phenomena of abundance. Freud's psychology is a psychology of want. He defines pleasure as the satisfaction resulting from the removal of painful tension. Phenomena of abundance, like love or tenderness, actually do not play any role in his system" (*Escape From Freedom,* [New York: Holt, Rinehart, and Winston, 1941], pp. 294–95).

Although caution is very much in order here, particularly in applying this to individual cases, I shall try to show in the next chapter that this very point is intimately bound up with the true function of Christianity within the human race.

22. R. Shaull, "Christian Faith as Scandal," p. 134.

23. S. Galilea, "La fe como principio crítico," p. 157.

CHAPTER EIGHT

Mass Man—Minority Elite
Gospel Message

The previous chapter has, I hope, pinpointed the weak spot that induced theology to give in to ideological mechanisms. It was the felt need to keep the masses within the bounds of Christianity at some minimal level of participation. This meant that the masses had to be provided with a conception of religion which dovetailed with that aim. In this way theology became more and more subject to the manipulation of the mass mechanisms at work in the various societies of the Western world.

Wittingly or unwittingly the Church sought to apply to Christian membership the same mechanisms that helped to secure membership in civil society, hoping thereby to achieve a parallel result. If one looks at the day-to-day work of theologizing with a realistic eye, it soon becomes obvious that this activity, however speculative it might seem on the surface, remained under the domination of this purpose even in its most abstract conceptual content.

One proof of this, already noted, is the claim to possess in divine revelation a moral code that is total, absolute, and unaffected by time. The data of the gospel message could have shown clearly and explicitly that any moral code extracted from divine revelation varies in accordance with the maturity of man; that it varies with the openness or closedness that man displays in his perception, judgment, and creative potential. The data of the Old Testament could have proved the same principle with countless illustrations. The message of Paul could have elaborated the same point in'and through its theology of history, the latter ranging from Adam right down to Christ.

But another fact, more critical and decisive in the social realm, exerted the decisive influence. The masses need an absolute code so that they can be integrated solidly and completely into the overall society. Here freedom becomes an intolerable burden, and only a "heroic" minority can bear its weight.

For of course there does exist a minority that knows and that does try to manipulate the relativity even without saying so. And it is to be found at both ends of the political spectrum. In Latin America, for example, we see democracy being invoked to forcefully suppress "nondemocratic" alternatives on the one hand, and to pave the way for the dictatorship of the proletariat on the other hand. Is that hypocrisy? Not exactly. It stems rather from the need to relieve the masses of the burden of relative options. If they try to face up to a complex reality and act consistently amid all its relativity, they are bound to fail. So the burden must be lifted from their shoulders.

It is right there that we find unexpected confirmation of, and new support for, the hermeneutic circle which we discussed in the first chapter. All speculative thinking is conditioned by a more decisive and concrete reality, generally an economic one. But this conditioning becomes particularly clear and powerful when we are dealing with a line of thought that is to be incorporated into mass awareness (or lack of awareness) and mass lines of conduct. All thinking has its ideological linkups. But one does not think exactly the same way when one is pondering the direct impact of some line of thought on the masses as when one is contemplating ideas that are to be grasped and implemented by minority groups.

So there is an essential methodological issue to be faced by Latin American theology and, in general, by any theology that has liberation in mind as a goal. Was the original Christian message aimed at masses as such, so that it must be thought out and propagated in those terms; or was it rather aimed at minorities who were destined to play an essential role in the transformation and liberation of the masses?

As we noted briefly at the end of the last chapter, the problem would not be very serious or merit great discussion here if the transition from minorities to masses were merely a gradual one involving numbers. Such would be the case with teaching people to read and write, for example.

It is not easy to teach the masses to read and write through the "mass communications media." But even when that approach is used, it presupposes the creation of a minority that is expert in educational approaches and procedures. Thus the process of bringing literacy to the masses begins with the preparation of minorities. Once the process is carried through to the end, of course, the qualitative result (i.e., literacy) is shared by both groups: by the teaching minority and the learning masses. Thus something that was a minority feature at the beginning becomes quantitatively a mass characteristic at the end, without losing anything of its qualitative nature.

Now the same does not hold true when we shift from literacy training to *conscientization* (or "consciousness-raising"). That is why the well-known approach of Paulo Freire poses problems in the political sphere, as is becoming more and more clear. Partly because his approach was bound up with literacy training and partly because it was pictured in political terms, conscientization and its results were viewed after the model of literacy training. But concrete experience and Freire's subsequent theoretical formulations pointed up essential differences between the two processes.

The very term "literacy training" alludes to an acquired skill, a usable mechanism: the ability to read and write. It presupposes what we might call a "net benefit." In other words, knowing how to read and write opens up new doors to the skilled person and does not shut any doors behind him. What is more, the possession of this skill or mechanism is facilitated by its very use or exercise. It is a low-cost project.

Consider the case of *conscientization,* by contrast. As practical experience and Freire's terminology indicate, we are not dealing here with a skill or mechanism that is "possessed" once and for all. Instead we are dealing with an indefinite process. The most indicative summary of the process is the statement that the person involved becomes an active subject rather than merely a passive object of history. If at some point this person were to regard the mechanism as something he "possessed," he would return to being a mere object of history. The process of conscientization has two features that make it very different from the features to be found in the process of learning to read and write. To the extent that one acquires and accepts the status of being an active subject in history, life becomes more complicated, the resistance of society grows, and one must face more threats and sanctions from the social system that seeks to perpetuate itself and to reify its members. Moreover, the exercise of this new capability does not become easier with use, as a habit usually does. Indeed it becomes more complicated and difficult. The more "consciousness" one acquires, the more difficult it becomes to translate its growing demands into the complex and objectified social reality around one. In short, it is a high-cost project. The process of conscientization, then, confronts us once again with the problem we touched upon in the previous chapter. To state it briefly in terms of our examples here: unless there is some change in the numerical proportions between the easy and the difficult on the human level as such, literacy training can be a mass process but conscientization cannot. To push people towards situations that are more complex, difficult, and intermediate is to create minorities.

Whether we label these minorities with the pejorative term "elites" will depend on whether or not they place the newly acquired and difficult skill at the service of the masses. Medical doctors, for example, will always be a minority. Whether the medical profession will be "elitist" or not will depend on whether it develops as a privilege for those who possess the skill in question or is placed *at the service of all,* though of course medical skill and knowledge will never be a capacity shared by all.

Masses and minorities: is this a basic constant in humanity? If it is, which processes are proper to Christianity—those akin to literacy training or those akin to conscientization? The present chapter will try to tackle these questions and to point up the implications of our answers for theological methodology.

I. THE ECCLESIASTICAL FORMULATION OF THE PROBLEM

Strange as it may seem, the Christian Church has lived with this central problem for twenty centuries without giving it any satisfactory solution. It has tended to ignore the issue or to resolve it in a contradictory way.

In his letter to the Romans and in his first letter to the Corinthians, Paul highlighted a typological parallelism between Christ and Adam. Adam communicated sin and death to *all human beings.* Christ communicated justice and life to all. This parallelism itself is rather difficult to conceive. Paul complicated the matter by indicating that the work of Christ *far exceeded* that of Adam. His communication of life and justification outdid Adam's communication of sin and death.

Paul's point is curious and rather mysterious since the "extra" in Christ's work is susceptible to many different interpretations. Indeed Paul's assertion seems downright contradictory because Adam's work really did bring sin and death to all human beings whereas the work of Christ brought justice and life only to a portion of mankind, indeed only to a minority.

Now what does Paul see as the role of the Church, of the Christian community, in this victory of Christ over Adam, in this even more effective communication of justice and life as opposed to Adam's communication of sin and death? Particularly since the latter seems to be so effective and automatic?

In one passage of Mark's Gospel (Mark 16:16), faith and baptism seem to constitute restrictive conditions governing any possible share in Christ's saving justice and life. Even if we disregard this passage as a later interpolation, the fact remains that both Mark and Matthew[1] attribute to the nascent Church the task of going to the whole world to convert human beings to the teaching of Jesus. So we might paraphrase our previous question this way: What exactly is the relationship between the supposedly universal victory of Christ over Adam and the function of converting human beings into disciples of Christ? Is it a one-to-one relationship, a relationship of identity?

Right at the start we feel that there is something odd going on here. It seems to us, and indeed to Paul, that Adam did not have to convert anyone in order to make all men sinners. Hence it is very hard to picture any universal victory of Christ over Adam that would entail the conversion of the very same people who had been affected by sin and death. The Church falls within certain historical limits, and countless millenia separate its foundation from the historical or mythical Adam. Quite aside from that fact, we would have to explain how a process calling for a personal decision could ever be quantitatively victorious over a process operating automatically.

And then there is another curious fact. The newly founded Church believed in a total victory of Christ over Adam vis-à-vis humanity as a whole. Yet, at the same time, it tended to identify those who had been converted to Christ with those who had been saved. Paul himself says in his first letter to the Corinthians that God *"chose to save those who have faith by the folly of the Gospel"* (1 Cor. 1:21).

Now it might be very natural for a small community that had only recently come into being to equate salvation with community participation. But it could not have failed to notice the contradiction involved in its assertions. On the one hand it was proclaiming the unrestricted victory of Christ's grace (see Rom. 5:18 or, in more general terms, Rom. 5:15–20). On the other hand it spoke about the rejection of this grace by, and the consequent damnation of, the vast multitude who refused to join the ranks of Christ's disciples (see 2 Cor. 4:3; 1 Cor. 1:18; 2 Cor. 2:15).

So on the one hand we are given the universal victory of Christ as a picture of the goal, and on the other hand membership in the Church and conversion to the gospel message are pictured as the means to this goal. The contradiction necessarily implied in this picture may help to explain the ambivalence that has marked the twenty centuries of church history. On the one hand the Church has laid down heroic and even superhuman demands, calling them essential and indispensable elements of the Christian message and pointing to *the cross*. On the other hand it has desperately and unscrupulously used any and every means to ensure the participation of the masses, that is, of all human beings, in some minimal level of adherence to the gospel message, the faith, and the sacraments; and so we have had the system known as *Christendom*.

It has become customary to divide the history of the Church into two major periods, the pre-Constantinian period and the post-Constantinian period. Now some would suggest that we are entering a third period, or perhaps returning to the hallmarks of the earliest period of the Church. But even though it may be true that the period since Constantine gave the Church the means and the opportunity to stress the second alterna-

tive in a disproportionate way, the basic problem transcends any chrono-
logical or periodic division. So true is this fact that it took a twentieth-
century theologian, Karl Barth, to take clear note of this basic ambivalence or contradiction. And it led him to break with one of the most
fundamental, if not *the* most fundamental doctrine of Luther: the doctrine of justification *by* faith alone. In Barth's eyes, a universal victory of
Christ over Adam implied that even faith ceases to be a precondition for
justification and salvation. For him faith is not *a human disposition for
winning divine salvation* but rather a *recognition of the fact* that redemption
and salvation have been granted to all.

Here I am not interested in criticizing or evaluating that specific
dogmatic position. What does interest me is the impact exerted on theological methodology by the governing supposition that the number of
those converted to some minimal participation in the Church has a direct and proportional relationship to the universal victory of grace and
salvation over sin and death.

Today a directly contrary supposition is steadily gaining ground.
The Church has officially accepted the notion of a salvation plan operating both inside and outside the boundaries of the Church (see *Gaudium et
spes*, n. 22 and *passim*). But the opposed line of thought is now so customary that the new thrust has not freed ecclesial activity from the weight of
an exaggerated sense of responsibility; instead it has provoked a paralyz-
ing crisis regarding the missionary or expansive activity of the Church.
If it is true that the number of those converted to Christian faith and
practice has no direct relationship with the number of the saved, then
why go out and convert people? Why have faith and the Church at all?

We are far from having reached a new consensus on the matter,
which itself proves and points up the ambivalence that has surrounded
the activity of the Church for centuries with respect to masses and
minorities.

Our main interest here is to focus on the historical results of this
age-old vacillation between two irreconcilable poles: a universal plan of
salvation on the one hand, and an inculcation of what are essentially
minority obligations on the other hand. The first historical result was
that the pastoral attempt to identify the number of the faithful members
with the number of the saved totally failed. It could not help but fail.
That was in the cards, so to speak. As the Christian message was more
and more turned into a *mass* reality, it became easier and easier; but at
the same time its value diminished. Christianity became a devalued cur-
rency, as it were, and there was a growing tendency to bolster it with
other values from the outside: e.g., social integration or the secular
benefits of society at large. This approach had only relative success. It

was also evident that as soon as these secular benefits could be won without having to pay heed even to the most minimal exigencies of Christian membership, then the tendency of the masses would be to take the easier way out. This and nothing else has been the origin of what we today refer to as secularism or the process of secularization.

The second historical result was that the continual undermining of what was supposedly an absolute value and goal (salvation) necessarily led to excessive and extreme defensive measures, both in theory and practice. The concepts used to deny or conceal the slippage and the means used to reverse the trend could not help but tend towards a cancerous autonomy. This attempt to find excuses for the defeat of a Christianity that was supposed to be universally victorious was waged heartily *on the theoretical level*. The doctrine of predestination and the Augustinian notion of the "condemned masses" (*massa damnata*) are not so much an interpretation of the Bible as a theoretical reflection of a pastoral defeat. The Church had failed to give Christ a quantitative victory in and through its membership.

Even more than the age of Augustine himself, the Middle Ages in Europe and its cultural system known as Christendom seemed to epitomize a successful attempt to deny the contradiction between minority Christian exigencies and majority numerical membership. But even then the contradiction could only be overlooked, not really overcome. The way to effect this oversight was to disregard the many non-Christian peoples that surrounded Western Europe. And even though the Mediterranean coast helped this process along, some peoples did not let themselves be forgotten so easily. The Muslims, for example, could hardly be expunged from consciousness.

Thus it is not surprising to find curious attempts to rationalize the situation in the Middle Ages, and indeed to convert seeming defeat into an odd sort of victory. The surrounding non-Christian world was minimized and regarded as merely a temporary obstacle. Christianity was pictured as being coextensive with the world itself, or at least with the real civilized world—the Western world. The universal victory of Christ came to be pictured in terms of separation and exclusion. Notice what this medieval hymn to the Archangel Raphael does to the image of Christ as the universal shepherd (John 10:16):

> *Auferte gentem perfidam*
> *Credentium de finibus*
> *Ut omnes unus unicum*
> *Ovile nos Pastor regat.*

> Carry away the infidels
> From the territory of believers,
> So that one Pastor may guide
> Us all, his one and only flock.

This contradiction, even on the theoretical level, continues right down to our own day.

On the practical level, pastoral exasperation is evident in all the unjust, violent, and inhuman means used by Christendom—in some areas at least—to maintain a satisfactory balance between the number of human beings and the number of church members. The Inquisition, the Crusades, and the numerous ghettos are clear indications, not so much of violent or primitive habits, as of a twofold moral criterion and a schizophrenic incoherence. They bear witness to a situation that is known in psychology as the *double bind,* a situation in which one loses all sense of direction because he is compelled to follow two opposing lines of motivation. *The (absolute) end justifies (all) the means:* long before this principle was attributed to Marxist morality, it guided the normal conduct of the Church and those who sought to defend it.

When I said above that the Church used *inhuman* means and justified them in the name of an absolute and universal goal (i.e., salvation), I gave examples that translated "inhuman" into unjust, violent, and barbarous. But the fact is that the inhuman nature of the means used in the pastoral activity of the Church was much more universal, and that it shows up even in countries and ages regarded as highly civilized. And that would of course include our own day. For if we define "inhuman" as anything and everything that diminishes the person and turns him or her into a domesticated one-dimensional being, then the worst contradiction imbedded in the praxis of the Church is the fact that it has tried to achieve liberative ends like those of grace and salvation by mass means that are intrinsically opposed to liberation.

In the United States today, for example, there is growing evidence and growing Christian awareness that a country that contains only six percent of the world's population but annually uses up to forty percent of the world's resources constitutes *by that very fact alone* one of the most inhuman and dehumanizing mechanisms on the face of the earth. But working against this awareness is the fact that the Catholic Church has long used a particular approach to keep up its membership among the successive waves of immigrants. That approach has been to integrate them as fully and completely as possible into that awesomely dehumanizing mechanism which a consumer society represents. So true has this been that the material ostentation of the Catholic pastors caring for these immigrant minorities came to be admired and defended as proof that they had acquired real citizenship and status within the United States system. What is more, one of the most important factors for social adaptation, education, has been employed extensively and fiercely at every grade level to keep up Catholic membership and at the same time provide access to the proper channels within consumer society. Now, in the face of the evident dehumanizing factors, there is a tendency to try to recover the deeper values of critical awareness, justice, and liberation *by using the same educational process.* The assumption seems to be that a means which adapts people to the system can also work in the exactly opposite direction. Thus no serious attention or consideration is given to the notion that Christianity is supposed to be a leaven in the mass, a minority factor in itself. People cling desperately to the old notion of numerical universality centered around the idea of salvation.

And so this basic contradiction has run through the whole history of the Church. It has preached a personal, creative, heroic style of life on the one hand, while utilizing mass mechanisms to ensure a church membership that is equally mass-oriented. Positive acceptance and utilization of mass mechanisms continues to be the guiding norm of its pastoral efforts and the key to any sound comprehension of them.

II. THE SOCIO-POLITICAL FORMULATION OF THE PROBLEM

Is it possible that there is a basic and permanent difference between masses and minorities, between mass lines of conduct and minority lines of conduct? Is it possible that the difference is not one of *mere accident and degree?* This basic issue is a relatively new one that has not been deeply studied as yet. Although people have for some time now been using such terms as "mass man," "elite," and "the masses," the terms seem to apply to new realities spawned by such recent innovations as the mass media, ideologically coercive programs, and coercive political systems.

Be that as it may, the fact is that as far back as 1901 Lenin, faced with the task of plotting out a Marxist revolution for Russia, felt obliged to criticize an overly simplistic view that was making the rounds. This view, either derived from Marx or formulated by some of his "orthodox" followers, maintained that the revolution would be the natural result of the contradictions inherent in capitalism *plus* the spontaneous action (or spontaneity) of the proletariat, of the working *masses* produced by the industrial revolution.

The direction that Lenin would give the revolutionary movement in Russia (where there had been no industrial revolution) was based on the supposition that a *new and decisive factor* for any revolution had appeared on the scene between the time when Marx wrote his books and Lenin was actually trying to bring one about. In his well-known broadside, *What Is To Be Done?* Lenin says this: "That *the mass movement* is a most important phenomenon is a fact about which there can be no dispute. But the crux of the question is, What is the meaning of the phrase: The labour movement will 'determine the tasks'? Either it means subservience to *the spontaneity of this movement,* i.e., reducing the role of Social-Democracy to mere subservience to the labour movement as such. . . or it may mean that *the mass movement* sets before us *new,* theoretical, political, and organizational tasks, *far more complicated* than those that might have satisfied us in the period before the rise of the mass movement." [2]

We are not concerned here with whether Lenin really believed in the *newness* of the mass phenomenon or merely used that as an argument against the claims of an overly literal Marxism. What does concern us here is the fact that Lenin's decision to go with the second alternative would prove to be of decisive importance in the history of socialist societies in this century. Even more important for our purposes here is to find out why the existence of mass movements implies new revolutionary tasks according to Lenin.

The first reason is this: even though Lenin takes for granted the economicist determinism maintained by his adversaries, he can no longer accept the notion that the *consciousness of the masses* turns revolutionary by virtue of the mere fact that it suffers the growing burden of exploitation and begins to feel its own numerical force. Faced with new facts and more recent developments, this notion seems untenable to him: "That is why the question of the relation between *consciousness* and *spontaneity* is of such enormous *general* interest."[3]

If we proceed to ask him why the worker class, as *the masses,* "is able to develop only trade-union consciousness,"[4] and why "the task of Social-Democracy is to combat *spontaneity,* to divert the labour movement, with its spontaneous trade-unionist striving, from under the wing of the bourgeoisie,"[5] he will reply by offering us an analysis of the mechanisms of consciousness and spontaneity on the mass level.

At first glance Lenin seems to localize (revolutionary) *consciousness* in the bourgeois intellectual class. This class possesses the (professional) training and capacity required to grasp the complexity of the social system and to realize that the true interests of the proletariat lie not with trade unionism but with a revolution that will radically alter the existing production system.[6] But if we explore his thought more deeply, we find that Lenin sees the possibilities of revolutionary consciousness associated with something else, with something that goes above and beyond the localization of its agents within the framework of class struggle. There is no doubt that "the theory of Socialism . . . grew out of the philosophic, historical and economic theories that were elaborated by the educated representatives of the propertied classes, the intellectuals. The founders of modern scientific socialism, Marx and Engels, themselves belonged to the bourgeois intelligentsia."[7] But upon closer analysis it becomes quite apparent that it is not class interest as such that makes possible this paradoxical and decisive attitude. In the bourgeoisie, as we shall see, there are what we might call almost "physical" possibilities of escaping from mass movements. In other words, what is essential to the rise of a revolutionary consciousness is not belonging to this or that social class but the potential for being immune to mass tendencies.

Thus Lenin describes mass spontaneity as regulated and determined by the "line of least resistance."[8] Here the physical image of inertia makes a crucial appearance and is applied to the masses. Lenin spells out what this line of spontaneous mass conduct means in the concrete: "Consciousness was completely overwhelmed by spontaneity . . . the spontaneity of those workers who were carried away by the arguments that a kopeck added to a rouble was worth more than socialism and politics, and that they must 'fight, knowing that they are fighting not for some future generation, but for themselves and their children.' "[9]

This particular description is applied to workers, since they are viewed as the ones who should have objective revolutionary interests. In fact it can be used to describe a much broader attitude of man in general. It can be summed up in two terms: *oversimplification*, which makes a kopeck and a rouble more important than socialism and politics; and *immediatism*, which places oneself and one's children above future generations. If the reader prefers, the two aspects can be summed up under one head: *oversimplification* both with regard to the means to be used and to the stages that must be gone through in seeking a solution.

It should not surprise us to find that in the end Lenin sees this mass mechanism present in every social class. Being an intellectual is no guarantee of possessing a truly revolutionary consciousness: "Are there not advanced people, 'average people,' and 'masses,' among the intelligentsia?"[10] Intellectualist predispositions and professional training represent at best a threshold beyond which one is in a better position to acquire the intellectual quality that is crucial for any revolutionary change: i.e., the ability to resist the lure of oversimplification and immediatism in one's conception of the social process. The model here, for Lenin, was undoubtedly Karl Marx—not precisely because he was a member of the bourgeoisie but rather because he was able to picture a revolution for the masses in terms that were not mass-based.

Just about thirty years after Lenin wrote *What Is To Be Done?* José Ortega y Gasset wrote a classic volume entitled *The Revolt of the Masses.* The fact that he used the term "masses" in his title has unfortunately obscured the fact that Lenin paved the way with his treatment of the same subject. And since a certain aristocratic sensibility is clearly evident in Ortega's starting point, this has fostered the misconception that merely posing the whole problem of masses and minorities is indicative of an elitist stance. This misconception might never have arisen if people had noticed the close parallelism between *The Revolt of the Masses* and *What Is To Be Done?*

Certainly one could hardly imagine two more antithetical starting points. Whereas the masses disturb Lenin because they are not spontaneously revolutionary, they seem to disturb Ortega because they revolt against the whole established order. Ortega is annoyed by the crowd, especially by a crowd that has lost all sense of respect for the age-old barriers that separated the qualified man from the man in the street, the aristocracy from the plebs.

Yet whatever our judgment may be on this reaction of Ortega's which serves as the starting point for his book, we must ultimately agree that his analysis of the mass mechanisms of human conduct is far more complex and profound than that; and indeed that he arrives at conclusions that are similar to, if not identical with, those of Lenin. The process of analysis is almost exactly parallel.

Ortega starts out by defining masses and minorities in terms of professional qualification: "Society is always a dynamic unity of two component factors: minorities and masses. The minorities are individuals or groups of individuals which are specially qualified. The mass is the assemblage of persons not specially qualified."[11] Ortega points out that this contrast should not be identified with the contrast between upper social classes and lower social classes. But, like Lenin, he is forced to admit that such qualification is normally bound up with social *status.* Cultural training, profession, and *status* shake hands with each other.

Exploring more deeply, however, Ortega is led to redefine the masses in terms that are more independent of social class. In this emerging type of human being he finds two essential characteristics: "the free expansion of his vital desires, and therefore of his personality; and his radical ingratitude towards all that has made possible the ease of his existence."[12]

To appreciate the thrust of this new definition of mass conduct, one must take careful note of the *neuter* phrasing in the second term: *"all that has made possible."* It is not a matter of being grateful or ungrateful to *those who* have made possible "the free expansion of his vital desires," but rather of being ungrateful to *all that* has made it possible. It is not that the masses do not show gratitude to *the elites,* but rather that they do not appreciate the long, complex, and delicate process that furnishes them with this possibility. And so, with their eyes trained on the future, they are prepared to sacrifice the things of the remote future for the things of the present moment, however critical the former may be.

Seen in this light, Ortega's redefinition of the masses coincides remarkably with the traits spelled out by Lenin: i.e., *oversimplification* and *immediatism.* The "free expansion of. . . vital desires" represents an oversimplification in the use of means as related to ends, and "radical ingratitude" towards the stages involved in the process leads to immediatism in decision-making.

What is more, the physical image of inertia crops up in Ortega's analysis as a parallel to Lenin's reference to "the line of least resistance." One of his chapters is concerned with "why the masses intervene in everything and why their intervention is solely by violence."[13] Ortega goes on to note: "As one advances in life, one realizes that the majority of men—and of women—are incapable of any other effort than that strictly imposed on them as a reaction to external compulsion. And for that reason, the *few* individuals we have come across who are capable of *spontaneous and joyous* effort stand out isolated, monumentalized, so to speak, in our experience. These are the select men, the nobler, the only ones who are active and not merely reactive."[14] Thus, in Ortega's analysis, the notion of social status is replaced gradually by the notion of nobility in his attempt to designate and describe the capacity to get beyond simplistic lines of conduct and engage in real decision-making.

Ortega's description of mass-dominated politics clearly points up the same two traits that Lenin noted, and which led Lenin to reject mass spontaneity as the sole basis for his own line of political action. Here is what Ortega says: "If we observe the public life of the countries where the triumph of the masses has made most advance. . . we are surprised to find that politically they are living from day to day. . . Public authority. . . exists from hand to mouth. . . Its activities are reduced to dodging the difficulties of the hour; not solving them, but escaping from them for the time being, employing any methods whatsoever, even at the cost of accumulating thereby still greater difficulties for the hour which follows. Such has public power always been when exercised directly by the masses: omnipotent and ephemeral."[15]

So Ortega, who had begun with a rather class-based definition of masses and minorities, ends up like Lenin saying almost the exact opposite. He comes to see that professional qualification is synonymous with specialization. And in modern civilization the specialists, with their limited vision and consequent inertia, may well be the ones most likely to propose simplistic, immediatist solutions. Lenin admitted that there were "mass-minded" intellectuals. Ortega is even more pointed: "And now it turns out that the actual scientific man is the prototype of the mass-man."[16]

Thus both Lenin and Ortega find that mass conduct is dominated by *inertia*. Quantitatively speaking, it cannot possibly arrive at the more complex and intermediate solutions that will truly contribute to the solution of social problems. Are they not both saying, by implication at least, that the proportion existing between masses and minorities constitutes an inescapable law governing the human world, just as the law of inertia in the strict sense governs the physical universe? We shall explore this suggestive question, this basic hypothesis, in the next section.

III. THE SCIENTIFIC FORMULATION OF THE PROBLEM

I said earlier that the problem of masses versus minorities was a relatively new one. Of course it has been considered many times in the past. The point here is that it is only recently that discussion of the issue has pointed towards some universal constant. This begins to show up more clearly when we begin to talk of the difference between masses and minorities in terms of such physical images as that of *inertia*.

People can certainly manipulate inertia. Indeed sometimes it seems as if they can actually do violence to it, forcing it to allow them to produce and even speed up movement. At first glance this would seem to represent a negation of inertia. In fact it is not, for such achievements do not really change the basic law symbolized by the term "inertia." No manipulation of the laws of inertia creates the least amount of *anti-inertia* in any absolute sense, such as that which would be embodied in initiating some form of perpetual motion within the context of known physical conditions, for example.

Of course we are using imagery when we apply a term like "inertia" to the realm of human conduct, and it is always hazardous to move directly from imagery to reality itself. But if we are going to envision the world in evolutionary terms, then it seems to me that we must assume that certain mechanisms valid in the realm of natural physics find at least analogous extension on the higher levels of life such as that of human living.

It is curious to note how we operate, or refuse to operate, with such ideas. The notion of universal evolution is now supported by a wealth of data, of indirect data at the very least. It would be rather anachronistic for anyone with some medium level of education to think in purely fixist terms or to deny that *homo* is the product of evolution among one or more branches of the mammalian class. Yet we are not often willing to accept the logical consequences entailed in such a view, nor is it very easy for us to develop and accept the mental attitudes that would dovetail with such implications.

For example, if one does think in terms of *universal evolution,* then it is logically impossible to deny that certain laws operative in the realm of inert matter can and do have an impact on the human realm also. It is equally illogical to acknowledge the impact of those laws in some cases but to maintain that certain spheres of human activity are immune to those laws—as if they operated on sources of energy coming from some different or antithetical galaxy. This obligation of consistency, of scientific consistency for sure, has nothing to do with a simplistic materialism that would reduce all existing phenomena to merely mechanistic processes. Teilhard de Chardin has made that very clear.

The way that most sociologists view the problem of masses versus minorities is a clear example of this lack of *consistency* in our thinking. Most sociologists view them either as two separate species existing as such since the appearance of *homo* or as the accidental result of a specific culture or social system.

The truth is very different. Masses and minorities have an intimate tie-up and relationship with the quantitative laws that are evident in what we, perhaps too loosely, call the realm of *mere* matter, of purely physical, inorganic matter. Three general facts hold pervasive sway in regard to the energy of this matter, falling under what is often called the laws of thermodynamics.

The first fact is the conservation of energy. The very same quantity of energy is present in every segment and in the totality of the evolutionary process. The world has evolved from inert matter to the most complex activities of man by employing the exact same *quantum* of energy. It has not received any injection of new energy, but neither has it lost the least unit of existing energy.

The second fact, a corollary of the first, is that the difference between *all* existing beings—ranging from rocks to persons—does not lie in the fact that the higher beings have a greater supply of energy at their disposal. The difference lies in the fact that the higher beings display a different distribution and specialization of the very same quantum of energy. Thus a human being represents a special—not abnormal —distribution of energy. Much of the energy supplied by molecules and cells is disproportionately distributed to the nervous system, and to the brain in particular.

Needless to say, this "unbalanced" distribution of energy undermines other possible functions and potentialities. Other beings, with different distributions of energy, seem to be clearly superior to man with regard to these deprived functions. But the complex and specialized concentration of energy takes its revenge. While a being who displays such specialization may seem weak in many areas, it manages to place the energy of other beings at its disposal and thus to overcome its weaknesses. Man cannot run as fast as a horse, but he can manufacture "horsepower" to transport him at much greater speed. Rather than talking about victory or revenge here, we would perhaps do better to talk about a certain dynamic complementarity, about an unstable equilibrium, about a dialectic. What should be clear in any case is that man's higher activities, however sublime they may seem, do not possess some peculiar energy of their own that stands over against material energy. They are grounded on the same general, constant quantum of energy; and they are conditioned by an elemental distribution of energy which psychologists might call "instinct" and sociologists might call "economic production." Henceforth even the grace of God and all the matters that concern theology should be contemplated in terms of the constant quantum of energy in the universe.[17]

The third fact, which also has gained general acceptance, is the continual *degradation of energy*, of the quantitatively constant supply of energy in the evolving universe. While the quantity of energy remains the same in absolute terms, we find on the qualitative level that the more simple and immediate sources of energy give out on us with use. We can explain this seeming contradiction as follows. With each use or exercise of energy, the quantum of energy remains the same in absolute terms but it is transformed into other forms of energy that are "degraded," that are more simple, diffuse, and unusable. Ultimately it is transformed into heat, the most degraded of all the forms of energy.

Consider, for example, the use of energy by a steam locomotive. The energy produced by the combustion of coal takes the form of steam expansion which ultimately moves the wheels of the locomotive. Some portion of the energy produced, however, is immediately degraded into heat. When all the coal is consumed, the energy in the form of steam and in the form of wheel traction also comes to an end. But the same quantity of energy is still at work, only now it has been transformed wholly into heat. This heat seeps out into the surrounding air and eventually becomes "irrecoverable." Similarly, if we are talking about a nuclear explosion, we can say that *everything* remains and that *nothing* remains after ten or fifteen years. In quantitative terms, everything remains: heat still remains, but it has been diffused far and wide. In qualitative terms, nothing remains that could move even the tiniest weight.

Thus energy, like matter (with which it seems to be identified insofar as science is concerned), evinces the same irreversible tendency or quantitative determinism towards simpler forms of synthesis that are mere aggregations of identical elements. This degradational tendency or determinism is readily translated into numerical terms: the more complex and specialized forms of energy, the richest forms of synthesis, are a minority in the universe. The energy combination that gives rise to a living being is infinitely more improbable and less numerous than the energy arranged in very simple forms and immediately available as inorganic matter. And man is an infinitesimal minority within the larger and seemingly infinite minority of living beings.

We cannot move right ahead and scientifically classify human beings as masses or minorities because this numerical law holds true within each and every individual as well. An obvious consequence of our remarks so far is that each human individual is subject to the same economy of energy that regulates the whole universe. The form of energy that characterizes man *as man* may be complex and very specialized, but it remains basically subject to the energy price that must be paid when one is dealing with a constant supply of energy. A genius depends on, and is subject to, his digestive system. Heroic conduct in politics depends on the mechanization of an infinitely greater number of lines of conduct in other areas.[18] In other words, no one can escape the basic law. We are all bound in solidarity to the quantitative factor as individuals, groups, and societies. Or, to put it another way, any *complex and mediate* solution is the apex of a pyramid made up of many *simple and immediate* solutions to the problems of existence at every level.

If we recall that both Lenin and Ortega decried *oversimplification* and *immediatism* in mass lines of conduct, we can readily see that the phenomenon of masses is not new or recent in itself. What is new is the manifold external manifestations of uniformity that have been made possible by the dimensions and the instruments of modern society. But the basic fact or reality is as old as the world. *Masses* and *minorities* are precisely what they are because they represent the two necessary poles of the economy of energy that rules the universe. They are the quantitative and qualitative poles present in any and every human group, *but equally present in the patterns of conduct of each and every human individual.*

Thus masses and minorities are as eternal as the numerical inferiority of life to inorganic matter.[19] And the same proportion will inevitably be found to exist between some form of love that represents a real synthesis of personal centers (hence a rich and costly synthesis of energy) on the one hand and instinctual, mechanical, one-dimensional lines of conduct on the other hand. In order to save energy for attitudes we value more highly in existence, *we choose not to choose* in most of the rest of our lines of conduct. Freedom entails a high energy cost,[20] and that cost brings us into fellowship with individual and group mechanisms.

On the basis of the data outlined above, I think we can proceed to draw four fundamental conclusions concerning masses and minorities:

1. *Quantitatively* speaking, the economy of energy operative at every level of the universe with a constant supply of energy determines that the vast *majority* of activities—ranging from physical to psychological—will follow *the line of least resistance.* This means that at every level statistics will indicate a majority of reactions directed mechanically towards the simplest and most immediate solutions. And when we are talking about *human* attitudes and lines of conduct, this same statistical viewpoint will inevitably be translated into the notion of *masses,* of a majority line of conduct aimed at the least possible expenditure of energy. Unless he or she were a "mass man" in some way and cooperated with masses, no human being could go on living or *advance* towards qualitatively rich, minority lines of conduct.

2. Without ruling out, on scientific grounds, the possibility of a total massification of man,[21] we can say that the majority of human beings accept the condition of saving energy for select fields of richer and more complex personal conduct: love, marriage, family life, professional work, and so forth. This economy can only be effected by letting one's conduct in other fields run in channels of low energy cost and seeking simple, immediate solutions for problems as they arise. Quantitatively speaking, what Ortega says of the masses is true of everything in the universe: we all live from day to day. Even when we deliberate, the result of that deliberation is usually a simple equation between available energy and external urgency. There is no scientific value at all in dividing human beings into masses and minorities *without specifying* what fields or attitudes or activities we are talking about. All of us human beings are, by definition, masses and minorities. "The people" are neither more "mass" nor more "minority" than the "elites" that govern them, exploit them, or give them expression.

3. Only this universal economy of energy makes possible the existence of *human sciences.* Only it enables us to translate statistical norms and forecasts to the realm of human decision-making, a realm from which a misguided brand of spiritualism thinks it should exclude scientific analysis for the sake of the freedom of the individual human being.

If a Gallup pre-election poll has a definite and high chance of predicting the future conduct of the electors, who are supposedly free, it is because the economy of energy tells us that the majority of the electors will not expend large amounts of energy to review and revise their political analyses and options unless striking new factors enter the picture. Without such a general underlying supposition of this sort, there would be no basis for any human *science* whatsoever.[22]

4. It should not surprise us, then, that the sense and value of our energy investments—the energy saved in more or less mechanized lines of conduct—depends on the level of mass mechanization. An important mathematical discovery, for example, is minority by definition. But the *probability* of its occurrence will be in direct proportion to the level of mass education in mathematics. There is always the possibility, of course, that some genius may live largely independent of his or her milieu; but it is not very probable. Even such a genius, should he or she wish to keep making forward progress, would feel a growing need for generalized knowledge data if for no other reason than to save time and energy in acquiring data that is needed. Thus the genius too would be obliged to get involved in shared solidarity and the services it offers—*not in spite of but precisely because of* its mass nature.[23]

Here is another example. If family love is to be fruitful, complex, and provident, it must entail the suppression of many primary reactions both inside and outside the home. In other words, it calls for the acceptance of a high degree of complexity and the rejection of much immediatism on the level of what is called "good education." And the latter is basically nothing else but a mass mechanism for saving energy, however much it may vary on different social levels or among different social classes.

To put this in more abstract terms, we can say that the whole theme of masses and minorities in no way leads to a canonization of "the survival of the fittest." It is not elitist, aristocratic, or antipopulist. Nor should it be erased from our thinking so that we might be able to think "for and with the people." We must not give it up for the sake of some antiscientific utopia that would purport to generalize typically minority patterns of behavior into mass patterns. A sound, integrated view of this whole topic would lead us to the conclusion that any and all minority growth simultaneously conditions and is conditioned by a rise in the level of mass conduct. And that signifies a *cultural revolution.* No cultural revolution is possible, by the same token, unless energy is expended by a minority that has distanced itself from mechanized thinking and feeling wherever the latter may be located, *perhaps even in "the people."*

Only if we keep these four conclusions in mind can we escape the verbal terrorism that surrounds discussions of the interaction between masses and minorities—in both the political field and the theological field. And the question of this interaction is one of the most crucial we now face.

The fact is that the "mass media" are used deliberately, along with other mass mechanisms, to keep the dispossessed classes passive and tranquilized. For this reason the political right usually refuses to get involved in this whole problem of masses versus minorities or to bring it up, since the logical conclusion would be that the same terms can be applied equally to the "elites" who hold power. Only in moments of radical crisis has the right appealed to these terms to justify, against all logic, its right to hold power and exercise it.

By the same token the left feels obligated to speak in the name of the people's interests as if the "silent majority" shared its own values and antagonisms. Hence the left is even more viscerally opposed to making a distinction between mass and minority lines of conduct than the right is. In circles that define themselves by using such terms as "vanguard" or "conscience" of the proletariat, the adjective "elitist" is used to automatically disqualify any attempt to make a careful and precise study of the interaction between masses and minorities in the revolutionary process. Paradoxical as it may seem, such circles prefer to assume and maintain—for outside consumption at least—that the masses will acquire the necessary "awareness" and join the vanguard through a gradual but steady process. But the fact is that any and every mass organization is based on very different assumptions, the latter being explicated by the leaders only behind closed doors.

Consider the leftist revolutionary processes that took place in Cuba and Chile, for example. (The latter is particularly revealing by virtue of the "spontaneity" that gave these processes legality.) Both show us the same thing. Whereas *the masses* expect the revolution to redistribute the wealth, to greatly diminish the most cruel features of work, and to provide greater freedom for discussion of such conditions among trade unions, the minority groups directing the revolution rack their brains trying to figure out how to bring this mass image in line with the harsh conditions entailed in any radical change of the economic system amid the realities of the international political situation today. In the first stages at least, success may call for state ownership of the national wealth, even harder work from the laboring class, and a diminution in the freedom and demands of trade unions.

It should be obvious that the "elite" groups who lead the revolution, and who are aware of the complexity and the stages involved, can easily *fall back into* mass attitudes. They may surrender to the conception that the masses have of the revolution, or they may take the other easy way out of merely prolonging and extending the coercion that was imposed on the masses in the first difficult stages of the revolutionary process. In the latter connection it is worth noting the turn that Lenin's own thought took. In *What Is To Be Done?* he sought to distance himself from mass spontaneity. In another work,[24] written near the end of his life, he called for a "cultural revolution" in the face of the new postrevolutionary massification. That might also explain the burning interest displayed in the discussions between Che Guevara and other Marxists regarding the possibility of introducing a radical transformation into the motivations of the masses for the work in Cuba. It seems Che Guevara could not decide *a priori* whether his position was an excessively minority stand (because it did not take due account of the human economy of energy) or a realistic forecast of the inevitable massification that would take place in postrevolutionary patterns of conduct.

But if this problem is a crucial one for any and every political process, it certainly is just as crucial for any liberation theology. Whether they realize it or not, theologies will be methodologically distinct and opposed depending on the way in which they tend to relate the Christian message to either mass or minority ideas and lines of conduct.

IV. THE BIBLICAL RESPONSE

If we make a quick survey of the Scriptures to find some possible link with the problem under discussion, we will find that the biblical response is clear-cut. It can be summed up in these words of Joseph Ratzinger:

> Essential to the one and only salvation plan of God is a correlation between "the little flock" and "the multitude." The two terms exist *for each other*. This correlation is one aspect of the way in which God saves the world; it does not represent a *failure* of the divine will. . . It is quite clear from Scripture that God divides humanity into two groups, one being "the little flock" and the other being the vast "multitude." The point is made repeatedly in the Scriptures: "The gate that leads to life is small and the road is narrow, and those who find it are *few*" (Matt. 7:14); "labourers are *scarce*" (Matt. 9:37); "For though many are invited, *few* are chosen" (Matt. 22:14); "Have no fear, *little flock*" (Luke 12:32). And Jesus himself gives up his life as a ransom for "many" (Mark 10:45).[25]

Ratzinger's conclusions dovetail with those we arrived at in the preceding section. This biblical division between "the many" and "the few" is not "elitist": "God does not divide humanity thus to save the few and hurl the many into perdition. Nor does he do it to save the many *in an easy way* and the few *in a hard way*. Instead we could say that he uses the numerical few as a leverage point for raising up the many."[26]

It must be pointed out that Ratzinger uses only a few explicit passages in Scripture dealing with this problem to formulate his position. He does not allude to other passages that are even more profound even though less explicit. Let us consider some of them here.

We know, for example, that the final redaction of the Synoptic Gospels postdates the main corpus of Paul's thought, and that the latter is centered around the *grace* of God. As Paul sees it, the whole life of the Christian depends on a *gratuitous* grant, a gift, a grace. This gratuitous gift, in turn, makes human beings capable of loving. And love, as John the Evangelist will spell out more fully later on, is the very essence and life of God. In other words, God's gratuitous gift makes human beings capable of something that is analogous if not identical: i.e., capable of gratuitousness (love = gratuitousness = grace).

Thus the term *grace* (Greek *charis*) and its theological import was already central to the Christian community even before the language and terminology of the four Gospels was fixed in written form. Indeed the Synoptic Gospels seem to offer clear witness that Paul's theological language on the matter of grace was not literally that of Jesus. Only Luke places the word *grace* (Greek *charis*) on Jesus' lips, and he was probably influenced by Pauline theology. Luke does so four times, and on three of them the term clearly has a direct relationship to the "extra" that Jesus demands of his followers above and beyond adherence to the legislation of the Old Testament: "If you love only those who love you, what credit [Greek *charis*] is that to you? Even sinners love those who love them. Again, if you do good only to those who do good to you, what credit [Greek *charis*] is that to you? Even sinners lend to each other to be repaid in full" (Luke 6:32–34; see also 17:9).

Whether the word "grace" was used by Jesus himself here is a moot point. The important thing is that Luke's passage serves to build a bridge between the theological vocabulary of Paul on the one hand and that of Matthew on the other. Matthew does not attribute the word "grace" as such to Jesus, and so it is interesting to look at the parallel text in his Gospel to see what term or expression he used in the same context. And the word he tends to use in the same context is "extraordinary" or other equivalent expressions: "And if you greet only your brothers, what is there *extraordinary* about that?" (Matt. 5:47). Furthermore, the people whom Luke describes as "sinners," that is, people who are capable of a love that is simplistic and centered around immediate returns, are described by Matthew as "publicans" and "pagans."

Synthesizing all this data, we can readily see that in Matthew's eyes "grace" is designed to turn the followers of Christ into "extraordinary" lovers. And the extraordinary element lies in the ability to get beyond the oversimplistic and immediatist mechanisms that are habitually used to solve problems posed by interpersonal relationships. The usual tendency is to reply to others in kind. In the Gospels this mechanical brand of love is regarded as a sin, as the hallmark of sinners, as opposed to a gratuitous, freely proffered love. In other words, Christians are asked to defy the statistical laws in this area, to be extraordinary lovers, to be a "minority" in this respect. They are asked to respond to the freely proffered love of One who is gratuitous giving itself.

Another passage in the Synoptic Gospels that classical exegesis tends to bypass too quickly is the one that recounts the meeting between Jesus and the rich young man (Luke 18:18–26; Mark 10:17–27; Matt. 19:16–26). The question of the young man is clear enough: "Good Master, what must I do to win eternal life?" The *first portion* of Jesus' answer is also clear, but it has often been interpreted as his complete answer when it is not: "You know the commandments." The young man replies that he has kept all of them since he was a boy. Accepting this as fact, Jesus then goes on to offer the *second part* of his answer to *the very same question:* "There is still one thing lacking." In other words, there is still one thing lacking if the young man wants to possess eternal life. Jesus is not offering a "counsel"; he is stipulating a condition that must be met if one wants to have eternal life! One must put love to work in very concrete terms, beginning with those who are in dire need and using all the means at one's disposal.

Neither Jesus nor his disciples regarded this stipulation as a mere "counsel." They saw it as a strict condition that had to be met in order to possess eternal life. The dialogue that follows in the Gospel account proves this clearly: "When Jesus saw it he said, 'How hard it is for the wealthy *to enter the kingdom of God!* It is easier for a camel to go through the eye of a needle than for a rich man *to enter the kingdom of God.*' Those who heard asked, 'Then who can *be saved?*' " (Luke 18:24–26).

Even the ten commandments alone seem to add tremendous complications to the life of the "mass man" who resides in each one of us. They seem to be an almost intolerable burden. But Jesus' demands begin *above and beyond* those commandments, above and beyond the level of merely mechanical fulfillment of the law.

Paul develops this point in his letters to the Galatians and the Romans. He pictures Christians as people who have been liberated from the law in order to carry out the complex demands of truly creative love. Since human society passes laws and expects almost automatic submission to them, Paul's view envisions a human community that will pass critical judgment on societal laws and structures instead of passively submitting to them. In terms of the economy of energy such a group must pay a high cost in energy expenditure and cannot help but be a minority. If *per impossible* its attitude were to become a general one, that would not be a miracle but rather a disaster.

An exegesis of the term "world" in John's theology will reveal the same antinomy between quantitative laws and qualitative laws in Christian conduct. In John's eyes, "the world" is a closed circle where mechanical lines of conduct prevail. Christ challenges these conservative mechanisms and tries to inject a creative crisis. He turns a spotlight on this sort of praxis, which involves only a low energy cost. He gives the same mission to his disciples, warning them that this conservative praxis will defend itself with all the means at its disposal and put the whole weight of its numerical superiority against the critical light of the gospel message. If Jesus can truthfully say, "I have conquered the world" (John 16:33), it is because his victory is a qualitative one. And the price he must pay for it is his own death—in other words, defeat on the quantitative level.

His disciples will be faced with the same equation in the future. While not belonging to "the world" (John 15:19; 17:14), they will remain in it—loving this "world" that is the dwelling place constructed by mankind (John 17:15; 17:18; 3:16). The tension between these two poles is something that only a minority can bear in a continuing way. Indeed it is what *constitutes* a minority as such.

We could look at other passages here (Matt. 10:16–37; 11:12; etc.). We could go into an exegetical analysis of such images as "leaven" and "salt" in the Synoptics, and "the flesh" in Paul's writings. But I think we have done enough exegesis to prove the following points:

1. The exigencies of the gospel message are *minority* exigencies by their very nature and definition.

2. This does not point towards the maintenance of the interests of a small, self-enclosed group but rather towards the liberation of humanity—of the masses.

3. The liberation in question does not entail destroying the quantitative proportion existing between masses and minorities, since that remains equally operative in the Christian life. Still less does it entail reducing the exigencies of the gospel message to some minimal mass level so as to win the adhesion of the masses.

4. This minority effort among the masses is not meant to impose elitist demands on the latter, nor is it meant to construct a society based on minority exigencies. The aim is to create, for oneself and others, new forms of energy that will permit lines of conduct that are necessarily mechanized to serve as the basis for new and more creative possibilities of a minority character in each and every human being.

V. HERMENEUTIC CONSEQUENCES

Systematic suspicion would seem to be an integral part of the hermeneutic circle of any liberated and liberating theology. Such a theology must ever suspect that theology, both in its academic and its experiential forms, has been sidetracked towards mass ends; and that this has led to a corresponding distortion of its content materials. Operationally speaking, therefore, a theology of liberation must feel some obligation to take on the task of restoring authenticity to the Christian faith. For the latter, thanks to the wayward tendencies described above, has been turned into mere infantilism and abject submission to the established order.

This latter point, however, is far from gaining unreserved acceptance, even among people who support liberation theology in Latin America. Some would attempt to set up a typology that would make a clear distinction between various brands of liberation theology; and the basis of distinguishing between them would be whether they propose commitments of a mass nature or commitments of a minority nature.

César Aguiar, a Uruguayan sociologist, thinks that the two basic tendencies can be clearly distinguished by asking oneself whether a given theology of liberation makes *a mature faith* a basic prerequisite or not. He writes:

> Another dividing line between groups of Latin American Catholics was that of differing convictions about the elites and the masses, the minorities and majorities, the faithful remnant and the people at large. Starting about 1960, certain advanced thinkers in the Latin American Church become convinced of the need for a personal, "adult and mature" faith. Their strong views on the crisis of Christianity and the need for a freely accepted Catholicism made them focus on the formation of elites, small nuclei of slowly and carefully prepared Christians, solid in their faith and aware of its theological implications. . . . Their stress on communitarian life, and on maturity, led them to emphasize the training of small groups, usually somewhat apart from the Church's official pastoral programs.[27]

Several points can be seen in the passage just cited. The first is brought out explicitly. It is clear that Latin American liberation theology did not arise as a new (pastoral) approach to the masses. It was a new way of exploring the political content of the faith and the risky commitment entailed. The second point is implied in what Aguiar says. The relatively "small" and "marginal" character of the groups who were influenced by this new theology was not due to their own choice. It was the logical consequence of another factor that should be added to the one noted above: except in rare and exceptional cases, the official Church did not adopt as its own pastoral programs that had liberation content in them. Even the declarations of the Medellín Conference did not produce any decisive changes in this respect. That accounts for the small and marginal nature of the groups, to which Aguiar alludes. The Church ambitiously hoped to be liberation-oriented on the one hand, and to be able to rely on mass adhesion on the other. In practice this came down to opting for the second alternative. With the passage of time and a change in overall circumstances, the numerical proportions might well change. But the point is that the "elitism" to which Aguiar refers above was not deliberately desired or chosen by those who opted for liberation theology.

And here I should like to add a third factor of my own which I think should be taken into account. The ambivalent position of liberation theology vis-à-vis ecclesiastical structures, its uncertain position between acceptance on the one hand and mistrust or neglect on the other, meant that the groups influenced by this theology developed *within* the Church rather than outside the Church as heretical groups. There was no break or rupture. These groups sought to grow, and for their growth they took advantage of all the means supplied by a Church that was structured for the sake of the masses and directed towards the latter.

This point is important because Aguiar uses this fact to label Gustavo Gutiérrez as the leading proponent of the "mass" faction of liberation theology—simply because Gustavo Gutiérrez has been sensitive enough to take note of the undeniable reality of the situation. In support of his view, Aguiar cites these words of Gutiérrez: "Certain criticisms can be raised about those pastoral programs devoted to minorities. The masses were less important—maybe because in our continent two other pastoral efforts were directed toward them: that of 'Christianity' and that of the 'new Christianity.' . . . One might wonder, though, what that pastoral attitude would have done about the masses if nobody were caring for them. It would seem that in some cases that attitude was a parasite on the others."[28]

As a sample of the "elitist" faction of liberation theology and how it thinks, Aguiar refers to one of my books. And he says: "The political stance of militant Catholics of this elitist mentality varied from person to person. In any event, some of them were wary, skeptical about Christians being involved in political activity because politics is a matter for the masses."[29]

Aguiar's argument to prove the existence of a dividing line between two basic tendencies in liberation theology is grounded wholly on a misunderstanding of both my position and that of Gutiérrez. Gutiérrez, for example, simply points up an evident fact: that liberation theology grew up in a Church with mass-oriented tendencies, structures, and pastoral activities. But this conditioning factor does not imply, in the eyes of Gutiérrez, that liberation theology has something of a guilt complex about dividing up the energy supply which was once wholly directed to maintaining the religion of the Latin American masses. The antiliberation impact of this mass-directed energy is clearly and force-fully criticized in his book entitled *A Theology of Liberation*. And anyone who reads his book can see that the theological development of which he speaks, and which he supports, will entail a maturation of faith. It will not come about simply through mass contagion.

As far as my own position is concerned, I think the reader can readily see that Aguiar has misunderstood it. There is no politics without mass-es. But neither is there any politics without minorities. The fact that the gospel message is not in itself an instrument that the masses can use politically to achieve their ends does not turn Christians into apolitical beings who focus their narrow gaze on purely nontemporal values.

These remarks should show that Aguiar is off the track. The dividing line that he seeks to draw between various theological and pastoral methodologies connected with the rise of liberation theology simply does not exist. Indeed there is a touch of irony in the fact that the very same Gustavo Gutiérrez, whom Aguiar sees as the leader of the mass-oriented faction of liberation theology, has recently been attacked as an "elitist" by a young Argentinian theologian named Ernesto López Rosas. He speaks from the standpoint of liberation theology, calling for its "further de-velopment and deepening in and through the Peronist experience."[30]

There is much more than irony in his article, however. Indeed the irony applies only to the typology that Aguiar attempts to set up. The fact is that the article written by López Rosas provides us with a clue to the real dividing line here, linking it up specifically with the matter we have been discussing in this chapter. The only really new thing in his article is his boldness in passing judgment on the theological work of Gutiérrez. His own position is not original in itself, and we have touched upon it earlier when we discussed the position of Adolfo Büntig.

In a key passage relating to his critique of Gutiérrez, López Rosas complains that "nowhere does Gutiérrez spell out an adequate concept of the people."[31] Here I would like the reader to remember that Büntig did not so much set store on popular *religiosity* or popular *Catholicism* as see value in the *popular* factor as such. Thus the religion of the masses is valuable in his eyes insofar as it is "of the people."

The point here is that in certain parts of Latin America,[32] and par-ticularly in Argentina thanks to the Perón phenomenon, there is de-veloping a "theology of the people." This theology is subsumed under the more general heading of "liberation theology" and is regarded by its proponents as a further and deeper development of the latter.

This new phenomenon should not be regarded as mere ecclesiastical demagoguery. To fully appreciate it, one must take note of certain im-portant political facts and events. Perhaps it is summed up best in the remark that President Perón made to the Movement of Priests for the Third World, and which the latter made its own: "For the first time the mass action of the people is coinciding with the gospel message."[33]

Now if we consider the gospel message as a "religious" element, then it is clear that the mass action of the people and the gospel message were tailored to each other in the cultural system known as Christendom. The importance of Perón's remark lies in the fact that he is referring to the gospel message as a political leaven. And he says that this leaven is coinciding with the mass action of the people *for the first time* in history.

Here Perón is apparently alluding not only to the present but to an ongoing tendency in past history. The implication is that one can prove that in the past the majority of the Argentinian people always followed those leaders who stood for the best potential of the nation—over against the small backroom cliques who wanted to keep a firm grip on power. In other words the (numerical) majority instinctively followed the most fruitful and promising long-range tendencies, whereas the governing minorities followed the simplistic and immediatist line of least resistance.

Does this view give the lie to what we have said about the economy of energy that pervades the universe? Be that as it may, it certainly seems to represent some form of "popular messianism" that parallels the "proletarian messianism" of Marx. And it stands directly over against the notion of a "false popular awareness" that parallels the "false proletarian awareness" which forced Lenin to have reservations about the spontaneity of the masses. The assumption is that once this latent popular majority finds a leader to carry it to power—Perón in this case—the same sound instinct that guided it in the past will keep it on the right track in the future. Only now it will operate in and through the leader who gave it expression and who has provided it with the instruments of power that will allow for fulfillment and complete expression.

I think that this chapter has provided the reader with enough data to form a judgment on the credibility of that position. What I want to do here is to point up certain methodological consequences for theology that flow from this viewpoint or position. Three points should be made.

Firstly, this position or conception proves, by a *reductio ad absurdum,* the point I was trying to make when I refused to follow Assmann all the way in his claim that there was no "specifically Christian contribution" prior to the revolutionary struggle itself. Suppose that one is somewhat doubtful that Peronism as such is to be equated *à outrance* with what Assmann calls "the one and only revolutionary process." Indeed I think Assmann himself would be the first to entertain such doubts. Well, in that case there are only two possible ways to decide the matter. Either one commits the sin of having recourse to some *a priori* ideological "contribution," be it Christian or not. Or else one takes the equally sinful tack of deciding the issue on the basis of minority or elitist motivations, not by merely tuning in to the people.

If, on the other hand, we take for granted the participation of Christians in this revolutionary process, then how can we call it a unique or unitary process when the dissensions are clearly visible? The "specifically Christian contribution" not only ceases to be *prior;* it ceases to exist at all. If the criterion governing an authentic revolutionary process lies in the qualities of the people, then only two pathways are open to us. On the one hand we can make an act of faith, which is hardly scientific much less Christian, and decide that Christianity is to be borne along by the numerical majority of people through some sort of "pre-established harmony." We must have faith that this majority will ever remain immune to bourgeois tendencies, deviant thrusts, and corruption by their leaders. Or, on the other hand, in the name of Christian values we must voice pertinent criticisms *against* the popular majority and their spontaneous feelings—which would call into question the very basis of one's adherence.

Secondly, from a more strictly methodological viewpoint, a "theology of the people" would seem to lead us towards a hermeneutic circle that could very well enrich such a theology and keep it vital. For one of the most fruitful suspicions from the methodological standpoint results from comparing a culture that is logically and conceptually structured in a tight-knit way with the wisdom of the common people, the content of their rituals and imaginative creations, and the internal logic of their strangest attitudes.

Thus we have reason to believe that we are confronted here with a hermeneutic circle that is rich in promise. If that promise fails to be realized, it will be due to the fact that we have wholly identified the exigencies of the gospel message with the popular wisdom and thus ceased to hold before us a *twofold* norm—which Cone rightly insists upon for any black theology of liberation. If the Christian message is wholly identified or equated with a specific cultural wisdom, then it will be reduced to the point where a serious, creative return to its own sources will be entirely ruled out. For these sources will cease to be normative, since they logically cannot be wholly identified with popular awareness as such.

Thirdly, and finally, from the preceding remarks it should be clear that the methodology of an ever more liberated and liberating theology is not an emotional sinecure. One cannot simply utter the word "liberation" and then link it up with the Scriptures in more or less slipshod fashion. Neither is it an ingenuous approach that allows the theologian to take the easy way out that is often taken by academic theology. For it does not allow theologians to set aside the great problems of today on the pretext that they belong to other fields or disciplines. Instead it forces them to confront the major problems of history, biology, evolution, social change, and so forth.

NOTES

1. In postpaschal passages which in themselves would call for more detailed exegesis: Matt. 28:16–20; Mark 16:9–20; Luke 24:47.

2. V.I. Lenin, *What Is To Be Done?*, Eng. trans. (New York: International Publishers, 1929), p. 46.

3. *Ibid.*, p. 31.

4. *Ibid.*, pp. 32–33.

5. *Ibid.*, p. 41.

6. See *ibid.*, p. 33.

7. *Ibid.*

8. *Ibid.*, p. 42.

9. *Ibid.*, p. 38.

10. *Ibid.*, p. 122.

11. José Ortega y Gasset, *The Revolt of the Masses*, Eng. trans. (New York: W.W. Norton, 1932), p. 13.

12. *Ibid.*, p. 63.

13. See *ibid.*, Chapter 8: "Why the Masses Intervene in Everything and Why Their Intervention Is Solely by Violence."

14. *Ibid.*, pp. 71–72.

15. *Ibid.*, pp. 52–53.

16. *Ibid.*, p. 120.

17. See Gordon D. Kaufman, *God the Problem* (Cambridge: Harvard University Press, 1972), especially Chapters 6 and 8.

18. This same basic ambivalence between the qualitative and the quantitative can be found in other realms. Mircea Eliade finds it, for example, in the realm of religion. There man tends to fashion "centres of the sacred." "Although the 'centre' is conceived as being 'somewhere' where only the few who are initiated can hope to enter, yet every house is, none the less, thought of as being built *at this same centre of the world.* We may say that one group of traditions evinces man's desire to place himself at the 'centre of the world' *without any effort*, while another

stresses the *difficulty*, and therefore the *merit*, of attaining it" (Mircea Eliade, *Patterns in Comparative Religion,* Eng. trans. [New York: Sheed and Ward, 1958], pp. 382–83).

Eliade does not have anything to say as to which tradition is the more pristine and original one, but he does say this: "Man's desire to place himself naturally and permanently in a sacred place, in the 'centre of the world,' was easier to satisfy in the framework of the older societies than in the civilizations that have come since. Indeed this result *became harder and harder to achieve.* The myths about 'heroes' who alone are in a position to enter a 'centre' became commoner *as the civilizations producing them became more developed*" (*ibid.,* p. 383).

19. As the notion of the superego suggests, reason can extend and confirm this inorganic, regressive tendency of the instincts. For an example of this in the realm of religion, consider this remark of Eliade concerning the human tendency to facilitate the construction of, and entrance into, "centres of the sacred." "Almost everywhere in the history of religion we have come across the phenomenon of an 'easy' imitation of the archetype which I have termed *infantilism. . .* Infantilism almost always has a character of *facility*, of *automatism. . .* But there is something else: *the desire to make all creation one and do away with multiplicity.* This desire is also, in its own way, an imitation of the activity of reason since reason also tends to unify reality—a tendency which, carried to an extreme, would *abolish Creation;* however, the creations of the subconscious and the infantilization of hierophonies are rather more a movement of 'life' towards rest, *towards a return to the original state of matter: inertia*" (*Patterns in Comparative Religion,* pp. 454–55).

20. See the remark of Erich Fromm cited earlier in note 21 of Chapter VII.

21. Here we run into the problem that Freud described in terms of the two opposite thrusts of one and the same instinct: *Eros* and *Thanatos.* (Since he eventually came to see only one instinctual force, a libidinal one, Eros and Thanatos are not really two different instincts.) The latter is the regressive tendency of the instinctual life *as a whole,* the tendency to regress to the inorganic level. With this concept Freud permits us to reunite two notions that had been separated by Western thought—with truly tragic psychic results: i.e., the notions of *guilt* (as regression) and *death.* Scientifically speaking, it is impossible to exclude the possibility of a total regression from the human level to the animal level, or from the animal level to the inorganic level. Physical death itself bears convincing testimony to that possibility. But even in that case, according to the later Freud, *Eros* would still be present in the fact that this regression towards death is "always" impeded and made difficult. So it seems that it would be an intrinsic contradiction to talk about a *total* massification of a human being, that is, about a constant, total, and irreversible victory of quantitative laws without any qualitative revenge (to use Teilhard de Chardin's terms) or without some victory of grace over death (to use St. Paul's terms). See Segundo, A Theology for Artisans of a New Humanity, Vol. 2, *Grace and the Human Condition,* (Maryknoll, N.Y. Orbis Books, 1973), pp. 162–67 (Chapter IV, Clarification III).

22. "In fact it is only possible to make predictions at all insofar as limitations on freedom are present" (R. Waelder, "The Problem of Freedom in Psychoanalysis and the Problem of Reality Testing." [*International Journal of Psychoanalysis* 17 (1936) 104]).

23. "An absolute prohibition that is automatically followed by all, and especially when it is applied without any exception to all the members of society, *saves us a good deal of psychic energy.* The unconditional formulation of the prohibition 'Thou shalt not' is much simpler than lengthy reflection on the pros and cons, on the possible risks and responsibilities versus the potential gains. Compared with the person who acts in an automatic way, the self-deciding person is freer and bolder in his efforts to obtain happiness. But precisely because of his greater freedom, his risks are also greater than *the average normal person* of today tends to accept. . . So the next question is, of course: How can we educate people to be free in the future without jeopardizing the authentic values of civilization?" (Michael Balint, "Sexualidad y sociedad," in the anthology edited by Th. Adorno and W. Dirks, *Freud en la actualidad,* Spanish trans. [Barcelona: Barral, 1971], pp. 187–88).

24. Lenin, *On Cooperation.*

25. Joseph Ratzinger, *Le nouveau peuple de Dieu,* French trans., (Paris: Aubier, 1971), p. 140.

26. *Ibid.,* pp. 140–41.

27. César Aguiar, "Currents and Tendencies in Contemporary Latin American Theology," in the anthology edited by L.M. Colonnese, *Conscientization for Liberation* (Washington: Latin American Division, United States Catholic Conference 1971), p. 43.

28. *Ibid.,* pp. 43–44.

29. *Ibid.,* p. 44.

30. In *Revista del Centro de Investigación y Acción social* (Buenos Aires), April 1974, pp. 5–27.

31. *Ibid.,* p. 14.

32. Notice this formulation by Frei Betto in Brazil: "The function of the theologian is to systematize the critical reflection *which the people makes* of its practice in the light of faith. What is rational knowledge in the theologian is wisdom in the people. The theologian helps the people to uncover the liberative dimension of their faith. This faith is lived amid the abundance of the Spirit's gifts, and its discernment enables *the people* to espy God's designs in the events of real life. . . Hence theology, as a scientific discipline, can only be worked out by someone who is participating intensely in the forward march of the people of God. . . In this connection pastoral activity must adopt a methodology which is capable of liberating the powerful elements latent *in the faith of the people.* And it must take care not to suppress the rich resources of popular religiosity, which are not always comprehended in scholastic formulas and concepts. There is a whole range of factors and traditions in popular religiosity which are eminently capable of liberating man's deepest potentialities and aspirations. Sad to say, they

are often taken to be mere superstitions and folklore elements" ("Deus é o ultimo dos homens," in the anthology edited by Leonardo Boff, *Experimentar Deus hoje* [Petropolis: Vozes], 1974, pp. 12–13).

33. Cited in the "Documento del grupo de Capital Federal del MSTM (Movimiento de Sacerdotes para el Tercer Mundo), April 29, 1974, in *Centro de documentación* (Buenos Aires), n. 16, p. 3.

General Conclusions?

The question mark is very much in order. As the reader probably realizes, my aim in this volume has not been to dissect a dead corpse but to examine the living organism known as theology. The methodological problems that we have been studying here are certainly the most salient ones in present-day Latin American theology of liberation. This does not mean, of course, that they are the only ones, or that the future will not furnish us with others even more relevant and critical.

What should be obvious is that the pathways traced out in this book will take us on a long journey. If theology in Latin America or anywhere else chooses to follow them, my book and liberation theology itself will probably be forgotten long before the new tasks outlined here have been carried out as thoroughly as those undertaken by other methodologies in the past history of theology. It will take centuries to match the latter in seriousness, range, and results.

Whether they are followed or not, the pathways opened up here lead into a long and unforeseeable future. The only thing that can be said for sure is that they take their cue from flesh-and-blood human beings who are struggling with mind and heart and hand to fashion the kingdom of God out of the human materials of our great but oppressed continent.